IT TAKES BLOOD AND GUTS

SKIN

WITH **LUCY O'BRIEN**

IT TAKES BLOOD AND GUTS

**SIMON &
SCHUSTER**

London · New York · Sydney · Toronto · New Delhi

1 3 5 7 9 10 8 6 4 2

Simon & Schuster UK Ltd
1st Floor
222 Gray's Inn Road
London WC1X 8HB

www.simonandschuster.co.uk
www.simonandschuster.com.au
www.simonandschuster.co.in

Simon & Schuster Australia, Sydney
Simon & Schuster India, New Delhi

A CIP catalogue record for this book is available from the British Library

Hardback ISBN: 978-1-4711-9491-7
Trade Paperback ISBN: 978-1-4711-9492-4
eBook ISBN: 978-1-4711-9493-1

Typeset in Bembo by M Rules

Printed in the UK by CPI Group (UK) Ltd, Croydon, CR0 4YY

MIX
Paper from
responsible sources
FSC® C020471

CONTENTS

BOOK THREE: THE TROUBLE WITH ME

BOOK FOUR: WONDERLUSTRE

For Lady . . . forever.
To Mum, there's lots of swearing,
please read with earplugs.

FOREWORD

This is not a woeful tale of past loves lost and won, but a book about the trials and tribulations of how a skinny black girl from Brixton grew up to shake the world of rock. How the fuck did I do that?

As a child I always felt weird inside, like something was out of place. Little did I know that it was me who needed to find her place.

This book is about the fits and starts, wrong turns and giant mistakes, along with the hilarious and magical moments that it took to get to the top of the rock tree.

Please pull up a chair, pour yourself a glass of something nice and enjoy my tales of the truly unexpected.

INTRODUCTION

I first met Skin in 1995, when I was a young music writer sent to Los Angeles by *Vox* magazine to interview Skunk Anansie on the set of Kathryn Bigelow's sci-fi thriller *Strange Days*. I was excited to meet the band. There had been a lot of interest in the press – this young incendiary female lead singer with a quirky punk style. Over four days I got to know her, going from a Rage Against The Machine gig to clubbing at the Viper Room on Sunset Boulevard, to the *Strange Days* film set, and back home. We stayed in touch, and ever since then she has been a strong and constant friend. As well as being an insightful, inspirational speaker, she is a great listener. I always remember her, at the peak of her solo success in the early 2000s, giving me a lift 60 miles home on the tour bus after a gig in Oxford, and coming in at 3am to eat Marmite on toast. I was a frazzled new mother having a rare night off and, despite her insane schedule, Skin took the time to see me home.

Over twenty-five years I have witnessed her highest points – headlining Glastonbury, riding a white stallion into the Teatro La Fenice opera house in Venice, performing an emotional set at Cadogan Hall for the *An Acoustic Skunk Anansie: Live in London* album – and her most challenging times. The soul-searching when Skunk Anansie split for a while, the endless touring and its personal toll on her relationships and – despite selling millions of albums, modelling for fashion designers and touring world-wide – the long fight to be recognised in her field.

Along with singers like Annie Lennox, Dusty Springfield and Kate Bush, Skin is one of our great British female artists. Skin takes what is happening in her life – rage, emotional pain or joy – and uses it as fuel for how she creates. That is why she touches people. As her close friend, the dancer/choreographer Richelle Donigan, says, 'It's not just entertainment. When you are in a concert with Skin, if you allow it, you are being trans-formed. You walk out a different person from when you walked in. Skin gives everything . . . she lifts you up.'

Skin is known not only as a fiercely talented vocalist, but also for her involvement in fashion, her charity work doing music therapy with young asylum seekers and campaigning against female genital mutilation, and as a socially conscious icon at the forefront of LGBTQ+ visibility.

Her importance as a cultural force was recognised at 2018's Women in Music Awards hosted by *Music Week*, who defined Skin as 'one of the most iconic and unforgettable stars of her generation', and handed her the Inspirational Artist award. I have written extensively on female artists, publishing biogra-phies of Dusty Springfield and Madonna, and the book *She Bop*, the definitive history of women in popular music. In my work I have always foregrounded the female voice, asking questions that don't often get asked, letting women speak deeply about their personal experience. Many stories of the 1990s place Britpop at the centre – a British music scene that was very white and male – but Skin's experience was very different, and is an alternative narrative of that decade. Emerging from a poor childhood in a Brixton marred by riots to becoming a huge rock icon, her story is extraordinary. I wanted to help her tell it, and for her to gain the recognition she fully deserves.

This memoir has been co-created from hours of interview time, not just with Skin but also close friends and members of her family.

This is her story.

Lucy O'Brien
London, 2020

BOOK ONE

100 WAYS TO BE
A GOOD GIRL

ONE

BRIXTON ROCK

But I don't want your charity
Twisting me round
I don't want your charity
Keeping me down . . .

'Charity'

No matter how far I travel, I'm always a Brixton girl. I can be drinking mezcal while listening to Bob Marley in Mexico, or eating a pizza in Napoli at 4am, but in my head I'm that child back home in Brixton Market, skipping between market stalls catching snippets of 'big people' conversations. Brixton is my barometer – always has been, always will be – not just for Caribbean delights but also for music, people, politics and, most importantly, attitude. I grew up two minutes from the market; two minutes from mothers pausing to gossip outside the local shops, with one maybe taking a breath to shout at her bored young child for wriggling too much, attempting to escape her vice-like grip. It was loud and buzzing with accents from every country in the world, and music was everywhere.

In a minute's walk through the market, you could hear all types of reggae music, from '60s ska to lovers rock, Ace Cannon's bluesy sax, loved by the old-timers, and the latest dancehall hits. There were stalls piled high with precariously balanced fruit, and stallholders selling the best avocados in the world. Massive and sweet with a thin green skin, you could scoff them like apples they were so tasty. We'd slice them up and eat them with bammy flatbread, ackee and saltfish or rice and peas on the side — always on the side, people!

Mum would do a lot of her food shopping there, especially for meat, and usually at the same stalls because she was very loyal. She and her friends knew who had the best quality and best price. This information was like a market Bible, except no one wrote it down; you just had to be in the Jamaican wives' club to get the lowdown. Then she would cook on Saturday and we'd eat it the rest of the week, except for Friday, when she gave herself the day off and we had fish and chips like English folk. My mum had a huge chest freezer in the kitchen for over fifty-five years full of things she had cooked and frozen. A few years ago it finally broke and, when she defrosted it, I asked if she'd found a leg of dodo at the bottom! They don't make appliances like they used to, that's fo' sure. She eats Jamaican food most days. Even when she comes to my house she brings her own food, not because I can't cook but because she knows I like her cooking better.

Local traders used to spread out along Atlantic Road and Electric Avenue — so called because it was the first street in London to be lit by electricity, also made famous by Eddy

Grant – and opposite, on Brixton Road, was Red Records, a legendary shop that specialised in music of black origin. Brixton Market was always the blood-filled pumping heart of south London, while around the edges it was a little rougher with streets and corners you'd avoid, like the alleyway to Brixton Academy, which we called 'muggers alley'.

The top of Railton Road was a no-go area for us, Coldharbour Lane was a maybe, and the high street was safe as long as you didn't act naïve. When I was a kid there always seemed to be at least one person with mental health issues screaming full volume outside Brixton tube station, which was completely normal to us. We'd walk past them holding onto the backs of our necks because the rumour in the *Daily Brixton* (our imaginary newspaper filled with child truths) was these 'maddup' people loved to bite you on your neck. We'd also cover our foreheads just in case. We kids had to be careful never to catch their eye, and if you heard one of them say, 'I see you, demon child!' it was time to run like Daley Thompson! Of course, most of them were completely harmless day patients from the mental health facility of nearby Landor Road hospital in Stockwell.

But there was one character we knew to stay well away from – an old guy with massive white teeth who always wanted to show us his willy. He'd be in dark corners or unlit parts of the street, so you learnt to be streetwise – even now my peripheral vision is always on high penis alert.

At the turn of the twentieth century, Brixton was already established as a posh part of London with busy department stores and two large theatres – the Brixton Theatre and the Empress Theatre of Varieties. It's why there are so many lovely houses there, as well as the massive St Matthew's Church in the centre of Brixton, built in 1824 for a congregation of two thousand parishioners. Brixton gradually became a place for post-war migration, attracting refugees from war-torn areas of the world – what used to be called a multicultural 'melting pot'. Now we use the word 'diverse', which is a much better description. That's what made it such a lively, special place, with a mixture of actors, anarchists and Black Panthers living alongside African-Caribbean and Irish families. However, by the late 1970s, there was growing unemployment and poverty. At that time, 40 per cent of the community in Lambeth was black or mixed race, 65 per cent of the unemployed in Brixton were black and the crime rate was one of the highest in London.

The police would send special patrol units though the neighbourhood, and in April 1981 alone they stopped and searched over 943 people, mainly young black men. The sus law (the so-called 'suspected person' law) meant police could arrest members of the public if they were 'acting suspiciously', not necessarily committing a crime, and this fuelled a deep feeling of resentment in the community towards the police and the Conservative government. Stop-and-search tactics made life hell, and people who were arrested might get beaten up in police cells – 'resisting arrest' they called it. The police looked at us with accusatory eyes, always assuming we were doing something illegal. My brothers and their mates use to wind them up. They'd walk past a policeman, hunch their shoulders and start walking faster, looking as shifty as possible. When they heard an 'Oi you!', they'd bolt because they knew the police dude wearing the Batman belt and truncheon could never catch them on foot. My brothers would run through our front door laughing and giggling, and I knew what they'd been up to again.

There was feeling of foreboding in the air, and finally riots ignited the weekend of 11–12 April 1981 between the police and black 'youths' (I've always hated the word 'youths', which feels like a polite way to say 'black criminals'), with bricks, bottles and petrol bombs thrown at lines of police behind riot shields. Shops and police cars were set on fire and there was widespread looting. We were living on Nursery Road at the time, just off Brixton Road, so our street became an escape route for all the looters carrying stolen TVs and being chased by the police. At the top of Nursery Road was a massive housing estate that for us was a dangerous no-go area where we might get mugged. It was an intricate web of corridors and dark staircases with many dead ends. Unless you knew the place like the back of your hand, you could get lost and trapped. So looters ran straight for the estate, chased by police trying to catch them before they got through the thin metal gate. I'd only seen scenes like this in movies, but now my backyard was burning on national TV.

I was thirteen and really into photography. I had a Pentax ME Super camera that I loved. I went out that weekend because my child brain thought it would be good to take pictures, but it soon turned scary. I nearly got my head kicked in by a crowd of about twenty kids because someone shouted that I was from the press. I talked my way out of it. I was lucky, unlike the photojournalist David Hodge, who went into a coma and died after he was beaten up during the later 1985 riot. I was foolish, but I learnt something valuable from it: that a crowd mentality is a very dangerous thing, like the wind that can change direction in a second from gentle swaying to ripping you off the ground. That moment taught me to not follow the masses or the mob, and I remember thinking for the first time, *I gotta get out of Brixton.*

Brixton came to be seen as a riot zone. A lot of shops were boarded up for months afterwards and never reopened. It felt like Margaret Thatcher's Conservative government just left us to rot. There was no investment in the community, nothing was repainted and everything was underfunded. There was nothing to do and nowhere to go; we felt like a forgotten generation.

Later, during the late 1990s, though, a lot of money started to come into the area. Pavements and potholes were fixed, benches and a new 'chill zone' appeared outside Brixton Library. As the area was 'regenerated', yuppies and hipsters began buying Victorian houses at bargain prices, and by the 2000s super-rich property developers were buying up rundown buildings and turning them into luxury flats. The New Labour government at the time could say they were investing in Brixton, with money flooding in and roadworks everywhere, but the investment wasn't for traditional Brixtonites or their families. It was for the new gentrifiers, who liked Brixton because it was cheap, had an edge and the diversity made it cool.

Even now the older generation like my mum are being put under pressure to sell up for below market value. As the years pass, fewer people in her family live nearby because no one can afford to. The most beautiful houses in Brixton are owned by black people, but there is an estate agent's word, a derogatory term referring to the practice of buying high-value houses from the older black generation. It's called 'uplift'. As if the gentrifiers are somehow better, more deserving of these five-bedroom havens. With their foot-long beards and fixed-wheel bikes, they still like *their* kind of atmosphere, to feel *their* kind of 'safe', and are financially able to do this, living in a privileged bubble.

Tings change, tings must evolve – I get it. Who wants to stay on the dancefloor when the needle is stuck on 'Redemption Song'? Eventually you have to play another tune. Brixton has always had a transient culture; new people moving in from exciting countries bring with them new life and fresh perspectives. I love hearing all kinds of accents exclaiming how good Brixton avocados are. But there should be space for them to mix with the people who were born and bred there. Second-generation Brixton locals are also open to fresh ideas and cultures, and it's sad to see one group of folk being pushed out to make room for other folk. Call me idealistic, but if there's a will, there should be a way to make room for everyone.

I remember my grandad, Bertram Wilson Wright (Bertie for short), as a large, beautifully dressed jovial man with a big laugh and a huge bushy moustache. He moved from Jamaica to England in 1948. He was part of the original Windrush generation, one of those who arrived on that small troop ship on the invitation of the British government. Jamaica was then still a British colony, and it was a common dream to come to the UK. In the aftermath of the Second World War, when so many town centres had to be restructured and rebuilt, and nurses were needed to work in the new National Health Service, people from Commonwealth countries were encouraged to come over to the UK and forge new careers. Mum remembers, when she was a little girl, Grandad Bertie picking her up before he left for England, blowing bubbles on her cheek and saying that once he'd settled he was going to send for her. He was such a lovable person and she really missed him, repeatedly telling her friends at school she was going to go to England, but waiting and yearning for years.

My mum, Patricia Dyer, was born in Manchester, Jamaica in 1944, and raised in the countryside in Clarendon. Her mother, Clarice, had a relationship with Grandad Bertie, but they never married. Soon after he arrived in London, Grandad Bertie met my step-grandma Wright and they had three children together. Still, my grandad always loved my mum, and wanted her to leave Jamaica and come to live with him, but Grandma Clarice was hesitant to send her. 'Who's going to look after you?' she would say.

When Mum was small, Grandma Clarice married my step-grandad Boysie and had five more children with him. She remembers a happy childhood spent running around with her half-brothers and -sisters in gullies that were full of fruit – oranges, tangerines, guava, naseberries, soursop and sweetsap, ripe and ready to eat. During the summer months, on the long walk to school, they would gorge themselves on fruit. On the way home too they'd fill their bellies, have no room for dinner and catch some licks for it. Because of all the fresh fruit they ate, children were rarely sick. In fact, inspectors would come to the school and say how healthy they were. Eggs and milk were less palatable – they used to boil eggs until they were blue, and give the kids milk powder, which my mum hated. She disliked the way it curdled in her mouth, and she jokes that maybe that nasty milk is why she has trouble with her bones now, all these years later.

As a girl, my mum was given a chubby pet pig that ate roots in the garden, and a chicken that laid eggs, which her parents would sell at the market. Grandma Clarice loved flowers, so my mum would help her with gardening. Clarice was also a legendary cook, making dishes with sweet pimentos, yam and sweet potatoes. She would make preserves from all the different fruits that grew in the garden and the countryside, and she would kill rabbits and sell the meat in jars at agricultural shows, sometimes winning prizes.

Mum's great-grandfather Pinnock was a Scottish man with blond hair who had bequeathed to Grandma Clarice's family a horse and carriage. Mum remembers riding to church in it as a child through Edgware and Epping Forest – Jamaican districts named after places in England. Times were very different then, and she and her siblings didn't dare disobey their parents or teachers otherwise they would get a lashing. At school, if they were late or talked during lessons, the teacher would hit their hands with a leather strap. If the children complained about this, the parents would just give a basket of fruit to the teacher! My mum says that a sense of harsh discipline ran deep in Jamaican culture, and was partially learnt from being a British colony and from the legacy of slavery, when violence was used to make people obey. 'That was our history, what we learnt about at school,' she said.

When she was seventeen, Mum was finally allowed to go to England by herself, so, in 1961, she arrived on a British passport. She flew BOAC, the British state-owned airline that later became part of British Airways, and, to this day, she still has the little blue suitcase she brought with her. Grandad Bertie met her at the airport, and the first thing that struck her about England was, *This country is coooold!* There was no central heating in Grandad's house, so he would light a big fire in the sitting room fireplace, or she would stand in front of paraffin heaters until her legs turned bright red. This was before the 1968 Clean Air Act, so all the buildings in London were covered with black soot. People still burned a lot of coal then, which created London's famous pea-soup fogs, and Mum remembers sitting on the bus on foggy days while someone walked in front of it with a lantern to guide the way, shouting, 'A bus is coming!' She found a job working in an office in Coldharbour Lane, in Brixton, for a general supplies company. A lot of Caribbean migrants did skivvy work because it was all they could get, so she considered herself fortunate, sitting in an office, processing orders, always beautifully attired.

Soon after arriving, Mum walked around Brixton with a friend and saw signs in people's windows declaring 'NO DOGS. NO BLACKS. NO IRISH'. This scared them, so they hurried back home. In reality, Britain was not the welcoming place they'd seen on the posters inviting Jamaicans to 'Come live in England'. In 1964, for instance, Peter Griffiths, the Conservative Party candidate for Smethwick, near Birmingham, campaigned with the slogan: 'If you want a nigger for a neighbour, vote Liberal or Labour', and there were demands for the council to make housing available to white families only. And in 1968, Conservative MP Enoch Powell made his infamous 'Rivers of Blood' speech, speaking out against immigration from the Commonwealth, saying that Britain was like 'a nation busily engaged in heaping up its own funeral pyre'. Quoting Virgil, he stirred up racial hatred and fear with his inflammatory line: 'As I look ahead, I am filled with foreboding; like the Roman, I seem to see the River Tiber foaming with much blood.' Faced with that kind of hostility, it's not surprising that black people lived in urban areas like Brixton where they had close networks of friends and family support.

Despite such fear and animosity in the UK at that time, Mum enjoyed living in Grandad Bertie's house with her cousins and half-siblings. He created one of the coolest drinking clubs in south London, the Effra Residential Club, in the basement of his house in Acre Lane. I've seen pictures of Muhammad Ali (when he was Cassius Clay) coming through the door, and musicians like Bob Marley and Peter Tosh used to drop in for a drink. Norman Manley, co-founder of the People's National Party and the first prime minister of independent Jamaica, went to the club when he was in London, and even had a conversation with my mum. He told her he was rebuilding Jamaica, saying: 'All the young people like you have to come back.'

In the post-war years, black people weren't welcome in night-clubs, so in urban areas like London and Manchester they created their own shebeens, an Irish word for private houses that sold alcohol without a licence. These places became an important way for people to meet and forge links in their communities, and in Grandad Bertie's club it was mostly African-Caribbeans and a few Irish people. Some of the Irish regulars would overdo the Guinness and end up starting fights, so my grandad would chuck them out and tell them not to come back. They'd always reappear after a few days, pleading, 'Can't we just have one drink? We'll be on our best behaviour,' and he'd let them in because he liked them – after all, they were suffering some of the same tribulations as us.

Years later, in 2012, the then Conservative Home Secretary Theresa May created a 'hostile environment' in the UK for people without 'leave to remain'. Although under the 1999

Immigration and Asylum Act anyone who had arrived in the UK from a Commonwealth country before 1973 was granted an automatic right to remain, if they couldn't prove this with documentary evidence they were denied access to jobs, services and bank accounts and offered 'voluntary deportation'. The policy was part of a strategy to reduce UK immigration figures to the level promised in the 2010 Conservative Party manifesto, and targets had been set by the Home Office for deportation of people considered illegal immigrants.

In what became known as the Windrush scandal, many older Caribbean-born people were targeted under this policy, with hundreds denied access to work, sent to detention centres or put on planes back to the Caribbean, to countries where they hadn't lived or worked for decades. Many of the original Windrush generation were affected, including people who might have lost proof of their British citizenship when, in 2010, the UK Border Agency destroyed thousands of landing card slips. In 2018, after a severely critical National Audit Office report, Home Secretary Amber Rudd resigned and deportations were 'paused'. At the time of writing, though, up to 3,720 people remain wrongly classified as illegal immigrants, and many are destitute, awaiting compensation from the Home Office.

This infuriates me. The Windrush scandal shows a callous disregard for Commonwealth immigrants, part of a wider lack of respect and appreciation for good, decent people like Grandad Bertie and my mum, who paid their taxes for years and who in their own way contributed so much to their local areas and Brixton cultural life. Grandad Bertie's club was a great place for Mum and her half-siblings to hang out. But it was also a vibrant, important social place for the black community that was not accepted into wider society. These Commonwealth immigrants were officially invited to the UK, but after decades of hard work and loyalty to the Crown, they were just kicked to the kerb like discarded cans.

When my step-grandma Mrs Wright went to Brixton market at the weekend, my mother and her half-siblings would sneak down to the basement where the club was held and whack the music up to full volume on the gramophone. Mum would dance and hula hoop, and she became skilled at spinning the hoop around her waist and doing tricks, like rotating it around one finger or around her neck. An Indian man came every week to empty the slot machines and the jukebox, and would give my mum a few shillings. She was thrifty; she saved the coins and, when she got older, bought a trunk that she filled with blankets and sheets for when she got married.

One day, in the summer of 1963, her cousin came to the club with two friends from the RAF. One of them was Kenneth Dyer, a handsome, light-skinned man sporting a full moustache. Apparently, the moment he walked down the stairs and saw Mum, looking stunning in a bright-red dress, he knew he was going to marry her. She liked him too and thought he was good-looking, with twinkly eyes and an easy smile. My mum and dad courted for a while before getting married a year later, in 1964, in St Matthew's Church in Brixton – the same church that we attended every Sunday and the place where my mum was later a churchwarden for decades. Afterwards there was a party at Bertie's club and a band called the Jubilee Stompers played ska and rocksteady.

Mum had four kids very quickly and very young, but she found being a new mother difficult. She was only twenty years old when she had my older brother Beavon. He was born premature, weighing barely five pounds, and had to spend his first two months in hospital. She said later that she didn't know what she was doing, and has no idea how she coped. My dad was stationed abroad with the RAF at the time, so Mum stayed with Grandad Bertie for a while and had to go to the hospital every day on her own to feed her new baby. 'He was so little,' she said, 'like a little pillow.' But once Beavon started growing he became strong, kicking a football almost as soon as he could walk.

I was born three years later, in Lambeth Hospital, on 3 August 1967. According to Mum, I was born just as the sun came through the window and kissed me on my cheek. I was given a religious name – Deborah. She was a prophet of God and the fourth Judge of Israel, the only female judge mentioned in the Bible.

Nineteen sixty-seven was a year of massive social unrest and cultural change around the world. There were race riots in Detroit, student demos against the Vietnam War across college campuses in the US, and 'be-ins' and 'love-ins', which were part of the psychedelic Summer of Love. It was the year the Beatles released *Sgt. Pepper* and the Jimi Hendrix Experience came out with *Are You Experienced?*. I like to think I absorbed some of that rebellious spirit, surrounded by the sounds of cultural shift. From an early age I was always driving myself forward, always curious, always pushing to try new things, even if it meant I was way out of my comfort zone.

I was followed by my younger brothers, Maurice in 1968 and Nicholas in 1970. When we were small, my dad's job in the RAF meant we lived on Air Force bases in different places like Brize Norton, Wiltshire and Herefordshire. My mum felt isolated because Dad was often away, leaving her alone with us kids. It was hard for her because there were few black people to talk to and it was difficult to get out – when we lived in Wiltshire, for example, the bus would come to the air base just once a day. Dad, meanwhile, was travelling the world and seemed to my mum to be leading a charmed life.

His father, Ashton Benjamin Dyer, had a farm in Clarendon, Jamaica, 40 miles from Kingston, and his mother, Mary Copeland, was a tall woman from a large family. Grandpa Dyer, however, was very short, and all of his eleven children were taller than him. Everyone in the family could sing, so when they went to church, about once every three months, they would all go to the front and, with vigour, sing all the hymns. According to my dad, Grandpa Dyer could be very funny, but he was also a stern, hard-headed farmer. All the children were expected to work hard on the farm because 90 per cent of what they ate as a family was grown on it. They reared pigs, cows and donkeys and had 3,000 chickens, plus 150 acres of land where they grew coffee crops and different fruits such as oranges, grapefruit and mangoes.

The farm was halfway up a mountain, so a lot of the land was unworkable, and in the 1960s Grandpa Dyer sold all his land to the bauxite industry. Bauxite is amorphous rock that is the main source of aluminium, and by the late 1950s Jamaica had become the leading bauxite producer in the world. Grandpa Dyer was a special constable, a pillar of society in his district, and the bauxite corporations knew that if he sold his land to them, others would follow. Bauxite mining had yet to take off in Clarendon, however, and, according to my dad, Grandpa Dyer didn't get paid what he should have.

My dad had a happy childhood in Jamaica and, as his mother's first son, he was given whatever he wanted – books, school trips; he even had a Mercedes at seventeen! He helped on the farm when he was forced to but, as he admits, he was a bit spoilt and unenthusiastic about menial work. Grandpa Dyer came up with a tough remedy for this, shaking my dad awake one Monday morning in 1960 to tell him, 'Instead of milking the cows, we are going to Kingston.'

When they got there, my dad had passport photos taken, and that's when his father told him he was going to England. Normally it would take eight weeks to get a passport, but Dad got his in twenty-four hours because Grandpa Dyer knew people in every municipal department, and by the Wednesday my dad had left Jamaica. Dad didn't want to leave – his ambition was to stay and become a doctor – but Grandpa Dyer told him, 'In one house there can only be one man.' Grandpa Dyer had to be obeyed, so Dad had no choice but to give up his dream of becoming a doctor. Later he discovered he couldn't stand the sight of blood, so maybe that was a lucky escape.

When my dad first arrived in England, he went to stay with his brother, who was already living in Tottenham. He worked as a lathe operator in Enfield and, after six months, in October 1960, he joined the Royal Air Force. He started as an RAF chef, learning to cook, but hated it, so he switched to the role of A-class air steward, flying RAF officers and their families to and from places like Singapore and Washington. Good-looking and charming, my dad was the only black member of an eight-man team flying out of Brize Norton airbase. He remembers working on the Queen's Flight once or twice – at that point, whenever the Queen went abroad long distance she went with her family on Air Force transport. He said the Queen was nice, but she was very concerned about protocol. 'If she spoke, you spoke to her, not otherwise,' he recalls. He liked Princess Anne and Princess Margaret, though; he found other royals easier to get on with.

Dad's unusual experience taught him a lot about the British class system. He was in the Air Force for six years, moving from steward on the Queen's plane to working in the bar in the officers' mess in RAF stations all over the world. He was often in Commonwealth trouble spots, like Borneo in 1963, when Indonesian forces were fighting against the creation of Malaysia. Despite his service in the RAF, he encountered a deep-rooted prejudice in a way that was hard to call out. Although he did well in his training, he was never promoted beyond the rank of corporal, even though he was qualified to be Warrant Officer, the highest non-commissioned rank in the RAF. It didn't occur to Dad that this was down to prejudice until long after he'd left the RAF and was reflecting on his career.

He regularly flew long haul, and each trip would involve flying from the UK to Singapore or Hong Kong, taking ten days to get there and another ten days to get back. The RAF flew DC10 planes, which had a poor reputation for safety – once, a hurricane blew out a window and the crew had to stay in Omaha, Nebraska for two weeks while the RAF kept sending the wrong parts from England. In the year my brother Beavon was born, Dad spent a total of six weeks at home. He missed his son, but servicemen were allowed only one trip home a year on compassionate leave. When we were young, he was sometimes only home twice a year, and so he became a distant presence in our lives. We didn't see him often, but when he did come home he was like Father Christmas; he always had a big smile and little gifts for us, and in hindsight that must have really irritated my mum!

TWO

I CAN DREAM

I caused a major war, just by talking
You flew into a rage, 'cos that's everything you know
Childhood of violence, filled with heartache
I flew into a rage, 'cos that's everything I know

'100 Ways to Be a Good Girl'

Alone, isolated and feeling insecure in her marriage, my mum packed some bags one day and left the Herefordshire Air Force barracks where we were living, and took me and my brothers to London. Dad says we just disappeared, and no one would tell him where we were. Although I don't recall the journey, I do remember being in a different place – in 16 Nursery Road, Brixton, round the corner from Grandad Bertie's.

Grandad Bertie's, at 33 Effra Road, was an impressive, tall house spread over five floors. One of my earliest memories is sitting at the top of the basement stairs watching everyone hopstepping to Prince Buster until we got told to 'get to your bed!'

But I loved watching everyone have fun, transfixed by the way they danced, my grandad laughing and mingling, making sure the night was running smoothly. He had charm, energy and the performance gene that runs in the family.

My step-grandma Mrs Wright, on the other hand, was a different kettle of fish. She was always a little bit removed and unaffectionate. I guess she was forced to recognise us as Bertie's grandchildren, so now, as an adult, I can understand her reticent feelings for grandchildren from another mother, but we were just little kids and we didn't understand why she didn't like us and why everything we did seemed to be wrong. Sadly, it meant we never became close, and I don't have many sweet memories of her. We were four tiny reminders of her husband's previous life, which must have been hard for her, but her indifference made it even harder for us.

I have much better memories of my Grandma Clarice back in Jamaica, a kind but strict woman who'd say to my mum, 'Give the kids a set of rules.' As a result, Mum was always shouting at us to stop doing whatever it was we were up to. You go to Jamaica and that's how everybody is – loud and shouty in a way that you get used to. I think you can run a straight line back to slavery, being shouted at by 'Massa', thinking that's normal and then shouting at your kids in turn. Children were seen as an irritation, and parents could be harsh and quick to beat them. Get any group of black friends together and we will laugh and joke about our tough parents, kidding about the many things they used to beat us with. The exception was my best school friend Carole, whose mum was the complete opposite, gentle and always laughing, so I knew there was another way Jamaicans could be.

Mum was keen to be independent. Ever since she had arrived in the UK she had been saving up and, with Grandad Bertie's help, she bought that small two-bedroom house on Nursery Road, behind the shops near Brixton Tube station, where we lived until I was twelve. My friend Sandra and her family lived next door, but they had a much bigger garden with a huge overgrown bush in the corner that to us was like a forest. My brothers and I used to play there all the time with Sandra. She had a much older brother who had learning disabilities, and was too big and strong to join in, but he would have fun watching us running around. The six of us in the garden would play 'forest' all summer, messing about till it got dark, with Sandra's brother screaming in delight. There was a wall between the gardens, and arches below the train track that ran from Brixton to Loughborough Junction, and we would run along the wall, using it as a pathway to the other gardens, and play in dere-lict houses. The trains were regular and loud, but to us it was normal, so when they stopped for a bank holiday the silence felt eerie. My partner reminds me that even now I find it difficult to live in complete silence. She's always walking into empty rooms where I have the radio blaring. I grew up with trains and planes passing overhead, brothers ranting, music playing, mother shouting – and I cannot sleep without an audiobook playing. I've lived a loud life.

Sometimes we'd go to the little sweet shop on the corner and spend two and a half pence, which in those days could get you five sweets. I always chose two black jacks, two fruits salads and a bubble gum. Around that time, I started to earn my first bit of pocket money sewing buttons onto strips of cardboard for Mrs Woollery, who lived opposite. She sold them to shops and I got

50p for each pack of five strips. But I hated every second of it, finding the work boring, repetitive and laborious, and I vowed that from then on I would enjoy whatever work I chose to do.

Mum did her nurse's training and got a job in the South London Hospital for Women and Children in Clapham. She worked long hours and we kids were left alone at home. At first, our great-uncle Maxie lived with us, but he mainly stayed in his room and drank. After he moved out, a family friend called Auntie Carmen, a sweet lady with a cute giggle, would occasionally come and look after us, but a lot of the time we had no babysitter; no one we knew did. Mum worked nightshifts at the hospital and she *had* to go to work whether we had a sitter or not. So we were home alone many nights and we ran wild.

We'd put our mattress and bedding at the bottom of the stairs and dare each other to jump onto it from the top – very dangerous but so much fun! My brother Maurice was fascinated by fire and wanted to be a fireman, so one night he scrunched up balls of newspaper, creating a large pyramid on the floor. Nicholas and I watched him from the sofa, thinking, *That's so pretty.* Then suddenly, to our shock, he lit a match, set the whole thing alight and, aided by the highly flammable 1970s carpet, the pile just went *woof!* We screamed, running to the kitchen to get jugs of water to douse the flames, and when we finally managed to put the fire out there was a huge burn mark on the carpet. We thought, *When Mum sees this we'll be in so much trouble*, so we moved the furniture around, putting the rug over the burn marks and placing a chair and table on top. Mum wasn't fooled; she smelt burning the minute she walked in the door and we all got the licking of our lives!

There were three cinemas in Brixton, so when we were a

little older and Mum was at work, me and my brothers and our little friends would sometimes go to the Ritzy, where they screened all-night horror movies, or we'd go to the Ace Cinema and see movies we weren't supposed to see, but as long as you paid for an adult ticket you could get in. We watched *The Rocky Horror Picture Show*, and everyone would get dressed up, throw popcorn and smoke weed; or we'd see funny B-movies that were more hilarious than they were scary. I loved horror movies when I was a kid – I didn't believe any of it; I could see the strings, knew it was fake blood, so it didn't affect me. Now, it's different; they are just too real and evil. The last one I saw was *The Blair Witch Project*, which, though I watched through a squinting side-eye, left me a jabbering mess.

One of my favourite activities was to go skating on Saturdays with friends at Streatham Ice Rink, gliding around to soul and funk and reggae music, a real 1970s craze. In America people were roller-skating, but we were ice-skating, and that's where we'd meet up with all our mates.

Growing up in Brixton, you had to strut your stuff and display big shoulders because if you showed any sign of weakness you'd be preyed upon. Nicholas was my smallest brother, so in some ways he had to pretend he was older and tougher, but ironically he's now the tallest and toughest in the family, and also one of the kindest.

One of my earliest memories of him involves a fight. We were always fighting when we were kids, driving my mother mad. Once, when I was twelve, and angry with him about something, I waited for him to fall asleep (he was a really deep sleeper), then slowly crawled up to him, curled the perfect fist and punched him full force in the face. *Bam!* Bullseye! In his sleep he jumped up, chased me down the stairs and gave me a kicking before I could get out the front door, then he slowly crawled back up the stairs, still asleep with eyes closed, and went back to bed! To this day he doesn't remember a thing, and had no idea the next day how he'd got a black eye. It gave my younger self great pleasure to know I got a full punch in that one time, even if I lost the fight.

Another time, the woman who lived next door accidentally left her gas cooker on while she went out. She came back, switched on a light and *BOOM!* – the back of both our houses flew sky high. We had to be rescued by firemen through the top front window, in our pants, in full view of the whole street. Nicholas was still half-asleep. For three months we had a toilet but no bathroom, so anytime we had a bath it was a long, laborious process of boiling kettles of water to fill a tin bath in the kitchen, with a tarpaulin as a makeshift roof. By this time, my grandad had moved back to Jamaica, so we had no choice but to stay in the house while it was being rebuilt.

One night, a ten-year-old Nicholas disobeyed Mum and decided he didn't want to boil kettles, so he filled a big metal bowl with cold water and put it on the hob. When the water had boiled he wrapped towels around his hands and picked up the bowl, but it was too hot to hold. Nicholas turned round and looked at me, and we both knew he was about to pour boiling hot water all over me and there was nothing either of us could do about it. I was standing in an alcove, so all I could do was jump upwards. He let go of the bowl and I jumped as high as I could, but the boiling water caught my ankle. All the skin immediately bubbled up yellow and peeled off. It was horrifying. I ran around the house screaming and screaming until

Mum caught me. She was a nurse, so she expertly wrapped and dressed the wound. I had a really bad scar for years, and to this day I still have the memory of the pain and the image of all the skin falling off imprinted on the inside of my skull.

As the boys got older it got harder for my mum without my dad. Beavon was exceptionally clever – the brains of the family, in fact – but that wasn't 'cool'. What was cool was being a box boy, for Sir Lloyd's sound system, one of the biggest reggae sound systems in London. They would hold competitive sound clashes with other sound systems like King Tubby's or Saxon Studio International, who have been going since the 1970s. Beavon would come home in the morning after a night working for Sir Lloyd and my mum would berate him for it.

Occasionally I'd say to Beavon, 'Just get home before she gets back from work and she'll never know.' But he never did it. He couldn't take the embarrassment of leaving early and not finishing his work. He had a clear choice: getting ribbed by his peer group in public, or getting licks from his mum in private, and he chose his mates. I thought this was silly, but I now realise that, like me, he had a dream – he'd found what he wanted to do and he's really good at it. Now he is a well-respected toaster and has his own setup; he just found his calling eight years earlier than I did. Still, in those days, I witnessed the same row over and over again. This memory eventually became the inspiration for the song '100 Ways to Be a Good Girl'.

When Beavon was out, I was the eldest, so I'd get home from school and pretend I was looking after the other two, but really, they looked after themselves. There was no way my brothers would let me tell them what to do; we were all too close in age and around the same size. Even though I was the only girl, Mum didn't treat me differently from the boys, and now I think that was very liberating for me. We all had to do the chores – all had to wash up, clean our rooms, iron our own clothes, hoover the carpet, clean the bath. I have no memories of my mum telling me I had to do housework because I was the girl; we all had to do it equally.

Being the female lead singer in a band of men was such a natural dynamic for me because it mirrored my childhood. I often played with the boys, joining them for five-a-side football when they needed an extra person in the team, and we all slept in the same bed together when we were little. I grew up a proper little tomboy, and whatever the boys did I did too, even wearing nothing but our underpants all day like they do in Jamaica. I wasn't subservient to my brothers, and the one time my dad tried to get me to iron his shirt, when he moved in for a while, I refused. He wasn't around when we were growing up, so I began to feel resentful and rebellious – no way was I suddenly going to start ironing his shirts, the cheek of it! Iron your shirt because I'm the girl? Being around boys meant I understood male psychology, but I missed out on all the girly things like messing around with hair and make-up. None of my POC friends at school wore it. In fact, I never wore a trace of make-up till my first gig at twenty years old.

My brothers and I went to Stockwell Primary School, an old Victorian school on Stockwell Road, half an hour's walk away, that had about thirty kids in each class. In those days, my brothers and I went everywhere by ourselves, either by bus or walking. There was no school run, we had no car, but we felt totally safe because we were in a group and we were streetwise. We had little bottles of milk every morning (before the then

Education Secretary Margaret Thatcher put a stop to free milk in schools and became known as 'Thatcher the milk snatcher'). I loved primary school because learning felt like playing, but my secondary school was a different matter.

St Martin-in-the-Fields High School for Girls was a strict Church of England ex-grammar school affiliated with St Martin-in-the-Fields church in Trafalgar Square. I had to sit an entrance exam. I passed the first time and started in 1978. My best friend Carole says I always wore the correct uniform: *the* brown jumper with red piping, *the* school skirt, and *the* Donny Osmond-style cap (I can recall everything but the cap), an old-fashioned uniform that came from a little shop in East Dulwich. My mum took me there and bought everything on the list, including the summer dress, hockey skirt and PE kit, for £105. I've never forgotten that price because it was the most I'd heard someone spend on clothes, and because Mum spent so much money I had to wear it. I remember being freezing cold in winter, because as I grew taller the skirt got shorter and shorter until it was more like a mini-skirt. My knees froze but I was so happy because I liked the idea of looking good. I guess my school uniform was my first real fashion moment; the first time I made the internal connection that looking good means feeling good. It also saved me, because we all looked the same, rich or poor, so no one could show off. I was part of something – proud of the fact that I was a perfectly dressed St Martin-in-the-Fields' girl. It was the best school in the area, with the choicest uniform and, because of that, the Dick Sheppard schoolgirls always wanted to fight us, and the lads from the all-boys Tulse Hill School were always trying to chat us up – and by 'us' I mean everyone but me. Maybe the boys twigged that this girl liked her bread buttered on the other side.

I found secondary school hard. St Martin's was imposing, although I don't think that was really about the school. It was more about becoming a teenager and sharpening my awareness of the real world, where bad things were happening. I was learning that the world was a scary place – there were IRA terrorist bombs in London, a hole in the ozone layer, and some old guy felt up my friend. Around the age of thirteen, adults stop shielding you from the madness of the world. It began to dawn on me that this was my life and that I had to take responsibility for it. And the very first thing I had to do was get a good education.

St Martin's was a rude awakening, and everything got very serious fast. Some of the teachers were warm and loved the job, some were vicious and clearly hated it, and others just didn't seem to care, plodding along until retirement. My English teacher, Miss Ruth Webb, however, was an exception. For some reason that still mystifies me, I understood Shakespearian poetry, an archaic language that made complete sense to me. Miss Webb spotted this and gave me extra attention, encouraging my love of words. One day, the actress Judi Dench – who was part of a Royal Shakespeare Company touring ensemble – came to our school to perform *Macbeth*. They had no props; they were all dressed in black, standing in a circle, and that was it. I was transfixed watching her play the part of Lady Macbeth. At one point she let out a scream that was like a kettle. It went on for about a minute. That moment, that blood-curdling scream, changed me forever. I was struck that she was able to let out such a raw sound that seemed to come from the bottom of her soul, and part of me wanted to express myself in the same unfettered way. I've never forgotten the way I felt at the end of her scream. My nerves sparkled.

I wanted to express myself like her but didn't know how – I was too quiet and shy. I compared myself to my three handsome brothers who got lots of attention and seemed so much more confident than me. I felt ugly and invisible, a painfully skinny tomboy with humongous lips and hair that never grew. I was treading water, waiting to be noticed, waiting for someone to see me. I was raised to be a good girl, and was scared of getting into trouble. My mum was under a lot of stress raising four children on her own without enough support. Working as a nurse doing the nightshift meant she needed to sleep in the day, so she was always shouting at us to be quiet because she was exhausted. As the second eldest, I was old enough to be aware of how difficult the situation was for my mum, and so I was the quietest. Sometimes, the person who is the best behaved receives the least attention and is the most overlooked. I tried to be good, not causing my mum any more grief, but in doing that I tended to make myself disappear. At home in England I was often subdued, but when we went to Jamaica I felt carefree and happy and able to express myself in a completely different way.

THREE

IT TAKES BLOOD AND
GUTS TO BE THIS COOL

I can dream, I can dream
I can dream that I'm someone else . . .

'I Can Dream'

I adored going to Jamaica. I went at age six and fourteen. Grandma Clarice lived in the countryside in a tiny house at the top of a hill in Clarendon. She grew bananas, coconuts, plantain and vegetables on the land behind the house, and harvested this to take to market and sell. The first time I tasted coconut drops (cubes of coconut covered in homemade molasses and left to set) was when she made them outside in the back yard, and they were the best thing I had ever tasted in my whole life. Grandma Clarice did all her cooking in a Dutch pot on coal and rocks outside the back of the house. I'd never seen that before, and I used to love watching her cook nearly everything in this one thick-walled black pot. It was a very long, steep walk down the hill to the market – we were knackered every time we had to walk back, but Grandma did that climb every day until just a few weeks before she died aged eighty-six.

I would spend my days running around with my cousins, totally free and unwatched. They would climb the Maypan hybrid palm trees to cut green coconuts from the top branches. Before I went to Jamaica, I thought coconuts were small, dark brown and covered in a hard, fibrous husk, but these were bigger than your head and green. After picking them, my cousins would skilfully make a hole in one end so you could drink the juice – wait ... coconuts had juice? I had no idea! And it was so tasty, sweet. Then they'd chop them in half with a giant machete and spoon out the insides with a piece of the outside husk. I'd never tasted anything better than fresh coconut from the tree, and we did this every day! The countryside was green and full of new sounds and smells, and the market at the bottom of the hill was so vivid, with people shouting, selling all kinds of meat and vegetables. People sold every part of the animals they reared – chicken back, or chicken foot or cow foot. Nothing was wasted. Even the bones were sold to be boiled and made into a wholesome soup.

I love that feeling when you step off a plane in a tropical country and the heat hits you; that rich smell of warmth reminds me of visiting Jamaica as a child. We went to places like Dunns River Falls, visited my Grandad Bertie, and sometimes stayed a few days with aunts and uncles on my dad's side of the family. A lot of those first Windrush migrants just wanted to make some money and then go back to Jamaica and help build the newly independent country. Grandad Bertie always knew he was going to return home, so, in 1972, when he was in his seventies, he moved back to the Caribbean, taking all the sound equipment and vinyl from the club and recreating it in his house in Jamaica.

When we visited Grandad Bertie, we would all drive around in his ancient jeep. It had a huge crack down the middle of it, so whenever it hit a bump the crack would open and close. I was convinced that one day it would split in half and we'd all go rolling off the cliff in opposite directions, *Tom and Jerry* style – stressful and thrilling at the same time. The first time we visited Jamaica, we stayed for weeks and weeks over the summer, and I remember crying when we had to go back. I wanted to stay. I loved it with all my heart. There was a tradition in Jamaica of giving children symbolic gifts. For example, when someone was born, people might give you a tree, like an orange tree, so once it was planted it could grow with you. Or a child would be given a little chick so it would grow and provide eggs. On one of those trips I was given a chick and a goat. I was so happy because I thought I'd be able to take them back to England with me on the plane.

Then, one morning, one of Grandad Bertie's farm workers called me over. He had an old black dustbin with a piece of flat wood across the top. He gently took my chicken, carefully laid its neck across the wood and chopped its head off. The head fell into the bin, and I screamed blue murder and ran away, but the man threw the headless chicken at me, it landed on its feet and chased me around the back yard, its headless neck flopping from side to side spurting blood everywhere while the worker let out a deep belly laugh. I was being chased by a headless bloody chicken, *my* headless chicken, that I'd reared from when it was a yellow fluffy baby chick. Eventually it fell over dead and became our Sunday dinner.

But I was so traumatised by the experience that I didn't eat chicken for years afterwards.

In London, everyone in our community spoke patois, especially when we were cracking jokes, but in Jamaica I couldn't understand a single word, not one. Real Jamaican patois was a completely different language. I was mystified by it – patois in London had mutated into an English version, a new black British dialect, but the fact that I couldn't understand it in Jamaica was a real culture shock. Up until then I saw myself as a mini-Jamaican; nearly everyone on my street was black. We weren't encouraged to socialise with other cultures outside of school, and the fact that there were very few black people on TV or in films compounded the feeling of being separate and in our own tight community. I'd always imagined Jamaica to be my real home, so it was a shock to realise that I wasn't Jamaican in the same way as Mum and Dad. Growing up in England, white people would always ask me, 'Where are you from?' I was already aware that people in Britain didn't see me as British, so I always said 'Jamaica'. I felt proud to be Jamaican, but now what was I? I was thrown into a full-blown identity crisis.

Many Jamaican parents and grandparents felt homesick, like they were biding their time in England. The Windrush generation were church people, all immaculately dressed in their Sunday best with white gloves and beautiful clothes they'd made and sewn themselves. Then they came to England and were treated like inferior citizens; the British never noticed the cut of their clothes, all they saw was their race. They weren't allowed to go to certain places and landlords wouldn't rent them rooms. It was also biting cold and, when they first arrived, none of them had clothes for the chilly weather. They were always talking about going back home to retire. That raised the question: *If my parents go back, do I go too?* In the words of The Clash, *Should I Stay or Should I Go?* After Grandad Bertie left in 1972, my mum considered it, and my school friend Carole's parents eventually went back. My generation felt like we belonged in two worlds – we were not considered British, but we also felt like Jamaicans once removed.

When I went back to Jamaica as a teenager, I walked into Grandad Bertie's nightclub room and got chills down my spine. The vibes were exactly how I remembered it as a child; all the furniture was there but the energy was different. The Effra Road club had been in the basement of a terraced house, all dark and cool. But now the Jamaican sun came streaming through a brightly lit upper-floor lounge, the lace curtains making perfect patterns on the carpet. I mean, lace curtains . . . in a club? But then it hit me that maybe it was supposed to be like that – maybe it was more like a shrine for my grandad, with everything perfectly preserved, stuck in time, somewhere to store the pieces of his old English life. Nothing in the room looked like it had been used much; his party days were over. But he still had a load of records packed in boxes, and that shocked me, because by then records were like diamonds to me – there was nothing on earth I valued more. I confess I took some of the titles I liked, some seven-inch ska and reggae and some 'last dance' records. I brought them back to London and replaced their tattered sleeves. I really wish I'd known Grandad Bertie properly. I feel like I inherited a lot of good traits from him – a love of music, a love of making people happy and, of course, my love of a good party. When he died, in the late 1990s, he left me a shiny Parker fountain pen, but it's the records that really remind me of him.

When I was twelve, my mum told Grandad Bertie, 'Deborah needs her own room.' She was hinting that she needed some help to pay for a new house. We lived in a tiny two-up two-down and were all growing up fast. Three boys and one girl hitting puberty in the same room was not going to work. So, in 1981, we moved to Tulse Hill and I finally had room to breathe.

Imagine: one minute we were crammed into a small terrace in the centre of Brixton, then suddenly we were in a five-bedroom house on a leafy street in Tulse Hill. It was magic. I was ecstatic! For some inane reason I was obsessed with Pierrot the Clown, so Mum bought me the curtains, the pillows, the duvet cover and finally the wallpaper – in lilac and pink. In the gay barometer of my life, this was and shall remain my girliest moment. It looked like it had been decorated by a psychotic five-year-old child who'd eaten *wayyy* too much sugar. I instantly regretted it, but was too proud to say, and it remains like that to this day.

My dad came back for a year when we moved to Tulse Hill, but it just didn't work out between him and Mum. After he left the RAF in the 1970s, he always chose jobs that took him away somewhere. He took a welding course, for instance, and worked in Manchester as a welder, then in Preston on an oil pipeline. From there he worked on oil rigs in northern Scotland, beyond Aberdeen, then had a stint in Iran before working on the rigs out at sea near the Isle of Skye, and a pumping station at Bathgate near Edinburgh. It was like he could never settle down. Even when he came back to London in the early 1980s, and got a job with the Post Office, he ended up sorting travel post on the night trains from London to Carlisle.

One Christmas, I asked Mum and Dad for a tape recorder so I could record my favourite songs off the radio. I got one tape recorder from my mum and a second one from my dad. This spoke volumes to me; their relationship was so bad they couldn't even have a conversation about the kids' presents, so I knew it was over. My dad admits that he was never there when we needed him, and my parents finally divorced in the early 1980s, after having lived separate lives for years.

I said to my dad recently, 'We grew up short of money. We had a black-and-white TV. We didn't know how the other half lived. You worked oil rigs in Iran. You must have been loaded. What did you do with all the money?'

He looked me right in the eye and said, 'I partied.'

I laughed – *that* I understood! At least he was honest and didn't give me some bullshit story. My relationship with my dad hasn't always been easy, but now we get on fine. He's funny and a great conversationalist with a million stories.

In some ways he'll never change, but he's my dad and I like him. A few years ago, he had a stroke and could've died. It struck me that if he had I would've wasted his last few years being resentful and distant towards him. I've learnt that as an adult you just have to suck it up and accept your parents for who they are; sometimes life literally is just too short.

My mum hated working nights as a nurse and, as soon as she could, she left and got a job working for Lambeth Council. She was always studying, and was very disciplined about it. I learnt that from her. She went to night school to do secretarial courses and further training, working her way up to become a Principal Officer in the housing and environmental department. She was politically active, taking me on demonstrations and rallies against the 'sus' laws and police brutality. My political awareness really began with the Brixton riots, and afterwards, going with my mum to local community meetings – some in St Matthew's Church and Lambeth Town Hall, or in the street – where twenty or thirty people would gather and there would be speeches and talk about the need for youth clubs and providing the kids with something to do.

After the 1981 riots, Mum was part of a consultative group for Lambeth Council, visiting Brixton Prison to look in the cells and check the conditions for all the inmates. She was one of the few people who could turn up at any time and demand to check the cells. The police were so aggressive in the 1980s. My brothers, for instance, were always getting stopped and questioned over nothing. I once saw three grown policemen interrogating a young boy, making him take his trousers down in the street to search him – deliberate humiliation. The atmosphere in Brixton then was like a powder keg, but no one cared – it took two riots where people burned everything to the ground before the council, community and church began working together with a police force that wanted to listen.

In her role as churchwarden, Mum took care of St Matthew's – the big church where she and Dad were married. When I was growing up, about forty or fifty people would sit in a service, and you could hear the police sirens echoing around the road outside. We spent every Sunday in church, going to a two-hour morning service at St Matthew's, followed by Sunday school. Then we'd go home for a big family lunch before me and my brothers were sent to a Pentecostal church in Clapham in the afternoon. Mum was very religious, but she stayed at home and rarely went to the Pentecostal church. Secretly I knew it was because she wanted some time by herself without us noisy kids, so we spent our Sunday afternoons in the only Pentecostal church with no gospel choir.

As a child I found Anglican worship to be quite dry and, to be honest, mind-numbingly boring. You would go to church and read the same prayers in exactly the same way for 120 minutes, and then you left. I loved the hymns, still do, but to me as a child the stories seemed far-fetched and unbelievable, in the same way I never believed in Santa Claus or the Easter Bunny. There was no real study and examination of the Bible; everyone just seemed to be going through the motions, and that was enough for them, but I'm naturally the world's biggest sceptic. I was inquisitive and good at sciences, and I applied the same practical analysis to religion. The idea that you were supposed to believe without asking any questions made me even more suspicious. Now I see much more interaction with children in church. Adults realise you have to make it fun or the kids will stop going the minute they can. By the time I went to Sunday school, the only thing I was interested in was filling my pockets with gummy bears from the sweet jar on the way out.

As an adult, I now see the Bible as a collection of stories about ethics governing how you could or should behave. I also understand how religion has been a well of strength for black peoples over hundreds of years through the most adverse conditions and heinous circumstances. Many times in the past, all people of colour have had is their faith, with the church at the centre of black communities when we needed it. I have a lot of respect for that view, and I also adore gospel music, which has so much life. Its foundation in blues is the basis for nearly all of the music and singers I love, from Sister Rosetta Tharpe, the Clarke Sisters, Billie Holiday and Aretha Franklin to Nina Simone and Stevie Wonder. I think if I'd been raised in a 'clap hand' church, where the congregation danced and sang from their souls, it would have changed the course of my life, and I probably wouldn't be a rock singer now, so I don't regret anything. But as a child, I had no real attachment or soulful connection to religion. We had to go to school five days a week, then church all day Sunday? It was too much, I resented it and I had no time for myself. As I reached my teens and asked questions, I was told I just had to 'believe'. My experience later fed into some of Skunk Anansie's most intense songs, like 'Selling Jesus' and 'God Loves Only You'. At fourteen years old, I was done. I simply refused to go one Sunday and, to my surprise, my mum didn't even argue with me. By then I had my own life, my own friends, and I was growing up.

The minute I was legally allowed to, I got a Saturday job. Pocket money was not my reality. That was a Hollywood thing I saw American kids get in films – if we wanted money we had to go out and earn it. So, at fifteen, I got my first job at Woolworths in Brixton, earning about £11 a day. You couldn't do much with that even in those days, so after a few months I went 'uptown' and got a job at British Home Stores (BHS) on Oxford Street, which was a real upgrade! Working at BHS was seen as the cream of the Saturday jobs because it was a nice department store with reasonable rates of pay. After a while I was promoted to running the home furnishings department, and my job was to make everything look beautiful on the shelves (otherwise known as folding towels all day). But everything changed when I quietly asked if it was necessary for BHS to keep selling a lot of South African goods during a boycott.

From 1948 to the early 1990s, the white supremacist culture of apartheid in South Africa ruled by a process of horrific racial segregation. It sparked global opposition and a trade boycott, and I thought anything that perpetuated the regime was very wrong. There was decades of resistance but police dealt with it in the most brutal way. In 1976, the government tried to impose the language of Afrikaans for teaching in schools. On 16 June that year, over 20,000 Soweto students began peacefully marching against that, and police opened fire on protestors. Many people were killed, including children. The official number of deaths was 176, with over a thousand wounded. I was only nine years old, but I can recall being so shocked by images of the Soweto uprising in the newspapers, and the fact that police killed unarmed schoolchildren, as I was just a schoolchild myself.

It was so easy for me to go to school in my uniform, getting a free education in safety, whereas if I had been born in South Africa that could have been me being killed. Remembering the Soweto uprising six years later, as a teenager, those images still haunted me and pushed me to support the boycott. The British Anti-Apartheid Movement had called for a consumer boycott since 1959, and by the early 1980s the boycott campaign was huge, with people refusing to buy Cape oranges or Outspan grapes in the supermarket, or South African brands at clothes shops like Next. Shops were picketed, and anti-apartheid stickers declaring 'DON'T BUY APARTHEID' or 'BOYCOTT SOUTH AFRICAN GOODS' were everywhere.

I went to my head of department and was sent up the chain to meet someone in management. I stated my case, and I was very polite about it: 'I identify with the boycott and, as a store that has so many black people working in it, we should support it.' I was a naïve, idealistic fifteen-year-old. I thought if I asked them, then maybe they will stop selling South African goods. They allowed me not to handle the goods, but still stocked them, of course, and after that the management were very wary and chilly towards me.

Because I felt less welcome after that, I left my £14 per Saturday BHS job and struck gold when I landed a Sunday job at B&Q and got paid double-time because it was a Sunday. Twenty-five pounds a day for a fifteen-year-old in the early '80s was good money. I was rich! I felt like Liberace! That's when I started going to clubs, heading up to the West End with my friends. You were meant to be eighteen, but the doormen didn't care as long as you dressed up. At the time, I thought it was because we looked so mature, but I looked nowhere near eighteen. I didn't even wear make-up. Now I know that young girls can always get into clubs, we were literally just prey for older men. We went to the Wag Club, danced to funk and soul upstairs at Ronnie Scott's, and to parties in Camden behind the market. In the summer there would be house parties all over London around the time of Notting Hill Carnival, with people from sound systems like Freshbeat, who would break into abandoned houses, steal the electricity from a lamppost and fling on a rave. I loved music, all music, and I loved to dance.

I went to Red Records on Brixton Road religiously and would just hang out in the shop. The guy running it was super-tall and friendly, and was the first person I could really discuss music with. He would play records for me to see what I liked, and test new tracks out on me. I was inspired, so I started writing lyrics to my own songs in a yuppie leather Filofax that someone had given me as a present. I'd work on my songs, singing different versions of them into my tape recorder, and when a song felt finished I'd rewrite a perfect, neat version on a page of A4, fold it into quarters and place it in the front pocket of my Filofax.

They were properly structured songs with the verses and choruses in the right place; tiny little pop songs questioning my life and what I was going to do with it. Songs about how odd I felt – but no love songs, and no rambling poetry. The choruses always had questions like, 'Where do I go from here?' They were more like a song diary of my life to that point – a little life, but it was a start. I worked hard on my secret songs and told no one I was writing them. I knew one day I would sing them to someone, but I wasn't ready just yet.

The first time I realised I had a good ear was during Christmas holidays in Jamaica one year, when I played a Christmas carol for Grandad Bertie's father. There was something magical about my great-grandad – he was the oldest person I knew, with no teeth, glistening eyes, a full head of snow-white hair, and he only ever wore pyjamas. He told me he loved the English carol 'Once in Royal David's City'. There was an old upright piano in the living room, so I recreated the carol from memory, secretly practising it every day, my left hand playing the bass notes, the right the melody. I played the piano and sang it for him on Christmas Day to make him happy. He loved it and gave me a toothless smile even when I hit bad notes.

If a child of mine did that, I'd be, 'Get that child some piano lessons!' but those were different times. My parents' generation was all about survival, getting food on the table and giving their children a better life, and music was not seen as a proper career. There wasn't the time to step back and take a look at your children and think, *What are they really good at?*

My musical journey started with some towering influences, like my first musical hero, Bob Marley. In the beginning God made reggae, and in my house there was no other sound. Alton Ellis, Dennis Brown, Third World, Peter Tosh, Ken Boothe, Jimmy Cliff – these were our idols, our titans, and Bob Marley was king of them all. My mum would play Marley *all* the time. My grandad knew him, and we were really proud of the fact that Jamaican reggae, our music from this tiny island in the Caribbean, was a sound that became huge all over the world.

The only other genre I remember where the groove was not on the offbeat was country music. Shock news: Jamaicans adore country! Check out the copious slide guitar on Bob Marley's records, for instance. My mum had a string-laden John Holt record called *1000 Volts of Holt*, which I must have heard a zillion times. I still love it, and it was only when I got older that I discovered his songs on that album were all covers. Country stars like Jim Reeves and George Jones would have huge worldwide hits, then Jamaican artists would cover them, but with a reggae drop for Jamaicans. Occasionally the original country version would be so juicy that Jamaicans would love that too. I remember 'Islands in the Stream' by Dolly Parton and Kenny Rogers being a Jamaican Number 1 for months, and my mum would play Tammy Wynette's 'Stand By Your Man' till the needle went on strike. And in the evenings we'd hear saxophonist Ace Cannon play 'last dance' covers of popular songs. It strikes me now that maybe that's where my hatred of the saxophone comes from, and I wonder, historically, if any other instrument has churned as much Stilton.

When we were kids we also loved watching *The Jackson 5ive* cartoon on telly. They were all so cute, and they were black! This was unheard of. We sang along to the songs and thought Michael Jackson was perfection. I was also mad about '70s boy band the Bay City Rollers, tartan-wearing Scottish boys with ankle-swinging trousers and funny accents, but I knew I was the only one of my friends that liked them, so I kept quiet about that. I convinced my mum to buy me a tartan scarf for £10. Imagine, this little black girl on her own with a tartan scarf, religiously watching *Top of the Pops* every Thursday at 7pm. I never missed it. For me it was like a window to another world – *Who are these people? What is this music? Why do they dress like that? They look so free.* I was fascinated because I hadn't seen anyone like that in my manor, so *Top of the Pops* became like a secret imaginary friend. Sometimes I would even talk to the telly. I loved Adam Ant but again I kept schtum about it because I knew my family and my crowd of black friends weren't into white pop stars and I'd definitely be teased; people might find out I was weird!

I'll never forget the first time I saw Blondie on *Top of the Pops* and Debbie Harry wearing that black-and-white striped dress. Something fizzed and popped in my brain. I must have been around eleven years old, thinking, *I wanna do that.* Whatever *that* was… I had no idea! I just knew I wanted to do what Blondie was doing, but my way. Why did Blondie do that to me and not Bob Marley? I guess reggae was too close, too familiar, and I knew instinctively that I didn't have a reggae voice. I wanted to create something completely different. I already knew I could sing, but watching Blondie was the first time I wanted to *be* a singer – she lit the spark!

I was always trying to develop my musical skills, and would have loved more tuition. For years I told everyone in my family I wanted a guitar, until one day, when I was fourteen, my mum's cousin turned up with an acoustic guitar for me. I was so excited, I couldn't believe it. I ran upstairs to play it but it had two strings missing and the machine heads were either stuck or broken, so it couldn't be tuned. I was gutted. I guess she didn't play guitar, so how would she have known it was broken, but I was so disappointed. I wanted that guitar to work so badly. I had all these dreams and ideas but I felt like I was invisible. It made me aware that whatever I wanted to be I was going to have to do it myself.

At St Martin's there was a very good music department and we were encouraged to take up an instrument because the school had a full orchestra. The choices were all classical, no guitars. I was desperate to play piano but there weren't many spaces, so I got stuck with the violin. At first, I hated it, but I still had to practise. For the first three years my playing sounded like a cat being skinned alive but, to the credit of my family, no one ever complained. I passed my grades and got quite good at it despite my brilliant but miserable tutor. Oh, she was awful! And clearly hated the job. I eventually became a soloist and was one of only five kids who played in the chamber group at the front of the orchestra. After six years I was pretty good, and had fallen completely in love with the instrument, but it got to the point where I had to buy my own violin and give mine up to a first-year student. I just couldn't afford it, so that was that. It wasn't until years later that it struck me what a wonderful training violin had given me. Having an instrument so close to my ear meant I had to hit the strings at the correct point, and that gave me an invaluable ear for tuning later on, and fuelled a love of orchestral music that has never left me.

After having to give up the violin, I began to work out how to take control of my life. My best friends were Carole Walker – the one with the lovely mum, who was a head girl like her brilliant older sister Viv – and a girl called Marie who was a bit of a school bully. They didn't get on at all, and it was like they represented the angel and the devil, reflecting two opposite parts of my character. Marie was naughty but charming, so we got on well. I had three brothers and was more than used to defending myself, so I guess she didn't smell any fear on me. Whenever I was around her, though, I seemed to get into trouble. There was a pear tree in the staff car park, and to get the fruit we had to climb up on a car to reach it. One day we were jumping up and down to reach the pears and, when we finished, we realised the whole of the car roof was sunken in. The teachers never caught us, they didn't know who it was, but they held a special assembly asking whoever had done it to own up. No one was going to tell on us because they knew Marie would have beaten them up. Marie and I would also sneak out a lot at lunchtimes to buy sweets from the corner shop, and one of the teachers would hide behind a car to try to catch us. At the time that seemed normal, but now the thought of a fully grown adult hiding behind a car to catch fourteen-year-old girls seems hilarious.

I chose my O level exam subjects thinking that I had to

grow up and start taking myself seriously or I would be stuck in Brixton. I had dreams. I was gonna leave and see what was beyond my Brixton bubble; be around people who didn't know me so that I could reinvent myself. I had to escape, and the only way I could do that was through education. I had a plan.

The first part of my plan was to choose my friends more wisely. Marie's reputation as a bully was getting worse, and I didn't want to be tainted by association. I spent more time with Carole and her mum, who as well as being a happy, warm, spirited lady was also a great chef. Mrs Walker had a small catering business that sold cakes and catered for mainly Caribbean weddings. Carole, my brother Nicholas and I worked as wedding waiters. The bride and groom would often order food for 250 people but then 400 would turn up. They'd expect her to provide all that extra food, last minute, at no extra cost, so it was always totally mad and loads of work, but Mrs Walker made it great fun. We'd predict the speeches, which were always the same ('I know she fram wen she was a lickle gurl . . .'), critique the dresses, try not to trip over fifty toddlers, and dance around in the kitchen to the classic songs at the end. The Walkers lived around the corner from me, so I'd go there sometimes after school and hang out. They were loving and fun, and always cracking jokes, especially Carole's quick-witted brother, Curtis Walker, who went on to become a highly respected actor and stand-up comedian.

The second part of my plan was to get good O levels, so I could go to college, then university, and then I could maybe make a living doing something creative like photography. I knew how to work hard and I had discipline. At school we had a careers officer, someone who was supposed to help you work out what you wanted to do with your life, then help you achieve it. Everyone was required to go to at least one session.

At the age of fifteen I loved photography. I had been developing my own film in the school darkroom, and I carried a camera around with me all the time, shooting anything that interested me. I also loved current affairs, and had this romantic, crazy image in my head of myself in a khaki jumpsuit being a foreign correspondent, jumping out of helicopters while dodging bullets, camera permanently on my shoulder, ready to film at a moment's notice.

I told this secret to the careers officer while she listened very carefully. *Great*, I thought. *She knows what I'm talking about.* I showed her all the information I'd collected about becoming a photojournalist or camerawoman, and when I finished talking she carefully put it to one side and slid an application form in front of me.

'While you're thinking about that, there's a full-time job going in Woolworths,' she said. 'They're looking for people like you. I'm sure you'll get it.'

I was astounded. I'd just poured out my dreams to her, the first person I'd told them to, thinking she understood me, but the whole time she was just waiting for the right moment to show me that Woolworths application form. I was hurt because I hadn't been listened to, I hadn't been seen and I knew exactly what she meant when she said 'people like you'. I knew all about Woothworths. I'd already had a Saturday job there. I picked up the form out of politeness, then left disgusted.

At that point I didn't think a career in music was an option. I didn't have the confidence. I had five O levels, but knew I needed more to go to a good university, so I opted to take three more, including Design Technology at Tulse Hill School, a boys' school with a mixed sixth form. I was the first girl ever to study it there, so it was a shock and a great feeling when I got an A and came top of the class. The subject felt brand new and exciting, and made me realise what I could achieve when I really enjoyed something. From there I studied for a diploma in Interior Design at the London College of Furniture on Commercial Road, east London. This was the beginning of my rebirth.

The first thing to change was my sense of style. I was raised a Christian, with a dress code that was smart, conservative and old fashioned – dresses that went all the way up to the neck, down to the wrists, and fell below the knee, topped with no make-up and a wet-look curly perm or straightened hair. It was important to look like a modest, perfectly behaved girl, which I was. We all bought our frilly church-friendly crêpe dresses from a shop in Brixton at the end of Railton Road. The dresses had pleats – the tinier the better. I had a white one that I wore to church and I hated it. Those tiny pleats were hell to iron. You had to try and line four of them up at once then make sure the iron was exactly the right temperature, but once you sat down they would crease and never fall the right way again. I hated that shop because the clothes made us all look the same. By this time, The Kids from *Fame* were on TV, and we were *obsessed*. We all wanted to be those leg-warmer-wearing, somersaulting dancers in the show. We also had our minds blown when Jeffrey Daniel of Shalamar body-popped on *Top of the Pops*. That was a revelation to us – a completely new style of music, fashion and dancing. The next day we were all trying to 'pop'. Watching this, we knew our *Stepford Wives*-style God dresses had to go!

College introduced me to proper fashion. I went from Christian gal to black soul-goth in about two weeks flat. I completely changed my look, wearing big, baggy yellow trousers with black detail, black crêpes, black socks and a black skinny T-shirt, and I cut my hair down to a flat top and put kohl round my eyes. I remember arriving home one day and my mum saying, 'What do *you* look like! Where you get dem colours from?'

'It's fashion, it's trendy.'

'I jus' don't understand dese kids . . .' she'd mutter to herself.

My personality was starting to come out. Christian clothing was no longer my style. I liked clothes that were functional, cool but with an edge. I would get them from Brixton and Roman Road markets, where they'd have all the designer copies. It was tat, but to a seventeen-year-old it was the top of the designer tree, the height of sophistication. I was really skinny, so I wore baggy clothes to cover myself up, especially my twiglet arms. Also, tight clothes weren't cool in our gang. I wasn't trying to be a 'sexy girl'. I liked club-boys with earrings and fluffy hair who did the latest moves. I didn't want to look like a Page 3 model and get attention from the kind of man who'd catcall you when you walked down the street.

I became the DJ at college discos, mixing all kinds of records from my collection, from indie bands like The Cure to soul music and New Romantic pop. I got the job because I had the biggest record collection and I played all kinds of tracks to keep everyone happy, not just the soul heads. My yellow brick road to rock started with ska-flavoured bands like The Specials, The Beat and The Selecter. Ska was familiar music to me – Prince Buster was the soundtrack to my nappy changes – but those 2 Tone bands from Birmingham and Coventry sped it up to sound punkier and a bit nutty. They all had something strange going on: The Specials were darker and political, The Beat had that driving eighth-note bassline, and The Selecter had Pauline Black in a suit. But what really caught my interest were the guitar riffs, with an edge that was different from sounds I was used to. They had a prominent, stabbing melody, and they weren't just about showing off chops and musical virtuosity.

In the world I came from there were strict divisions between black music and other genres, with little diversity. Radio was king but we only listened to pirate radio where DJs chatted all over the tracks, triggered sound effects like car horns and explosions, and, of course, gave the classic shout, 'Rewind!' *Just play the record, mate*, I used to think. If you were black, you listened to soul, funk, reggae and David Rodigan, but *Top of the Pops* had shown me there was another world out there, and I was itching to get at it and make my way.

Despite my changing image, and the opening up of my world through music, at that time I had no inkling about my sexuality. I had crushes on boys and went on a date when I was fifteen with a sweet white church boy. We went to see a film, but then he never asked me out again. We liked each other but my mum said his dad had made a funny comment about us; he didn't like the match. Mixed-race relationships then were out of the ordinary, and we didn't have a strong enough attraction to fight for it. I was over-conscious that people were staring at us and not in a good way. It was more usual to see a black man with a white woman, but highly unusual the other way round, so he was quite brave.

My first real boyfriend was a Jamaican guy called Tony, who

was twenty-nine and a lot older than me. I was seventeen when we met, at the Pentecostal church. Every time I went to a service he stalked me so that afterwards, wherever I was, he would find me and start chatting. He got round my mum one night by giving us a lift home, so he knew where we lived. He then just turned up at our house one day with his car and said, 'Let's go somewhere.' I felt I had to be polite, that I couldn't say no, and that's how our relationship began. I guess he fell for me, but in the weirdest way he never expressed any love towards me, yet he wanted to buy a house, get married and have kids but without me having any choice or opinion about it. He seemed to think my thoughts on the matter were irrelevant.

I had rebelled against my strict Christian upbringing by changing my image. I was buying my own clothes and my mum couldn't tell me what to do anymore. But it was harder to rebel against Tony because he was twelve years older than me, and was very sure of himself, very possessive and much more intimidating.

During weekdays, at the London College of Furniture, I felt free to explore my new self, but at weekends when I saw Tony I softened my appearance. A change of look can happen quickly, but changing on the inside is a more gradual process. On the outside, I was a trendy college student, but in my head I was still the good Christian girl wanting to keep everyone happy. As I look back, I know that I had zero interest in Tony. The fact was I didn't know how to say no to him; it was that simple. We didn't do anything or go anywhere, and I don't recall him ever taking me to a restaurant or a movie like normal couples. He'd pick me up from my home in Brixton, drive me all the way to north London, and we'd watch telly in his room. That was our relationship. I was so meek I didn't have any voice at all.

One of the most important people in my life at the time was my dear friend Susan Okukenu, who has since sadly died of lung cancer. She was a little older than me; she had a lovely daughter called Michelle, so she was also wiser. I learnt a lot from her. She was no-nonsense, incredibly funny and totally non-judgemental. I remember once going out clubbing with her and our other friend (also called Michelle) not long after I met Tony. While they were on the dancefloor, a guy sat next to me and put his arm round me, trying to kiss me. Susan stomped over to us and slapped his hand out the way.

'You don't have to just *let* them!' she said to me.

'I didn't know what to do,' I said.

'You can say no.'

'I can?'

I didn't realise you could say no. I thought it was rude and that men would get angry with me. The idea that I could say no was a revelation!

One night, when I was out with Tony, we had a fierce row over the fact that I wanted to enter a dance competition with a boy from college. Tony told me I couldn't go, so I said, 'Why not? I can do what I want!' He drove me to an isolated car park, somewhere no one could hear us, and he punched me.

'See, no one can hear you scream here,' he said.

I looked at him in pure shock. I could not actually bloody believe it. Then, *BAM!* He punched me again, full fist, straight in the face. I was in such a rage it didn't even really hurt. Instead my brain buzzed, in simultaneous guilt and rage. *How the hell did I get here?* I thought. *How did I not see this coming?* I wanted

to scream, 'FUCK YOU! You will NEVER touch me again!'
But then it hit me that I was in trouble and I had to get myself
out of it. I thought, *What would Susan do? Say nothing, be clever,*
wait for your moment.

My survival instincts kicked in and I didn't cry, I didn't react.
He drove out of the car park and, when he stopped at the traffic
lights, I opened the car door, jumped out and ran. It was midnight, and I had no idea where I was. After a while I found a
bus stop where I could catch a bus back to Brixton, and that's
where he caught me. Bystanders watched as his car screeched
to a halt, then he got out and chased me down before I was
bundled into the car and driven back to his house. Now I was
in dangerous trouble, but to my surprise he changed tack and
started crying and apologising. I guess he realised he'd have to
either kill me or take me home. He couldn't leave me on my
doorstep all battered and bruised because I had family; there
would be consequences.

'I'm not going to do it again, forgive me,' he wailed.

'Just take me home,' I muttered. I repeated those same four
words for three hours until he had to take me home. I didn't tell
my mum. I was too ashamed – I had let some deadbeat put his
hands on me – but from that night my relationship with Tony
was done. This was the first time any man hit me like that and
I knew it must also be the last. I knew that I had to make a
choice. I saw it all laid out in front of me and decided I wanted
no part of it; marriage to Tony was not going to be my life. It
was time to escape him, and that meant getting as far away from
home as possible.

FOUR

MILK IS MY SUGAR

So here I stand, stand, s-t-a-n-d
So here I stand, stand, s-t-a-n-d . . .

'Here I Stand'

I have to be honest, I was never really into dancehall. In the mid–1980s that scene was a bit rough and the dance moves were 'dutty'. Also, I was a bit too young and innocent in the head for dancehall lyrics. Those choppy snares and ragga bass grooves were part of a new fresh style of reggae that came straight from the shanty towns of Kingston, Jamaica and everyone in London was going crazy for it. But my brother Beavon kinda put me off dancehall because in summer he would be out all night with Sir Lloyd, having a party, toasting on the mic before coming home and playing the tapes he'd recorded at full volume all day without a break. It drove me mad, and as we were now older and mouthy, we'd argue all the time. By then I was nineteen, had finished my diploma at the London College of Furniture, with grades I was proud of, and was going off to Teesside. The day I was leaving we had a huge physical fight and I got thrown down the stairs. I can think of better send-offs, and I was very happy to leave.

I ended up in Middlesbrough, at Teesside Polytechnic, in 1986, doing an honours degree in Interior Architecture and Design. At its height, in the early 1900s, Teesside Steelworks in North Yorkshire had over ninety-one blast furnaces and was one of the largest steel producers in the world, but by the 1980s, Teesside was a post-industrial area in decline. However, I loved being there, and it was a joy and a relief to be away from Tony. I felt free to reinvent myself again. I was five hours away from London and nobody knew who I was. Nobody knew my background, and I could be who I wanted to be.

I moved into halls of residence but lasted only a few weeks. It was gross and manic and full of excitable eighteen-year-olds who had never done the washing up. Me and my brothers would get a tongue-lashing if we didn't clean up after ourselves. Our Mum would say, 'You tink you have slaves in here?' I couldn't cope. Every time I went to make something to eat the kitchen was trashed and someone had eaten all my food. I moved out and rented my first crappy student house with three friends I met in the first week.

In my second year, I moved into 21 Romney Street with my new friends Patrick and Deborah, who were of Caribbean descent, and Kiran, whose parents were from India. The place was freezing and falling to pieces, and I'd often wake up in my ground-floor room to a carpet covered in slug trails. One night, desperate for the loo, I stepped on a giant slug and it squelched between my toes in long green tubes. I think that's the night

I became a soprano. After that, I made myself a salt path every night to dispose of them. As young, first-time tenants, we had no idea that we could complain – we had to pay the whole term's rent up front, so we had no leverage at all. God, it was awful, but we loved having our independence.

We housemates were so lucky to have found each other. They were three of the loveliest people you could have imagined, and without them life at university would have been a lot less enjoyable – we are still friends now. We noticed that African students in particular weren't very well looked after, and found England a culture shock and a hard transition, so we invited them to our parties. We started a Saturday night club at our house, with food, music and chatter. In those days, Middlesbrough could be scary for us students of colour, and we learnt very quickly how to stay safe. We all had racist abuse shouted at us in the street, and knew not to go to any local clubs, especially the black guys, who would never be let in anyway – only the Students' Union was safe for us. I remember walking along the street one day with a friend, and a guy shouted from a car window: 'Fucking monkey, go back to where you came from!'

I turned to my friend and laughed out loud. 'Monkey! He called me a monkey!' I retaliated: 'Nineteen fifty-two called . . . it wants its wanker back!' At the time, Middlesbrough was old-school backwards racism, whereas racism in the college environment itself was subtler – more about being perceived as different, part of a minority. On the interior design floor I was the only black girl on the course. That was why we started our occasional Friday dinners or Saturday night parties, to create a feeling of solidarity.

I passed my first year comfortably, but in my second year I relaxed and spent more time on my social life than my studies. I got called in by the head of department – a dry, sour man I found intimidating.

'You're only here as an experiment,' he said. 'You'd better buck up!'

As the only black student on the course, I knew what he meant. In those days there was no one to complain to, and if I had I would have been kicked off the course. My friend and housemate Deborah, who also went to the London College of Furniture, and joined the course a year after me, told me recently that the same tutor gave her such a hard time, down-grading her marks and saying her work wasn't 'ethnic enough'. In the end she had to leave Teesside, and said she was trauma-tised for years.

My new friends were a lifeline – they were all students from different countries who didn't know how to blend in with the 95 per cent white student body. Now we were looking after each other. On those Saturday nights everyone would make a dish and bring something to drink, and Patrick and I would DJ. In the end, our parties became so big we had complaints about the noise, and had to stop, but it provided a good support network and was great fun while it lasted. We went everywhere together. Patrick remembers that we were always dressed to the nines, like we had to make a statement everywhere we went.

I loved Middlesbrough. On the surface it was a grey, run-down northern town, but underneath it had a vibrant artistic culture surrounded by beautiful countryside. It was a small place, so I got to know it well and it felt like a home from home. I also loved my course. Teesside Polytechnic had cutting-edge software and design technology. Everything was fresh and new. I was discovering ideas in art, design and computing at the same time as developing my personality and learning who I was emotionally. My first reinvention of self had been at the London College of Furniture, where I'd studied for my Interior Design diploma and had become a soul-goth; and my second reinvention was at Teesside, where I realised I was a performer and where I also discovered my sexual identity.

In my second year I was heavily involved with the Students' Union and became Entertainments Officer, booking bands and DJs. I was always listening to music on my Walkman and would sing walking along the corridor between courses. Word spread that I could hold a tune, so I started getting offers to sing. A student jazz pianist asked me to sing jazz standards so he could practise his piano, and we would rehearse in a hall on campus. After a solid year of bugging from a guitarist friend, I also joined a covers band, a jazz/soul septet we named JASS. We practised with lesser-known songs like 'Blind' by Talking Heads, Rufus and Chaka Khan's 'Stop On By' and Hue and Cry's version of Prince's 'Kiss'.

Our first gig was in the Students' Union – it my first time on stage and it was terrifying. As I looked out to the packed crowd, all there to check out the Student Union band, every part of me was shaking. Because I was so nervous at first, I forgot all the words to the songs and just made up the lyrics. For our Talking Heads cover, for instance, I just sang, 'I'm blind, I'm blind' over and over because it was the only part of the song I remembered. Once I got over my nerves, though, watching that big crowd of drunken students dancing and jumping up and down, I thought, *I could get used to this.* We did a few more gigs in the Union and I played with the jazz pianist one night in a local club in Middlesbrough. I got a taste for being onstage ... and it was *sweet*.

As well as making music, I became involved with Student Union politics – whether it was going on anti-apartheid demonstrations or protesting about things closer to home, on campus. My friends and I were idealistic, wanting to change the world for the better. I clashed with members of the rugby club a lot – guys who stuck naked pin-ups from the *Sun* newspaper on the walls of the Interior Design department. All the girls hated it, and asked for the pictures to be taken down. We complained to the tutors but they did nothing, and in fact a couple of them were very creepy, saying the pictures weren't doing any harm. Eventually I got fed up with it, so one day I tore them all down, saying, 'This room is supposed to be for everybody. I don't want to see that.'

Over the space of a week, every time the boys put them up I'd tear them down again. In the end they stopped putting them up, but I earned the nickname 'Red', after the Russian communist flag, just because I didn't want their sexist pictures on the wall.

The rugby club were always up to no good doing something racist or sexist, dismissing any objections by saying, 'We don't mean it, we're just having fun.' One night they had a 'slave market' party off campus, with students dressing women up as slaves in blackface and being 'auctioned off' for a joke, so a group of us from the Students' Union picketed it. I stood outside the event holding a banner and shouting through a megaphone: 'Don't go in! This demeans women!' I was arrested for disturbing the peace, then put in a police cell for a few hours, and was later fined £200, which was infuriating considering the rugby club had been the intolerable ones.

As part of my reinvention of self, in my second year I also sampled Middlesbrough gay culture. I was still naïve when it came to relationships. I'd never heard the word 'gay' until I was fifteen. At Sunday school I'd read something in Leviticus about men lying with other men, thinking, *Well, that's just silly, who's going to do that?* Then I read the next verse about men lying with animals, and I thought, *They're just making it all up now.* It was just not in my mindset; as a kid these things were alien to me. In the 1980s, so many people were homophobic, and the prevailing view was, 'Ugh, that's gross, that's disgusting'. Lesbian relationships were invisible in society and the media, so there were very few out role models. During my first year at Teesside, I had a crush on a girl, but I didn't take it seriously, thinking it was just a phase and would pass. I was also getting a fair bit of attention from boys, which I liked.

In my second year I fancied another girl, a rugby player, but this time the feelings didn't pass and my 'crush' went on for the whole year, to the extent that it became very distracting. I didn't know what to do with my emerging feelings. One day I was sitting with some friends and they were discussing whether someone we knew was gay. Halfway through the conversation I suddenly felt a surge of white-cold heat from my chest to my head. I stood up, ran home and shut the door. *Gay . . . was I gay? I can't be*, I thought. *I like boys.* But the thought was now in my consciousness. I had a rush of memories. It was like that scene at the end of *The Usual Suspects* when special agent Dave Kujan drops the cup as he realises suspect Verbal's been lying to him the whole time. Was I lying to myself? I had to rethink my whole story. The evidence of my gay identity was there the whole time. How could I have been so stupid! The crush on the girl in my first year, the female rugby player in my second year, Pauline Black in a suit! I mulled it over for weeks, then decided I needed to confide in someone – someone who was also gay, bisexual, whatever I was. Someone not straight. So, one night I confessed to my friend Liz Daniels, who was head of the Students' Union. 'I think I'm gay,' I said.

She looked at me deeply. 'OK, come with me.'

We went out of the Union, down the road and knocked on her friend's door, a woman called Avril, who was an older lesbian.

'Meet my friend,' said Liz. 'She thinks she's gay.'

With that, I stepped through the looking glass into a completely different Middlesbrough. Avril was absolutely lovely. She took me under her wing, introducing me to all these other gay girls, and took me to the only gay club in Middlesbrough, a place that was open only at weekends. You had to bang on the door, a slide would go across a little window, and a suspicious eye would check you out and, if they didn't know you, that was it – they wouldn't let you in. It was like something out of a prohibition movie, as if the place was illegal and could get raided at any time.

It was rough – a dirty dive full of creatures of the night, with a small bar and a dancefloor. It felt like heaven. Friday night was mixed gay night, and the place would be full of all types of queers and other outcasts. I'd never seen anything like it. It was proper *ole skool*, with all the different gay subcultures together in one club. The girls were super girly, all heels and long hair with a red lip, and the butches were decked out in checked shirts and crew cuts, holding onto one beer all night with an ''ello gorgeous' smirk on their faces. The boys were either camp-as-Christmas high-pitched screamers, muscle Marys or Tom of Finland leather daddies. I do remember trans folk being there too – they were the nicest, always ready for a chat and a laff. Don't forget, this was Middlesbrough 1987 – they would have been risking their lives just stepping out the door. Personally I wasn't really into the butch or femme thang, and none of the girly girls or butchie butches looked like me. I was obviously a student, and the only one in there, so I guess I was in my own category, which was southern student tosser! The locals *hated* students – *hated* anyone from down south – but being black and with friends who were locals, I slipped in through the gay crack.

My experiences in Middlesbrough made me feel adventurous, so when I went back to Brixton for the summer holiday, I decided to try the London gay scene. I'd heard about Venus Rising, a legendary lesbian party at the Fridge nightclub, just down the road from my mum's house, which drew two thousand women every month. I tried to get a friend to come with me, but she said, 'Nah, I think it's all women,' so I went on my own, feeling shy and petrified. I walked in, got a drink and hid in a corner for two hours, watching all these gay women laughing, chatting and dancing. After about three vodkas, I felt stronger and went on the dancefloor, but kept my back to the DJ booth. Some girls noticed me and started chatting me up, and I swapped numbers with them.

With my new friends I slowly eased myself into the gay community that summer, getting invites to gay house parties in the local area. I heard from a friend that Venus Rising was looking for all-female security staff, so I joined the security team as a bouncer. Although I was still a little shy, and not a typical bruiser bouncer, growing up with three brothers meant I knew how to break up a fight. From afar my shyness could be mistaken for arrogance or over-confidence. The first night I was there, a tough-looking woman came up to me and said sneeringly, 'What do you need to work here, then?'

Putting on my best James Bond face, I fibbed, 'Three black belts.' I hadn't done any martial arts, but she looked shocked and wandered off. She must have told everyone because after that I was always instantly obeyed and continued working as a bouncer during the holidays.

My world was opening up. Back in Teesside, I made friends with women who worked at the Rape Crisis Centre, and I went there after hours a few times to help out with social events. I learnt so much in conversations there, absorbing new ideas about abuse, with women seeing themselves as survivors and not victims. I realised that abuse was not only about physical violence, and I heard terminology I hadn't previously been aware of. I thought back to my relationship with Tony, and how he used fear to control and dominate me, making it difficult for me to draw boundaries with him. Knowledge gave me strength, and now I had words to define what had happened to me, which I found very healing.

My social life was exciting but it didn't help me with my degree. At the end of the first year I had been top of the class, but by the end of my second I was swimming around the bottom, so it was indeed time to 'buck up'. In my final year I worked hard in pursuit of a good grade. For our final-year project we had to redesign a whole building, so I chose the legendary Bon Marché on Brixton Road. Opened in 1877 as the UK's first purpose-built department store, it was modelled on the Bon Marché in Paris, and in the 1920s was an upmarket store with more than forty-eight departments. By the late 1980s it was an indoor market operating at a loss and in need of regeneration. Being a local, I had the added advantage of blagging my way in to get special 'behind the scenes' access to help with my floor-plans. I reinvented it for my project, adding restaurants, a radio station and a community recording studio.

That project helped me get a good degree, and after I graduated I came back to London and got a job with an office design company called Interex as a design assistant. This was right at the end of the Canary Wharf building boom, when London Docklands was being redeveloped. I was good at putting together beautiful mood boards that showed exactly what an interior would look like, including samples of flooring, furniture, wall colours and even plants. I made the interiors look exciting to clients, but really it involved very little actual design, and was more about space-planning, seeing how many desks you could fit into a room. These boards would be shown in meetings to new clients who tended to be male, white and suited up. After a while they let me come into the meetings to present the projects myself, but whenever they had a question they'd ask my boss, who was white, who would then ask me, as I had the answers, which she would then repeat. That used to drive us crazy – again I felt invisible, just like I had as a child, and she hated it as much as I did.

By then I had left home and was living at No.1 St Matthew's Road, a house owned by St Matthew's Church and run by Tom Minney, whom I'd known from childhood. I had come back to Brixton after Teesside because it felt like home, but I also had my independence. 'Number One' (as we called it) was in the heart of Brixton, next to the vicarage, with eight massive bedrooms and only one bathroom right at the top of the house. In the late 1980s, the house was run down and in need of restoration, and Tom, who was on the church council at the time, offered to renovate it and make it available to African and black British students as a cost-effective way of living in London.

Tom was a journalist in his early thirties who had loads of energy and a huge kind heart. He was always smiling and cracking jokes, and when anyone was unhappy he'd charm them into forgetting their troubles. The place was full of Namibian refugees and black activists, and was a hive of political activity. This was when South Africa was still driven by the apartheid regime, controlling Namibia on its southern border, and somehow all the South West Africa People's Organisation (SWAPO) activists knew about our house in Brixton. A lot of Namibians who came to stay were students, and our house became legendary as a place to hang out and learn about the world. It became so famous that someone from Namibia even asked how they could apply to 'The University of Number One'!

The Africans were always cooking and organising, and there was usually a giant pot on the hob with something tasty bubbling away in it. People would pop in to discuss politics and eat fufu, African cassava or yam dumplings. It was very democratic living there – everyone contributed to the cleaning, cooking and washing up. We produced newsletters in the basement, and the whole kitchen was regularly full of banners because we were always going on a demonstration somewhere. There was a continuous anti-apartheid protest outside the South Africa House in Trafalgar Square. Students from Number One would go there to hand out leaflets, sing freedom songs and get the public to sign petitions calling for the release of Nelson Mandela who, as leader of the ANC, had been a political prisoner since 1962.

I remember Margaret Thatcher implied at a press conference at the 1987 Commonwealth summit in Vancouver that Nelson Mandela was a terrorist because she said the ANC was a terrorist organisation. I was really appalled by that, disgusted to the core. She and her husband Dennis had investments in South Africa and were friends with President Botha – under his leadership in the 1970s and 1980s thousands of people had been tortured, killed or detained without trial – so I wondered how anyone could support her as prime minister.

Some years later, I would go on a trip to Namibia to visit Tom, when he was then working for the newly independent government, and I would also meet Mandela after he became South Africa's first black president. But in 1989, I had no idea what my future would be.

FIVE

AUTUMN LEAVES

I'll be your sailor girl
I'll tip my cap to your parade
Life won't be dreary no
I'll be the waves inside your bed

'I Can Dream'

From the outside it looked like I had it all. I had a great job in a London design company, money in my pocket, and I was young and ready to take on the world. But in reality I was dying inside – this was not the life I wanted. I had put singing and songwriting on hold in my final year at Teesside while I focused on my degree, but back in London I grew obsessed with it again. I resolved in the autumn of 1989 to become a singer, and once I made that decision I realised that every hour I spent not doing that was a wasted hour.

I started looking at myself properly in the mirror: *what's wrong with me, why do I feel so awkward?* I took my head-wrap off. I had never been happy about my hair. By then I was wearing headscarves all the time because I didn't know what to do with it, and had no interest in spending time worrying about it. My old school friend Carole was going out with a guy named David, and one day he had a pair of hair clippers with him.

'Can you shave off all my hair?' I asked.

'I'll shave it down for you,' he said, 'but I'm not shaving it all off.'

I protested until he shaved off most of my afro, which at that time was a sad, grown-out curly perm. 'Lower, make it lower,' I said, and one more layer was gone. 'C'mon, David, take it down to the skin!' He was horrified, then point-blank refused.

'I'm just gonna go to the barbers,' I declared. And I went the next day. I *begged* them to shave my hair off, and reluctantly they did. I looked in the mirror, and for the first time in my life I loved what I saw.

I'd found myself. Once I'd shaved my head people would look at me, so I had to be confident, to let go of my shyness, and a bold new me emerged. Every time I went to the barbers they whined and complained. They were from a different era: 'C'mon, baby, you mus' leave a lickle 'fro fe de man dem' – they figured I wouldn't catch a boyfriend with such short hair – so eventually I bought a pair of clippers and learnt how to do it myself, backwards in a hand mirror, and I haven't needed a barber since.

I found my new look at the same time as I met my first proper girlfriend. I'll call her Sabrina. She was my first love and I was obsessed. First loves are awful: you don't have the mental tools to cope; you give every last tiny drop of yourself to the other person, and the relationship, and you believe with all your heart that it will last forever. When it doesn't work you're devastated, because you held nothing back, and so you have nothing left.

I met Sabrina at a party in Brixton in the summer of 1989. She came up to me and said hi but I was distracted. A few weeks later I got invited to a 'girl-party' on a council estate in Surrey Quays, south-east London. I walked into the living room and there she was, lounging, gorgeous, on the sofa. Sabrina confessed to me later that she had set the whole thing up. She got me invited to the party and waited for me in the perfect pose and perfect outfit. She was very cute – skinny with hazel eyes and long plaits. We exchanged numbers and began some sort of a relationship, though I never quite felt she was mine. She was slippery like an eel. She was an eternal rubberneck, always looking over my shoulder for the next prize until someone else showed interest in me, then she'd claim me.

It's hard to recall the positives about our relationship because it was laden with drama. We'd go out to clubs and have fun but she'd be flirting with someone else, and I'd walk around, chasing her round the club. When I was with Sabrina I felt stressed and anxious, always trying to get her approval. I was emotionally a lot younger than my years. After a while, but too late for my aching heart, I discovered she had a much older suga-mama in north London. In spite of this, I didn't split up with Sabrina because I was in too deep. I was consumed.

Sabrina used to smoke a ton of weed, always by herself, as I don't smoke. She talked a lot about writing a book. Every last detail was discussed, intellectually breaking down every article or book she was currently immersed in, and how and why hers would be better. But she had no discipline and could never stick to anything. She once told me that if she didn't feel like going to school, her mum would say, 'Just stay home, then.' For me it was the polar opposite: we *always* had to go to school and be on time. That was non-negotiable even when we were sick.

After about six months, with my help, Sabrina managed to move into Number One when a room became vacant. She was upstairs and I was in a room downstairs. One day, I got bored of all the chat with no action, so I said, 'Let's do a five-year plan.' My plan was to write better songs, put a band together and get a record deal. I had no idea how I was going to do it, so step one of my plan was to find a manager. I can't remember all the details of her plan but there was definitely an incredible book at the end of it. Straight away I started working on my plan by writing songs and hanging out in places where I thought other musicians and managers would be.

By then I no longer worried what others thought of my musical tastes. From my DJ stint at college, to my role booking bands as ENTS Officer at Teesside, I discovered all types of music, from A-ha to Aerosmith. I would read the *NME* and *Melody Maker* religiously every week. On evenings and weekends I sang with a jazz band from east London I'd met through an advert in the *NME* classifieds. I would also do small gigs with the band's guitarist in local bars like the Brixtonian. I learnt jazz standards like 'Autumn Leaves' and 'Summertime' that were a good grounding for my voice, teaching me how to sing properly. I learnt to sing by listening to the greats: people like Sarah Vaughan, Ella Fitzgerald, Nat King Cole and Dinah Washington; singers who had big, thick voices, wonderful phrasing and voice control, one-take kings and queens. I'd sing in my house, my kitchen, the street, everywhere. I wrote songs all the time, dissecting those I heard on the radio, copying the structure: verse, chorus, verse, middle eight, out. I recorded some melodies on my tape recorder, because my head was bursting with tunes.

After work I was a different person. I was out nearly every night, and there was always something exciting going on that I had to be in the middle of. With no social media and no mobile phones, everything was done via word of mouth. If you weren't in the know, you weren't cool enough, and if you didn't look good you weren't getting in. To find out where the best parties were, you had to be part of every scene. All the info was in your head. You had everyone's phone numbers memorised, you remembered addresses, you knew where all the clubs were, who had the best house parties, and how to get in for free. You could always find your friends, as they were usually in the same corners of the same clubs, bars and parties. I didn't drink that much, so I thought pubs were boring. We'd go to three venues in one night, so the thought of sitting in one place the whole evening talking to the same people? No way!

One evening, after a gig, a guy came up to me in the Brixtonian. 'We have a small label, and I'd like to talk about signing you,' he said. I thought, *It won't hurt me to go for a meeting*, so I met him with his two friends. They wanted me to do demos, and made me sign a couple of pages, but even though I didn't know anything about the business, they were nice guys, so I naively thought, *Why not?* They hired a little recording studio upstairs in Bon Marché and got me working with an engineer, but I quickly realised the guys had a lot of talk and didn't really know anything about making music. The engineer knew how to work the gear in the studio but it was all stock computer tones that made my songs sound middle of the road and bland, like cheap bananas with no flavour. I had no idea how to get the sound I wanted, but I knew enough to realise they didn't sound right. I didn't know how to use the microphone, and the sound that we ended up with wasn't soulful or black or white – it was like generic elevator music.

Those early studio experiences were constructive because they showed me how much I didn't know. I felt helpless trying to create my own musical sound and style, and I didn't like that. I hated not knowing how any of the gear worked. My instincts told me to get out of that record deal. I didn't know *how* I was going to do it; I just knew that I definitely needed a manager, and a good one.

I heard about a really popular club called Singers, near Tottenham Court Road, that was run by the musician Jeb Milne (who sadly died in 2013). You could put your name down, then give your music to the pianist and go up on stage and sing. It was a relaxed, buzzy atmosphere with lots of industry people getting drunk and having fun and looking for the next big thing. I went to Singers one night in early summer 1990. There were some amazing vocalists in the room, but I was determined to stand out. I had no cleavage and was as skinny as a plank, so I played that up by wearing a tight black catsuit, a short brown suede waistcoat that had tassels down to the floor, and high-heeled boots. My head was clean-shaven and my eyes lined with thick black kohl. I knew I looked good.

A handsome boy with long blond wavy hair and bright blue eyes came up to me and said eagerly, 'Are you going to sing tonight?'

'Yeah.'

'Okay, great.'

Then he wandered off. I kept my eye on him, but after a while I saw him leave. I was disappointed because I thought he might be someone I needed to impress. I felt deflated, but by then it was 2am and my turn to sing. I felt terrified and was physically shaking. I had awful stage fright but, if I really wanted to be spotted by a potential manager, I knew I would have to get onstage and do my thing. As I stepped into the lights everyone stopped talking and looked at me. *Shitttt,* I thought. My song was 'Autumn Leaves', the jazz classic. The pianist tapped out the first few intro notes, the whole room was quiet, expectant. I was so nervous I sang the first four lines really badly and everyone went back to their conversations. I knew I'd lost the room. I felt I had captured the crowd's attention with my look and now I was sure they were thinking, *She looks good but she can't sing.* I took a deep breath – I knew I could do better. I had to get the room back. So I closed my eyes and just went for it, and sang like I'd never sung before. At the end I got a standing, cheering ovation. It was my *A Star Is Born* moment, like a Disney movie on steroids.

As soon as I finished, a serious-looking young woman came up to me. She had a short red bob, kind hazel eyes and a pretty face that was set to intense. She got straight to the point and said, 'Do you have a manager?' She didn't say her name.

'No,' I said. 'But I'm looking for one.'

'Let's meet up tomorrow.'

We met up the next day at the Brixtonian. Her name was Leigh Johnson, and she was very different to anyone else I'd met in the music business. She was young, determined, driven and resolute. Right from the beginning she outlined exactly what she was going to do – no bullshit, no wasting time. I was very impressed. Leigh had begun her career in the A&R department at CBS Records, working with legendary producer Muff Winwood before branching out into management and working with artists like Neneh Cherry and Massive Attack. The boy with the blue eyes who had approached me at Singers club was Len Aaron, an aspiring guitarist, songwriter and soundtrack composer whom she was managing. She wanted me to team up with him. I liked her chat and said, 'Let's try it, then.'

We got off to a rocky start. I was way too chilled and undisciplined at first, turning up late every time we arranged to meet. Eventually, after arriving two hours late one day, she lost it with me.

'This isn't going to work,' she shouted. 'If this is the way you're going to carry on, I won't be able to work with you!'

I was shocked, but not intimidated, as I was raised in a blast-zone at home, and I just thought, *She's not my mother, she can't beat me!* In fact, I liked it, thinking, *She cares about me.* But it was a turning point, and it was the last time I was deliberately late. I didn't mess Leigh around again like that, and she's been my manager ever since.

The first thing Leigh did was help me get out of the record deal with the guys from Bon Marché, which freed me up to do session work and songwriting with Len. I was rapidly losing interest in my day job, and it showed in the clothes I was wearing. At first I was a proud, smart office worker in beautifully ironed crisp white shirts tucked into skinny jeans, or a 'sexy secretary' pencil skirt and a tiny heel. As I didn't drive, I had a company moped instead of a company car, so I had all the gear for that too. But after a few months I was called into the office to see the big boss. He was a proper East End type with a Tom Selleck *Magnum* moustache and a no-nonsense gruff but kind voice.

'What the heck are you wearing?' he asked.

I looked down and realised I had on a huge blue-green headscarf, big hooped earrings, a long red tank top that hit me mid-thigh, no bra, about twenty bangles on each arm and a pair of multicoloured ring-tights, which ended in unlaced Timberlands. I could see his point, though in my defence I had come straight from a club!

That summer I was headhunted by another interior design firm, so I left work early one afternoon and did a great interview with them, but on my way home afterwards I felt depressed. *What am I doing?* I thought. *This is gonna be a better job – why am I not excited about it? It's because it's not what I want to do. I don't want another design job . . . I want to make music!*

I realised that I had to give music all my time and attention. The job was paying my rent and bills, but I knew it was a safety net that was in reality holding me back. I told myself, *I've been the good girl, I've earned the money, I'm educated, I've got my degree. I'm going to stop doing things because I should and start doing things because I want to.* So I left my job and I didn't take the other one I'd been offered.

I had quite a striking look, with my shaved head and androgynous club style, so Leigh helped me get session work to put some coins in my pocket. I joined two other shaven-headed black girls and started doing backing vocals for UK soul artists Diana Brown & Barrie K. Sharpe. I did a short UK tour with them, which led to more session TV work on shows hosted by

Jonathan Ross and, my favourite, *Top of the Pops*. I even did brief stints modelling. I was writing and working hard with Len, but just when I began to get into my groove, something happened that stopped me in my tracks.

SIX

MAMA WILD

You're too cool to be smart, but that is what you are
You're too sane to be hard, but that is what you are ...
You don't have to run
You got to rise up, sweet woman child

'Rise Up'

My girlfriend Sabrina's book never materialised. In the end she ditched me and ran off with a poet. She was a mature, charismatic and talented orator who wrote the most succulent poetry. Looking back, I think Sabrina was always searching for someone to give her the life she wanted instead of creating it herself. I think the affair was one of those open secrets where everyone knows but you. If I'm honest, I had a feeling there was something going on, but I was blinded by love and so refused to see what was right in front of me. I mean, shit happens, but at the time I was devastated. I wrote the words to 'Hedonism', crying at 4am, reflecting on our relationship and her unfaithfulness.

The lyrics were bitter and a bit harsh but that's how I felt. Writing it was cathartic.

> *Just because you feel good*
> *Doesn't make you right.*
> *Just because you feel good*
> *Still want you here tonight . . .*

Being unfaithful is a kind of hedonism. You're so in the moment, feeling so good you just don't care about anything else. Years later, in 1997, 'Hedonism' would become a huge hit, and there's a moment in the video where I look straight into the camera and sing, 'I hope you're feeling happy now.' That was aimed directly at her.

After we split up I was comforted by two beautiful black boys who were regulars at the Brixtonian – a gay couple who were always happy and positive, giving out the love. They were generous with compliments, which gave my self-esteem a much-needed boost. For years I had been self-conscious about being skinny, trying to hide my body in baggy tops, but I started experimenting with cool, sexier clothes that accentuated my figure.

One hot August night in 1990 I went to Venus Rising at the Fridge, just to dance and take my mind off things. I was wearing a swimsuit with a deep V in the front, a tiny leather Katherine Hamnett skirt, a floaty see-through sequinned top over my shoulders and Timberland boots. It was a damn hot look and I was workin' it! I left with my friends at four in the morning. They offered to walk me home, but I said, 'It's okay, I live nearby.'

Number One was diagonally across from the Fridge, so it was a one-minute jog. As I ran across the street, I could hear someone behind me. I was a runner at school, so I upped the pace, but I could still feel him gaining ground. I turned into my street, sped to my door, then bounded up the steps but, as I got my key out, I realised that if I opened the door the man chasing me would just push me in. All the windows were dark. Was anyone in? I turned around to face him; he lunged at me and grabbed my breast, so I screamed and started fighting him, pushing him down the steps. I saw his face before I ran inside the house. I raced downstairs to the basement room where Sabrina was and banged on the door. She was with her 'new' girlfriend. 'I've just been attacked!' I cried.

'That's terrible,' she said, but the horror didn't reach her eyes. She sat with me for about five minutes then went back to her room, callously leaving me alone and in shock. I packed a bag and called a cab, heading for a friend's house, where I stayed for a while. Perhaps I had caught them off guard by turning up in a complete state, but it was a double whammy. Being attacked and then realising that Sabrina had already moved her new girlfriend into her room added to my feeling of utter desolation. Strangely, to this day, I have no memory of packing that bag. The mind scrambles when it's in pain.

I came back a few days later, but didn't leave the house unless I had to. The attack really affected me and changed my whole perspective. I was terrified to be out after dark, I lost all my confidence and I was fearful of everything. A few weeks later, I was walking along the street and saw my assailant. I called the police, he was arrested, and three months later the case came to court. I remember there was a black guy on the jury staring me down, as if to say, 'Why are you accusing another black person, you're shaming us,' and the attacker got off because it was my word against his, and he had a better lawyer. I found out afterwards from the police that he had previously attacked a thirteen-year-old girl. The defence lawyer intimated to the police that it was my fault because of the way I looked – that I shouldn't have been out that late at night wearing a skimpy top and a short skirt. I was furious. As we were walking out of the courthouse, my attacker whispered to me, 'I know where you live.'

He started stalking me, following me in the street. I saw him three times and it was terrifying. But then, one time during the day, he followed me and he said it again: 'I know where you live.' That became a pivotal moment in my life. I hurried away quickly at first, like I'd done before, panic-stricken, thinking, *God, this is going to be my life, this guy will always terrify me.* But as I walked I felt angrier and angrier and I slowed my pace. I thought, *Is this my life, running from this guy?* I stopped dead. A rage that I hadn't felt since I was a child surfaced, and I turned around and ran back to where he stood. I lost my mind, scream- ing at him in the middle of the street. People stared while I shouted at the top of my voice: 'That guy's a rapist! You tried to rape me, you raped a child, you're disgusting!'

He literally shrank before my eyes, hunching over in fear. I shouted, 'You stopped me from going out at night? *You?* Look at you, you little shit!' I followed him for a while, screaming – now he was running from me! Finally I stopped and walked away, head held high, shoulders back, and I never saw him again. For a while he'd taken my confidence, my power, my security, my Brixton, and he thought he could break me. I snatched my power back and healed myself by confronting him, the anger making me courageous. That day I pulled something out of myself, a fearlessness that never left, that I could channel into my voice, my music and my songs. I found my strength.

After the attack, I focused on my music in a completely different way. I had been doing a lot of work that involved looking good, dancing and singing backing vocals. I had been saying yes to everything, thinking that was the best way to get noticed and to get work. I'd been hanging out with the backing singers for the Rolling Stones, and one of them looked me in the eye and said, 'Don't do too much of that session stuff. In ten years' time you'll be ten years older and you won't even own your own house.'

There was a sadness to her words that hit me. I realised she was talking about her life, and warning me. It turned out to be some of the best advice in my career. She confirmed something I was beginning to feel: I was turning into a jack of all trades singing stuff I wasn't into, hoping for a lucky break, but it wasn't going happen that way. So I stopped all the session singing and the modelling and all the stupid bits and pieces I was doing that paid me £50 here and there.

I centred my life around songwriting with Len. That's what had kept me going through those dark months after the attack, travelling every day from Brixton to his home in a tower block in Deptford. We were very disciplined, setting ourselves targets. We had to write a song every day, and we would make ourselves finish it even if it wasn't good. Len originally came from Teesside, and started off on the music scene of the mid-1980s as a jazz guitar player, playing in quartets, when the jazz/soul sound was popular, capturing people's imaginations with films like *Absolute Beginners* and musicians like Courtney Pine and Sade. By the time we started working together in 1990, the sound had morphed into the funkier style of acid jazz. We had traces of that in our early songs, but were soon experimenting with different sounds. Len was a proper songwriter with a sixteen-track recorder and a studio desk crammed in the living room of his small council flat. It wasn't the best gear in the world, but he knew how to work it. I brought to him all the songs I'd been working on since I was thirteen, and he knew exactly how to structure them properly. I was always aware they could be improved, but I didn't know how, and I knew I could learn from him.

We worked five days a week for the next three years. That's ten thousand hours, baby! That's what it takes. Len gave me the discipline I needed. I would come over with lots of ideas and we would push each other to record original sounds, phrases and melodies. We were competitive with each other. Len said he felt the pressure to come up with something new every day. He told me later that our workdays were really intense, that from the moment I left at around eight in the evening he would make something to eat and then get tracks together for when I arrived the next morning.

I'd moved out of Number One after the attack. I was enjoying my new life working with Len and being managed by Leigh, and I'd relocated to Hackney, east London. I had a second-hand bicycle, which I used to ride through the park and down through Greenwich Tunnel to Deptford every day, so I was also feeling really fit. To top it off, I'd started a new relationship. I'd met Maxine while I was doing security at Venus Rising. She was a regular, and I thought she was lovely, and we had been friends for a while before we got together. She had grown up in west London and, like my family, her parents were part of the Jamaican Windrush generation. One night, at Venus Rising, we were flirting and started dancing close together, and I sang to her (slick, right?). Later, Maxine told me she thought, *This girl can hold a tune.* We kissed and exchanged numbers, and so began my first loving, caring relationship.

When we met I was sharing a house in Victoria Park, Hackney with an older lesbian who had an Alsatian dog at death's door and a no-man rule. Her dog had weak back legs and was incontinent, so she had to carry the poor thing everywhere and couldn't bear to put him down. She never cleaned anything, and there was always a black ring around the bath after she washed the dog. The house was owned by a gay housing association that forced her to share with me. She'd had the house to herself for years and she really didn't want me there, so I was delighted when Maxine suggested I move in with her into her flat in West Ealing. We got on really well; she's hilarious, highly intelligent and takes no bullshit. She says it as it is, which I love her for. I was happy and able to focus on my work instead of running around London trying to be at every party. I didn't need it – I had Max.

I've never hidden my sexual identity and, with hindsight, maybe I was a little naïve about that. I always remember a conversation I had with Leigh a few months after we met. In those days you had to be careful with new people – some would be cool in the moment but then judge you later. I wanted to see if I liked her, and if my sexuality was going to matter. One day we met in a café and I told her I was bisexual.

She paused for a second.

'Okay, do you want the world to know? This is something you have to consider: if you do want the world to know, that's the best for your mental health. But I believe there's a possibility you'll sell fewer records.'

'I think I'd rather sell fewer records.'

'Okay, fine, that's the way we'll go.'

I thought, *I'd rather be happier.* I was in my queer friend group bubble and I didn't understand how big a deal that would be, and besides, selling records wasn't important to me then. I just wanted to write, perform and be me. When you're from a working-class background, everything is a bonus. Later, after Skunk Anansie formed and we released a record, I didn't officially come out to the press. I just didn't pretend to be straight. Eventually it was an *NME* journalist who asked, 'What does your boyfriend think of your music?' and I answered, 'Boyfriend? You mean girlfriend.' And that was it, I was out. I didn't even think about it. Leigh was right – with hindsight I know we would have absolutely sold more records if I'd played the sexy straight girl, so much easier to sell, but she was also right about being a happier person if I was out. I was and still am.

It wasn't always easy being out, though. In my early twenties it led to me falling out with my mum, whose religious beliefs made her uneasy about my lifestyle. Her opinion was the only one I truly cared about. One day, I went with a group of friends on a Gay Pride march to Brockwell Park – thousands of people were there protesting against Section 28, the Tory government anti-gay legislation that prohibited discussion of gay relationships in schools. I got very drunk at the event, and enthusiastically said to my friends, 'My mum lives round the corner, let's say hello to her!' My friends were like, 'Are you sure, love?' but I insisted, 'My mum's cool!'

We walked to Tulse Hill, and when I turned up at the door, a little worse for wear, Mum said to me angrily, 'Where have you been? You been at that dutty place? Move from me doorstep!'

She just cussed me, upset that I'd been to Gay Pride. Looking back, I feel like a complete idiot. It was a really thoughtless way to tell your mum you're gay. After that we barely spoke for two years.

At that time, I didn't come out to my old friends or relatives. I just came out to my new friends. I knew my family wouldn't like it or agree with it. In 1990, gay marriages and civil partnerships were not yet legal; it was not an open society and the climate was very anti-gay. I don't care what my brothers think about my sexuality, it's irrelevant to me. We have an unwritten rule: I don't get involved in their relationships and they don't get involved with mine. We're not close like that. There are homophobic people in my family but, if I'd listened to them, I wouldn't have done anything with my life. I've never discussed my sexual identity with anyone in my family because I feel you either accept it, or you don't – and that's part of my survival as a black gay woman.

I didn't have an overtly gay look. I wasn't particularly butch or femme. I was just me. I'd hear coming-out stories: 'I knew I was gay at ten years old.' That wasn't my story. I had crushes on boys *and* girls, so I thought I was bisexual. Back then a lot of people thought that being bisexual wasn't a genuine identity, that it was just a gateway from straight to gay. But now I define myself as queer. I'm happy with that; it's really all I need.

Back in 1991, I was determined that nothing should hold me back, that I needed to live life the way I wanted, and that meant devoting all my time to music. During the second year of working with Len, I sat on the Tube all the way from Ealing Broadway to Deptford, two hours there, two hours back. I loved it. I'd watch the other people in the carriage and invent stories about them in my head. I'd imagine their lives, writing lyrics and making up melodies. I didn't have much money at the time; if I went out I would bunk the Tube, or in summer I'd just walk places. When I went out I always made sure I put my night bus fare in a separate pocket so I didn't spend it. I didn't need much money. I ate when I was hungry or when there was free food. I'd forget to eat a proper meal all the time, sometimes for days; it just wasn't important to me.

It took me and Len a year to write a great song – one we knew worked lyrically, musically and had feeling. In the beginning the plan was Len would be the songwriter and I was the singer. I gradually learnt from him how to structure what I wanted to say, and began to fight to share the writing with him and include my words.

'What point are you trying to make?' he would ask. His songs were beautifully crafted and well written, but I felt they didn't have the edge I was looking for. They didn't sound like me. I had good instincts and could tell when something was working or not. We argued all the time, and we loved it! It wasn't personal; they were creative arguments that were for the good of the song – that's where the best songs came from. I had good ideas that were underdeveloped, but I'm a Leo, so if Len told me I couldn't do something I would try to prove him otherwise.

We worked quickly – one of us would come up with a germ of an idea and Len would get a groove or a beat or guitar line going on while I sketched out lyrics. He was always big on choruses, saying, 'If it hasn't got a chorus, you haven't really got a song.'

By 1992, after two years of writing together, we had over 100 songs, including 'Hedonism', which was one of the first songs we finessed. I'd written the verses at 4am, crying over my break-up with Sabrina. When I brought it to Len, he said, 'Where's the chorus? The song needs a chorus.' At first, I was a bit miffed – I thought it was perfect! But then he said, 'You need to sum up your feelings, what you want to say, then make that the chorus.' He was right.

Initially we thought it sounded too sweet for me, so we were gonna send it to Mariah Carey! Thank God we didn't, because it ended up being our biggest hit.

Once we started writing good songs together, I realised I wasn't a solo artist. For years I'd had a recurring dream of me standing onstage holding a microphone with two hands, screaming into it, rocking out. That was the image I was going for, that's what I wanted – to sing in a band. At the beginning of my musical career, I had sung a lot of jazz. I was the perfect pretty thing dressed in polite outfits, doing acoustic Van Morrison-style numbers. But by then I realised jazz was too 'nice' for me, that I wasn't fully expressing myself. I had a vision of myself in a band playing overdriven guitars, in-ya-face music that was political and aggressive. By then I was hanging out in King's Cross and Camden, watching rock bands and listening to American groups like Tool, the Smashing Pumpkins and Nirvana, loving the sexy groove, fire and riffs of that sound. I decided I wanted to form a band with Len, and that's how, early in 1992, Mama Wild was born.

Len brought in a fierce rock guitarist called Elisha Blue, and an American guy called Malcolm Scott – musicians he'd already worked with on London's jazz/soul scene. Leigh then got word of a great bass player who'd just finished touring with soul singer Terence Trent D'Arby. Leigh and I arranged to meet him outside Ealing Broadway Tube station, and I had no idea what he looked like. Suddenly we heard a massive roar and this dude, dressed head to toe in tight black leather on a tricked-out jet-black Harley, parked right in front of us. He took off his helmet and long brown dreadlocks came cascading down his face, framing the biggest smile you've ever seen. This dude was slick!

Born and bred in Notting Hill, Richard 'Cass' (short for Cassius Clay) Lewis's parents came from Barbados. He came from a violent home and grew up fighting, sometimes involved in petty crime. In his early twenties he found an outlet for his emotions in music. His best friend, Culture Club's Mikey Craig, taught him how to play bass. As part of his rehabilitation, he ended up working for Chiswick Women's Aid. The founder Erin Pizzey took him under her wing, giving him a job preventing abusive fathers from snatching their children. Cass then joined Erin and her family when they moved to New Mexico. He spent a year there, building adobe huts in the desert for the locals, and that's where he began to seriously play music, writing reggae rock songs with Pizzey's son Amos. When Cass came back from New Mexico, he and Amos got a record deal with Virgin, but it didn't work out. After they were dropped by the label, he worked in a sports shop, and luckily an audition eventually came up playing bass guitar for an up-and-coming singer called Terence Trent D'Arby. Cass ended up touring around the world with him, earning enough money to build a recording studio to work with new artists.

We started doing gigs with both Len and Blue on guitar, and Cass playing bass. After a few gigs it became clear that although Len was very talented, he wasn't really a rocker. I was pushing him into something that was not his style. Len was calm and introverted; he didn't stalk the stage like an arrogant rock god. After a year, I had to make the really difficult decision of taking him out of the band line-up. That was really hard. We assumed he would be my guitarist, and had no idea it wasn't going to work, and he found it difficult letting go, but we continued writing songs together, including some of our biggest hits.

Our first Mama Wild gig was supporting Edwin Starr at a venue in Ealing Broadway. At the time we had programmed samples as part of the set, but they weren't mixed in very well because the sound levels were wrong. I came off stage thinking, *Those samples don't work.* But I was really excited when Edwin Starr went on stage. He was a Motown hero who had a huge hit in 1970 with the anti-Vietnam War protest song, 'War'. The first thing he said was, 'Now we're gonna play *real* music.' *What?* I thought. *You're Edwin Bloody Starr! Why are you slagging us off?* I was so offended. He was totally right, of course – we weren't very good and there were weird sounds flying all over the place, but the diss hurt.

Those early days singing rock were a little hairy. I hadn't yet found my people, so I had some bitter, negative comments from both white *and* black friends over me being a black woman singing rock music. One black friend cut me off because I apparently wasn't singing the music *of my people*. She said I was trying to 'sing with the oppressors', that she was actually ashamed to know me. I was shocked, this was an extreme reaction, but I knew she was wrong. It was clear to me that I was on the right path with Leigh and Len. I just had to keep going, keep getting better. I never hung out with that friend again.

Mama Wild lasted two years. We built up a small following and started playing venues like the Splash Club in King's Cross, but we made too many mistakes and remained unsigned for too long, and I felt something wasn't quite right. The songs were too bluesy and not strong enough, and we didn't have one killer song that shone. We still had the wrong line-up. I knew I liked Cass's energy, but wasn't sure about the other two. Malcolm was a sweet guy, a good solid drummer, but too soft and poppy in his playing, and not enough attitude. I could also feel that he didn't believe in me as a lead singer.

Blue, meanwhile, was a phenomenal player but a complicated man, and challenging to be in a band with. He played solos over everything and could never seem to remember the structure of the songs. During rehearsals Blue would forget his parts, or roll a cigarette just before he was supposed to play and mess up, so Cass would shout at him and Blue would shout back and I'd shout at the both of them. Malcolm, meanwhile, was in the middle with an anxious look on his face, stuck between three volcanoes.

An American label was showing interest in us, and when that happened I pictured myself on the tour bus with Blue, Cass and Malcolm and thought, *I can't do it*. We needed a major change, and the time was right to create a completely new band.

BOOK TWO

RISE UP

SEVEN

LITTLE BABY SWASTIKKKA

Skunk Anansie played their first gig at the Splash Club in 1994, the year that Britpop emerged as a media force. The year before, Blur's lead singer Damon Albarn had declared war on US grunge with the upbeat '60s pop influences of their album *Modern Life Is Rubbish*. His girlfriend Justine Frischmann, from punk-pop band Elastica, said that their music was 'a manifesto for the return of Britishness', whilst glam rock-styled Brett Anderson from Suede graced the cover of *Select* magazine, posing in front of a Union Jack flag, over the coverline: 'Yanks Go Home!' The scene was to explode later that year, with the release of Oasis's debut album *Definitely Maybe*.

Britpop music – guitar-led pop with catchy, insouciant song-writing – was inspired by '60s mod culture and '70s glam, and linked in with the emergence of London street fashion and radical YBAs (Young British Artists) like Tracey Emin, Sarah Lucas and Damien Hirst. 1994 was also the year that men's magazine *Loaded* launched, with the strapline: 'For men who should know better'. The magazine was devoted to sex, drink, football and the New Lad. The scene celebrated a Britishness that was very white, male-defined and harking back to Swinging London for its reference points. With their diverse, multiracial line-up, Skunk Anansie articulated a different narrative about Britain. And Skin, a black woman singing rock, independently created a style and sound of her own.

The Union Jack meant something different to us. Our first rehearsal space was run by a British Movement guy, and there was a massive British flag positioned just as you walked through the entrance. That's where, one day, I saw the baby swastika, a small, wobbly version scrawled on the wall only a foot off the ground. It looked like it had been drawn by a four-year-old, so when I got in the studio, I started singing about it. It started off as a whisper, low, over Cass's bassline, and then I spoke the lines that came into my head: *Who put the little baby swastikkka on the wall ... who put the little baby nigga-head on the wall ... the eyes were so big couldna been more than baby scrawls.* Then I scream: *You rope them in young ... so delicately done, grown up in your poison.*

Cass said he liked the way I attacked things. 'Fucking hell,' he said, 'you're singing about *that*. Go on, babe!' Cass really didn't realise who I was until we played our first gig with Mama Wild. I wore Dr Marten boots and gauzy scarves and had an alternative look he had never seen before. He thought I was quiet and unassuming, until I turned into a monster onstage. Cass got it; he recognised that anger.

I knew exactly what I wanted to do, and I was gaining confidence as a live performer. I could see which songs were working with the crowd, and I remember feeling secure and finally happy in myself. At the beginning of 1994, I broke up Mama Wild and started a new band. Cass suggested the name Skunk, but I objected because people would assume we just smoked weed all day, and I don't even smoke cigarettes. He reassured me that even though there was a nice double meaning, it wasn't to do with ganja. The name came from his time in New Mexico, studying shamanic medicine cards as a source of divination. In Native American culture, the symbolic and spiritual power of animals is understood as a way of connecting mind, body and spirit. Cass interpreted the skunk as a black-and-white animal respected by the whole animal kingdom, without being a predator. No animal will go near a skunk because they don't want to get sprayed by that smell. Not even a tiger or a leopard will try to kill a skunk. It's one of the smallest animals, but its power lies in its simple weapon.

The biggest bands at that time all had one name – Blur, Oasis, Pulp, Elastica. I wanted our name to have a different flavour, with another layer, a name that reminded me of my heritage. I remembered being a little girl, sitting in front of the TV in Jamaica watching poet and folklorist Miss Lou tell Anansi stories on the kids' show *Ring Ding*. Originally Anansi the spiderman from Ghana, in Jamaican culture Anansi is sometimes depicted as a black man with an afro and six legs. He was my favourite character in the jungle, always playing tricks on the other animals, and always getting away with it. I loved one particular story about three friends who each had a banana and felt sorry for Anansi because he didn't have one. 'Mi hungry, mi hungry, mi don't have banana ... give me half of your banana now,' he said, so they each gave him half a banana. Chuckling to himself, he ran with three halves of banana before they worked out they'd been had. That's the kind of thing Anansi would do.

The fact that he was the trickster really appealed to me, as anyone that knows me will tell you I love a naughty little prank. Anansi was a vivid childhood memory that meant something to me at a time when a lot of music felt meaningless, with many bands writing apolitical love songs. I thought: *I'm a black kid from Brixton, I've had a different life, I experienced the riots outside my front door. I'm not going to write insipid love songs – there is so much I want to express.*

I heard bands saying they had simple names because they were easy for people to remember, almost like a marketing ploy. At the time I read a quote from the actor Arnold Schwarzenegger, who said he never changed his name because he figured that once you learnt the name Schwarzenegger, you'd never forget it. For me it was, 'Yeah, let's make it difficult. Why should we dumb it down?' And so Skunk Anansie was born.

I also thought about my own name. As a child I was given many nicknames. 'Lippy the Lion' (from the Hanna-Barbera cartoon *Lippy the Lion and Hardy Har Har*) was a favourite because my head was little but my lips were the same size as they are now. I was called 'tree head' for a while, because my mum had an African friend who would twist my hair into long, skinny strands using thread, but they would fray at the top like mini baobab trees – nice! I was called 'Kunta Kinte' after the main character in *Roots*, a drama about slavery that shook the world in 1977 – luckily that didn't stick. But as I got a little older my friends would call me Skinny, because as some of them filled out and became womanly, I stayed the same stick-thin shape. Way before the 1990s fashion catwalk, 'skinny' was not a compliment. Jamaicans like a lot more flesh 'arn de bones', and as a child I was too 'marga' (meagre) and everyone was always trying to feed me up. I didn't feel like a Deborah, and hated its abbreviation Debbie even more, so when Skunk Anansie started I shortened my nickname Skinny to Skin, because I thought it was edgier, and I then used the name with pride.

Our look was British rock meets raver meets punk, which was anti-fashion, in itself a fashion statement. I wasn't into hairspray metal – too tight and shiny – or New Romantic, too beautiful and expensive. I preferred goth bands like The Cure or dark ska bands like The Specials. When grunge came along in the early 1990s, it felt like Year Zero. American bands like Alice in Chains and Smashing Pumpkins gave us something we could identify with. The bass groove on some of those records had a huge sound with a lot of black music influences, and that's what sucked us in.

The sound chimed with the way we dressed. We had no money but we would find clothes in charity shops: sturdy boots, oversized jumpers, old T-shirts and jean jackets. We were young, everything looked good!

There was an army surplus shop in Warren Street, known as Laurence Corner – we got a lot of our clothes from there. Anything that looked too slick or smart or too cool we rejected. We'd go to Camden to see what was new and goth. When we started Skunk Anansie, there was no sponsorship from Gucci; everything was home-made, rough, raw and thrown together. It was natural and honest – our own London take on US grunge.

The fat grooves and swaggering guitar riffs of grunge chimed with the image I had in my head, and my recurring dream that I was onstage screaming into a mic, raging to giant riffs. Then 'Smells Like Teen Spirit' landed on us all like a mushroom cloud obliterating everything else. Cock rock was dead, and out of the ashes flowered this beautiful wilted thorny rose called Nirvana. It wasn't pretty, it wasn't safe, but it was profound. I'd finally found the music that suited my nightly visions. Nirvana to me weren't about groupies and tight, bulging pants; they were honest and real and they looked like us. We recognised the same dark lyrical landscape, the same shy, painful outsider life. That was the music we were playing in London, but with a British style, heavy and riffy. We definitely weren't Britpop.

We hung out with Echobelly, another multiracial indie band, with singer Sonya Madan and Debbie Smith on guitar. But I didn't really spend time in Camden pubs with the other Britpop bands. Camden was cool but cliquey. There were certain pubs journalists would drink in, so if you wanted to be noticed you would get pally with them. King's Cross was a different scene – a rundown area where people with no money hung out and you could rent cheap rehearsal spaces for £5 an hour. They were converted from old office buildings, and you could hear people rehearsing in the next room.

In those days, King's Cross was pretty rough. It was the home of prostitutes and drugs, muggings and violence. You had to be careful. I would come out of the station and jog quickly to the venue, stopping for no one. The Splash club took place a few nights a week at the Water Rats, a pub at 328 Gray's Inn Road, that was a former music hall built in the late nineteenth century. Bob Dylan played there in 1962. Celtic punkers the Pogues had their first gig there twenty years later. Katy Perry even played an intimate gig there in 2017. There was a whole scene in that one pub. It was just down the road from the Scala, an art-house cinema in nearby Pentonville Road that screened trashy cult movies. I'd get the night bus home to Brixton, a journey that became a great source of songs. You had to be vigilant because some of your fellow passengers might be drunk, on drugs, or mentally unstable, and you'd *never* sit upstairs; too easy to get trapped. When I got home, I'd write down phrases and ideas that came to me on the bus, adding to the pile of diaries and notebooks I had stacked up in my bedroom.

It was at the Splash Club that I met a cool new guitarist called Martin 'Ace' Kent. Ace was tall, shaven-headed and skinny, a rocker from head to toe, and he had moved to London from Gloucester in the early '90s. His band Big Life Casino wanted to release a record, so they started the Splash Club in order to have somewhere to play and promote their music. Because they were booking other bands to play there, they got to know all the managers and agents. Ace used to do the lights, stage management and door, and he was DJing the night we met. He'd let artists come in free and I was one of them. I remember him DJing vinyl, and one of the first conversations we had was about Rage Against The Machine.

He had this shiny white label release, brand new, an advance copy. He put it on and said, 'Watch this.' The place went off – it was awesome! I'd never heard it before. It was riff heaven!

'What's this?' I shouted.

'It's a new band from America. None of these sounds are made by keyboards.'

'This is cool.'

'I've got Pearl Jam, Stone Temple Pilots, all this white label stuff,' he enthused. 'I'll make you a tape of all these bands.'

For us, the '70s was the last great era of rock. Sabbath, Led Zeppelin and Parliament and Funkadelic were our original inspirations but in the '90s along came Soundgarden, Tool, Nirvana – they all arrived on white labels from the US. The American invasion was so exciting to us, and it revolutionised our sound. The crossover came with Run DMC's *Tougher Than Leather* and the track with Aerosmith, 'Walk This Way'. Then, in 1988, Public Enemy put out *It Takes A Nation* and sampled Slayer on 'She Watch Channel Zero'. That was a game-changer. In 1991, Rage Against The Machine emerged from LA with a new kind of rap-metal. They were so solemn, totally unforgiving, but not alienating.

Ace's band Big Life Casino played alt-heavy rock and had a couple of records out mastered by Adrian Sherwood, who founded the distinctive On-U Sound label. Ace was connected to everybody, and knew it was about going out and hanging out, standing outside Camden Palace, the Orange or the Borderline at 2am to hand out flyers. He booked everyone from Oasis to Suede to Ocean Colour Scene. He organised the night when Ocean Colour Scene got signed and Paul Weller came down. He was also stage manager for Oasis when they did their first gig at the Splash Club. I was there, it was rammed, and they smashed it. They stood and played great song after great song with a sound that was really heavy and defined from the start. We remember them shooting the video for 'Supersonic' on the roof that afternoon in King's Cross, then doing the show in the evening. The Gallagher boys were cool, but with an edge.

Cass and I needed a guitarist for our new band, so our manager Leigh asked me to draw up a list, and Ace was my number one choice. I had a mini crush on him in those days, and there was always a bit of a lingering chemistry that later worked well onstage. I'd lick his head and kiss him – I was always trying to mess with his zone and make him laugh. I felt he was authentic, a real rock king. After being in a band with Blue, who was too difficult, and Len, who was too sweet, I thought, *Here's a proper rock god!* Ace looked cool, had natural stage presence, and the proper gear.

Seeing Motörhead at the age of twelve was a life-changing moment for Ace. He described Lemmy as 'a man of the people', and when we got to know him later he *was* that person. Motörhead were the big outsiders of that new wave of British heavy metal. Lemmy was like us, we had an affinity, and later on enjoyed many nights out with him. I loved his company. He used to come to our gigs if he was in town, and we played gigs with Motörhead too. What inspired Ace in particular was the raw power of their music, an elemental quality.

There is a photo of Ace taken in the early 1980s on Christmas Day, standing outside his home in Gloucester wearing a leather jacket, aged fourteen, with a Gibson SG copy guitar his dad had bought for £20 in a bric-a-brac shop. He didn't read music; he was totally self-taught, listening to records and learning to play that way. He identified all the techniques, then put them together and wrote songs, and his guitar playing was very simple. The *sound*, however, was a different matter. His philosophy was simple things played well, in the same way that U2 guitarist The Edge evolved a unique style that was a mixture of experiment, accident and pure passion.

Ace and I played a few shows on the same bill at the Splash Club, with me in Mama Wild, him with his band Big Life

Casino. I wanted my band to have a more contemporary feel, not bluesy at all, and Ace was into US grunge and hip-hop as well as Motörhead, Black Sabbath and British heavy metal. Problem was, he was already in another band, and it's bad karma to steal musicians from other bands. I couldn't ask him to be in mine, so I decided: I won't ask him, I'll just *tell* him I'm starting a new band. So I did.

'Who's your guitarist? I want to be your guitarist,' he said, understanding straightaway. He saw it, he got it and he was into it.

Cass had a studio in Ladbroke Grove, so we organised a rehearsal and started jamming. He played a complicated riff from our song 'Sucking Sugar Melons', but rather than say, 'I can't really match that,' Ace played chords with his pedal board and lifted the roof off with his mastery of effects. It was all about space – he helped to define that early Skunk Anansie sound, which is playing huge, fat riffs and filling the space. He got the job. Ace recalls afterwards ringing his mum, enthusing, 'This band is the one.' He also went to his fave guitar shop and said, 'This is the best band I've ever been in.' The guy behind the counter eyed him sarcastically and replied, 'Yeah, I've been in a few of those.'

Our early rehearsals as Skunk Anansie were in an old office block in King's Cross, with Malcolm, formerly of Mama Wild, on drums. A guy called Graham from Splash had bought the block and was going to convert it, but before he did that he allowed bands to use it, with all the office furniture still inside. There would be a band in each room – for instance, Feeder in one, us in another, and our friends Rub Ultra across the corridor. For £30 a week you'd get a key and a place to rehearse and store your amps. I vividly remember that first rehearsal, when we started jamming on a riff and within thirty seconds we knew the chemistry was there. We exchanged looks and started giggling with joy. Skunk Anansie was born! We were all so different, but there was a unity and understanding between us.

All of a sudden we were talking about different childhoods, different lifestyles, eating different food, listening to different music. It was brand new, like finding a new best friend. Ace and I went to dozens of gigs together. We went to the Garage in Islington, the Astoria, the Lock Tavern in Camden Town and the Bull & Gate in Kentish Town. We hung out as friends, sharing music and sharing clothes. One day I said, 'I like your coat.'

'You can have it.'

We still swap stuff with each other today, except now it includes cars and motorbikes, and even houses!

Ace said that he discovered himself as a player in Skunk Anansie. In normal life, as people, we couldn't fully express ourselves, but we did it onstage through the music.

I knew our band was good. I felt I was finally the person I was supposed to be. Our first gig was at the Splash Club in March 1994, and it was on *fire!* The gig was packed and there was a big buzz. Ace had booked us in a headline slot. All the regulars came mainly out of curiosity, because they'd followed Mama Wild and Big Life Casino, and together we were like an unsigned supergroup. As I ran onstage, all those years of working with Len in Deptford, all those lessons learnt in Mama Wild, came together and we rocked! Straightaway Ace and I had an amazing onstage rapport; we fed off each other. I'd punch him, jump on him, stick my tongue in his ear and rip his T-shirt off. The first picture in *NME* was of me jumping on his back while he played a solo.

Ace rebooked us a month later for our second gig on 8 April, and it was packed again. By then we had a new drummer, Cass's friend Robbie France, who had played with everyone from the Style Council to jazz saxophonist Jean Toussaint to heavy metal band Diamond Head. He was only thirty-five, with blond 'Billy Idol' hair, but looked twice as old as everyone else in the band. Personally, I wasn't too keen initially, because Robbie didn't seem to fit, but as he was such an incredible drummer I couldn't really argue.

We were getting ready backstage when we heard that Kurt Cobain had died, so during our set we dedicated a song to him. Fourteen A&R industry bods were there, lining the back wall, nodding their heads, while in front were 200 kids totally losing it in the mosh-pit. Every label showed up, ready for battle. Some labels loved us, some hated us – major record companies seemed scared of us – but the indie labels understood where we were coming from. Rick Lennox, A&R for the label One Little Indian, was upset about Kurt Cobain's death, and hadn't intended to come to our gig, but during the show he was blown away. He said to us afterwards, 'You took my mind off the fact that my favourite artist has died. I'm going to sign you.' It was like a rock 'n' roll fairytale come true.

We next played the Monarch pub in Camden, and again it was busy, but this time we didn't know anyone in the crowd. They were all new fans. The buzz was spreading. Labels started bidding and One Little Indian made an offer, but Leigh said it wasn't enough. The following month we went for a meeting at the offices of record label Beggars Banquet and, after negotiations over a potential deal, we came across Rick Lennox waiting in a car outside, ready to offer us what Leigh had asked for. He wanted us so badly he knew he had to make a grand gesture in a way that was impressive or he'd lose us.

One Little Indian Records was founded in 1985 by members of various anarcho-punk bands, and managed by former Flux of Pink Indians bassist Derek Birkett. Flux were famous for their 1983 album *The Fucking C**ts Treat Us Like Pricks*, which was banned by many UK retailers, and copies were seized by Greater Manchester Police. One Little Indian had an experimental ethos – by the early '90s, it had a varied roster of artists including Björk, dream pop duo AR Kane, anarcho-punk band Chumbawamba, and rave pioneers The Shamen. It seemed like the perfect home for us.

Leigh made sure we had creative freedom written into the deal. She said to them, 'You put the needle on the record at the beginning and take it off at the end, and what's on the record is nobody's business but my band's.' That kind of freedom was very unusual for a new band, but as we had a few offers on the table, we could demand it.

Our first promotional release was the song 'Little Baby Swastikkka' (spelled with three Ks, like in Ku Klux Klan). Leigh's friend Martin Mills, chairman of Beggars Group, said to her, 'You should go out heavy, because you can always go softer later.' That song was first played on the Radio 1 *Evening Session* with Steve Lamacq and Jo Whiley. The audience were told, 'You've a choice of three bands, and we'll print up seven-inch promos to give out of the one you like best.' We won! In fact there was such massive demand for the record, they had to print over a thousand copies.

We then signed to Epic in America, and were flown out to do a showcase set at the record company offices in Los Angeles. Word went round about the new signing. Before we did our showcase we were told Mariah Carey might come in and check us out, and if she did we were instructed not to look at her. We were hugely excited, and of course we looked at her – how could we not? It's bloody Mariah Carey, one of the most famous women in the world and the singer we nearly sent 'Hedonism' to. I might have scared her off though, because I sang right into that cherub face!

At the time Skunk Anansie took off, my girlfriend Maxine had set up the PR agency Red Rooster, and her biggest client was the fashion designer Red or Dead. Maxine's agency launched workwear and street styles from different labels, and was part of UK fashion reinventing itself. It was an exciting time. While she worked the agency, I was happy at home. I lived and breathed music, scribbling down lyrics and building on my ideas by drawing and sketching in my notebooks. Despite my prowess onstage, I wasn't quite comfortable playing the big rock star, preferring to be in the shadows, rather than the drama that enters the room first.

The early days of our relationship were great fun, and we absolutely loved raving. There were weekends when we would get in the car with a duvet, a change of clothes, a bottle of water, sunglasses and a few sandwiches and come back on Monday morning. In those days, you could go from club to club all weekend. We'd start at Bagley's, the legendary warehouse dance venue in King's Cross, then go to Trade in Farringdon at 4am and dance for hours to the tunes of Smokin' Jo, Alan Thompson and DJ Steve, then after a nap in the car it was DTPM at The End near Tottenham Court Road, which had the best wall of speaker sound in London. Then we'd finish off at Queer Nation in the Gardening Club, which was gay gay gay! Sometimes we'd fit in Heaven, or Body & Soul, or Ministry of Sound. It was madness, gliding in and out of the clubs, bumping into friends, DJs and UK club-kids. It all came to a grinding halt, though, after Skunk Anansie started.

We came back once on a Monday morning in 1995, after a weekend of clubbing, and went straight to a full day of press interviews. It was hell on earth. I hadn't slept or eaten properly and I could barely talk, let alone answer a million questions. I managed to make some sense to journalists, but I returned home to Maxine, saying, 'It's one or the other. I can't do that again.' That was the end of our mad weekends. It was time to take the band very seriously, as things were starting to happen.

At one point the power dynamics in our relationship changed. Maxine remembers a moment at the Splash Club, not long after we'd been signed, when I was singing 'Weak', our big ballad. I was wearing my Doc Martens and a slip dress. 'The light was on you,' she said, 'and you were looking really angelic, singing this song.' She stood in the middle of the crowd, hemmed into this small room, watching me. She felt nervous and vulnerable, scared that the band would become huge and that she would lose me. She told me later, 'I always remember that, because it proved to be true. But you can't hold that back; it was unstoppable.'

The more we played, the more our band gathered momentum, at a speed none of us could ever have predicted.

EIGHT

PARANOID & SUNBURNT

You go to church and light a candle
And then you're blinded by the light from the golden pews
The devil's snapping at your toes now
Because the angels can't be bothered to live to you

'Selling Jesus'

The song 'Selling Jesus' came out like a cannonball. I flicked on the TV one morning before a band rehearsal and caught an evangelist preacher. He was asking for big donations for the Lord, but as his hands moved all I could see was his humongous gold watch glistening under studio lights. I thought, *People fall for this shit?* I quickly scrawled in my notebook: *They want your soul, your money, your blood, your votes.* It was a testy song about how easy it is to exploit people's beliefs in order to gain money and power.

The late *NME* writer Steven Wells shot the video as part of his Gob TV production company. It featured me with a white cross daubed on my face screaming at the camera and a Christ lookalike being ushered by minders through a crowd of paparazzi. We loved Steven – he was a lovely loony with tons of evil ideas and he understood us. He wanted to shoot a scene in a room full of hanging meat carcasses, but Cass and I were vegetarian, so instead he got us a herd of live sheep that seemed gigantic to us! We city kids had no idea that sheep poo backwards, so we spent most of the time swerving thick streams of brown liquid. It was gross and hilarious at the same time.

The whole day was spooky, because the venue was an old disused mental institution that had been closed down in the 1950s. It had an eerie presence. We dared each other to go deeper and deeper into the unlit, dilapidated wards where all manner of hideous things must have been practised, from lobotomies to ECT. But the scariest moment was at 2am when the shoot ended and I was left behind. I was alone in the pitch-black institution full of creepy noises and echoes. The bastards forgot me!

A powerful song, with Ace's chunky guitar riffs and Cass's deep, frenetic basslines, 'Selling Jesus' was the first single from our debut album *Paranoid & Sunburnt*, which we recorded in the autumn of 1994 in Linford Manor, an expensive, state-of-the-art studio in the Milton Keynes countryside. We had delicious food cooked for us, and top alt-metal producer Sylvia Massy flew in from the US to work with us. She had just produced *Undertow*, the double platinum-selling album by Tool, which we loved, and she had come out of the San Francisco hardcore scene, working with punk groups like Verbal Abuse and Michael Franti's industrial hip-hop band the Beatnigs. She was a perfect choice for our debut album, but I found the experience traumatic.

The first song took thirty-two takes. I was appalled and disgusted with myself, my confidence completely undermined. I'd never recorded an album before; we'd only done live gigs. Cass had a studio in Ladbroke Grove but our demos were so horrific that we never played them to anyone outside the band. Our party line was, 'If you like us, come see us, we don't do demos'. Singing live was easy – one take and you're done. No one wants you to fix a word or re-sing a sentence because no one's listening that closely; they just want to rock and sweat with you. But studios were an unknown world to me, and I was totally out of my comfort zone. I didn't know how to get a vibe without an audience. On top of that, Linford Manor was, well ... really nice, almost too nice! We went from playing on sticky pub floors and eating dodgy food in the backstreets of King's Cross to having a private chef and en-suite bathrooms in the lush British countryside. Not one room had a penis drawn with a Sharpie on the wall! Not one!

Sylvia spotted our discomfort. 'We need to fuck shit up,' she drawled, so we deconstructed the space, making it more like a battlefield. We raided an army surplus store and, ever so politely, trashed the studio, building a vocal bunker out of soundboards with netting for a roof, covering it with slogans and rubbish so you couldn't see the floor. A lot of the songs were political, and it felt like war. I was fighting my own demons, but it was also an incendiary time in London. In 1994, for instance, there was civil unrest against the Criminal Justice Bill (which outlawed free rave parties) and a resurgence of riots in Brixton in 1995 after the death of Wayne Douglas in police custody. So, inside the bunker, I covered the walls with notes, lyrics, feelings, fears, thoughts and advice for myself.

When the energy felt right, we started recording drums, bass and guitar, but slowly the pressure started to build. I walked past someone and they said, 'Vocals next week – they gotta be good, like really good.' I took in this information, thinking: *Vocals are coming . . . you know this record is depending on your vocals; you really have to be incredible.*

Someone said 'Aretha Franklin standard', and I slowly began to freak out. With hindsight, underneath my bravado I was already terrified. My self-esteem crumbled, my throat became sore, I got headaches, ate less, stopped chatting and had very strange thoughts. I didn't know how to get a good headphone sound to sing to; everything was brand new and came with a learning curve steeper than Everest. I became anxious, convinced everyone was going to be disappointed in me. It seemed as if the success of the whole album was down to me and I was about to fail miserably. I wasn't sleeping and I felt overwhelmed. Finally I cracked and cried all night. It felt like a slow-motion madness. For some reason, I thought all the furniture in my room was in the wrong place, and that if I turned it upside down everything would be better. It wasn't.

Cass and Ace found me curled up in my room in a real state, eyes swollen, nerves snapped. I had to go home. But before I left, I insisted on recording '100 Ways to Be a Good Girl'. I instinctively felt that if I had gone home without singing anything at all, my anxiety would have defeated me, and it would have been harder to perform when I got back. I knew I would spend those days off just fretting about my vocals if I didn't master at least one song. I had to sing something really well in whatever state I was in. I *had to do it* to get my confidence back.

The song is about staying out of trouble, whatever the trouble is to you – everyone has their own interpretation of that. I went in, cried through a few takes in the bunker we had created, and then I got it. To this day, that song still reminds me of that moment. You can hear the tremor in my voice – but it's also one of my proudest performances. It was mentally exhausting, but I got over it by channelling my feelings into my voice. Stepping up to the microphone still makes me nervous, but I've learnt how to put that demon on a leash. Nerves are not always a bad thing, and they never really go away, but you can lessen them by being as prepared as you can possibly be, and that means practice. I went home calmer. A few nights in my own bed fixed me and made me feel like my old self again. When I returned, I joked that I just needed the stinking, rotting city smell back under my nostrils. 'Maybe I should draw a penis on my toilet door for comfort!'

I am fortunate, as mental health is not an issue I struggle with, but at that point I was overwhelmed by the pressure of recording our first album. I didn't feel I had the power to say, 'Don't tell me I need to sing like Aretha, you're stressing me out!' The music industry can screw with your sense of self because there are always so many people – from A&R to marketing to press and fans – with opinions about what you should do. After my crisis, everyone became more supportive and realised I was vulnerable. I learnt how to cope better by expressing myself when I felt too much pressure instead of pretending I was invincible. For me, it was the beginning of the realisation that I don't have to sound like Aretha or anyone else. I just have to sound like me.

When I returned to Linford Manor a week later, we recorded 'Selling Jesus' as if we were playing live, and the rest of the songs came more easily. The album was a vivid snapshot of our lives at the time. I have big ears, I'm a dirty eavesdropper, and I love stealing fragments of conversations I overhear – dialogue that's not meant for me but rings true in my life or sends my head spinning into fantasy land. That's why some of our song titles are super-long.

'It Takes Blood and Guts to Be This Cool But I'm Still Just a Cliché', for instance, came out of a bitchfest I was having with a friend about a press review that called us a cliché. How can we be a cliché if there's no one like us? We work hard! 'It takes blood and guts to be this cool,' I said to her, and then we cracked up laughing. I was being sarcastic but the line stuck in my head. It's arrogant, a little camp, and later, when it became part of a song, I sang it with a smirk on my face, a sneering top lip and a bored visage. I wasn't sure if anyone caught the irony, but I do remember that was when I stopped reading reviews, good or bad. I wasn't strong enough. I hadn't learnt how to process them. The good ones swelled your head, the bad ones stabbed you in the heart, and sometimes they were so personal and cutting they would take your breath away. It's just not worth the agony. Funny, that in those days you could ignore reviews – now it's near impossible not to know what everyone thinks about you. You can read a thousand wonderful things about yourself, but the comments you inhale into your very core are always the most negative.

'Blood & Guts' is a mess of a song; it shouldn't really work. The structure seems upside-down, there's a bloody complicated bassline, and at any point in the song, you might think, *Can you actually call that singing?* Still, isn't it glorious! It's like a rabid dog with schizophrenia. Len and I had one of our biggest artistic rows when writing it because he had this rule that you should *never* change tempo in a song. 'It messes with people's groove on the dancefloor,' he said, but I vehemently disagreed, simply because it was fun to argue with him, and it's a silly rule. The song worked and we loved it, especially on T-shirts we had made up with the song title in my scraggly writing. It was our first go at merchandising, and became an instant hit. It also became a bit of a Skunk Anansie motto and gave us strength.

That press review calling us a cliché was like a warning shot from the music press establishment that the honeymoon was *over*: 'Piss off, Skunk Anansie, your time is up. You're too weird, you're too shouty, political and aggressive. You're not cool enough. We can't fuck, fight or fit you into any of our nice boxes, and we don't know what to do with you because you didn't play the game.' It marks the day we became outsiders, and we had yet to discover that was the best place to be.

Our debut album was very personal, even autobiographical in places. Our standout song was 'Weak', which I wrote reflecting on the relationship – if you could call it a relationship – I'd had with my first boyfriend, Tony. Now, as a grown woman, I could clearly see what I had been through with him. I understood my steps to recovery, ending the relationship by leaving London, and by having long conversations with people who worked at the Middlesbrough Rape Crisis Centre, who helped me move through it.

I may be weak, I wrote, *but I've no tears for you. I'm no one's fool.*

I blanked out the assault for around nine years, until a conversation with a friend in my twenties sparked the memory out of nowhere, and I recalled that awful, terrifying night when Tony punched me. The night before a songwriting session, as

I jammed on my guitar, I had an idea for a song that mirrored the feeling I'd had at the time. I had felt scared and vulnerable, but I was determined not to become a victim and channelled that into strength. I wrote everything but the middle eight to 'Weak'.

Initially I didn't think much of the song, assuming it was a quiet B-side, but when I took it to the band and Leigh they loved it, and we finished off the middle-eight section, polishing the rough parts and giving it a groove.

That song gave me a lot of confidence, as it was the first one I composed solo on my new mahogany £300 Wishbone acoustic guitar, which was the first thing I had bought with my One Little Indian record deal cheque. It was about the idea of not letting one 'weak' moment define my whole life. No matter how scared I was, or how much he cried for forgiveness, I had no tears for Tony. I felt sorry for myself, even angry with myself, but I had no sympathy for him at all.

In a strange way, I regret nothing. It was something I needed to go through to become me – a lesson I needed to learn. I was letting life happen to me, and I needed to toughen up and take control. For me, the only way to deal with bad things is to confront them and then conquer them if you can. Writing the lyrics to 'Weak' drew a line under that experience, and I feel safe in the knowledge that I will never let myself go through that again.

'Weak' turned out to be one of our biggest and most powerful songs, and one that I still love to perform. For years I've done what Cass calls a 'Jesus walk' across the hands of the fans to this song because it's a lovely bit of drama.

Rod Stewart later recorded a cover version of 'Weak' for his 1998 album *When We Were the New Boys*. I truly loved that, because anyone who loves Rod Stewart knows he has impeccable taste for a strong song. Other artists have rarely covered our songs because, when you break them down, they are quite weird and complicated. Rod changed one word, from 'weak young heart' to 'weak old heart', which made me smile.

Another slow song on the album was 'Charity'. *I don't want your charity twisting me round* is about the times I've felt vulnerable but expressed it to the wrong person – someone who either just pitied me or who didn't care. I suppose that's the only way you learn who the right person is, by getting it wrong. Traumatic things have happened to me but I don't see myself as a victim. It was those conversations at the Rape Crisis Centre that gave me a clearer understanding of the impact of trauma, and how it's possible to not be treated as a powerless victim. I don't want to be pitied. I'm very uncomfortable with that. I want options and opportunity, and I want to be listened to and respected. I don't want anyone to do all that for me because then I'll never learn how to do it for myself. Songwriting is very cathartic and provides a method for doing that. In those days, I couldn't find the words in conversation to express how I felt, but strangely I could sing them.

But I also realise each listener has their own idea of what our songs are about, and that's okay. Once we've recorded them, they go out into the ether, and in some ways they don't belong to us anymore. I actually love hearing other people's interpretations, even if they're far removed from our original intention. The power of a song is in how it makes someone feel.

Some of the songs on *Paranoid & Sunburnt* are like rallying cries. 'And Here I Stand', for instance, is about being black and British, referring to the identity crisis my friends and I faced being the first generation born in England to parents from the Commonwealth. We were like a bridging generation, made to feel that we weren't British by the British, even though we were born in the UK, but also not feeling very Jamaican – something I realised in the country markets of Jamaica, when I couldn't understand a word anyone said to me. 'And Here I Stand' turns that around, claiming England as home. No more identity crisis, no more being made to feel we weren't welcome – we were standing our ground.

That song drew on my experience with Sauda (Swahili for 'dark complexion'). Sauda was a monthly, black-women-only performance event at the Women's Centre in London that we started in the early '90s. During the first part of the night there would be singers, musicians, comedians, dancers and spoken word performers, followed by a dance party with DJs till 4am. We got together a group of seven brilliant friends with a variety of skill sets, and threw our own party. The initial idea came from my friend Richelle – we were so tired of there being nothing in the gay scene for black women, so we decided to do it ourselves. The cabaret lasted for three years and it was rammed every time we did it. Soul II Soul vocalist Caron Wheeler came to sing, as did Carleen Anderson from acid-jazz band Young Disciples. I put together an a cappella group called Sauda Voices, and helped out with art direction and stage production, learning a lot about putting on a show. We created a place where we all belonged – somewhere we could feel at home. It was an exciting time, a moment when my black British generation developed our own culture, which came out so strongly in the music and the hybrid collisions of soul, jazz, rock and rap.

'Rise Up' is also a song about identity. Strangely inspired by Guns N' Roses' 'Sweet Child O' Mine', the lyrics stemmed from a conversation I had with some female friends, one of whom had split up with her boyfriend because he felt she wasn't paying him enough attention. She was filled with self-doubt, and I felt like she needed a positive message. With its blues riff sound, it's one of the few songs that survived the Mama Wild days. It was also a massive favourite when we performed those very early gigs, a fist pump of a song that we would play as an encore, but as time went by we realised it was too bluesy for Skunk Anansie; it was a song from another era.

Songs like that age badly because it seems they're of a moment, yet they never quite evolve into the next moment. 'Intellectualize My Blackness', for example, was left out of our live set for about twenty years because it just didn't fit. The idea for it came from that 'good friend' of mine who told me I shouldn't be singing 'the music of our oppressors'. Seriously? Just because black artists dominate genres like soul and reggae, that doesn't mean that's all we can do! To me, music has no boundaries, and what's really important is authenticity, empathy and respect, whatever genre you play.

When we recorded 'Intellectualize My Blackness', it was late at night and it was loud – like, Motörhead loud. I had black warpaint on my face and was dressed in camouflage, jumping around the studio like a kangaroo while the boys were going nuts, strobing the lights. We recorded the song like it was a gig in a war zone. You can hear the boys shouting at the beginning of the song because it was recorded through the pick-up wires on their guitars. Pete Winkelman, the owner of the studio, came down in his pyjamas.

'Shit, we're in trouble again,' said Ace.

'What the heck's going on?' he asked. 'This sounds amazing!'

Phew!

Sylvia was so much fun to record with. She loved anything unconventional, and no idea was too crazy. Skunk Anansie worked by two mottos: 'leave your ego at the door' and 'you never know until you try'. That way, everyone was free to criticise anyone else's contribution, and no one was allowed to kill an idea without trying it first. Some things sound awful in your head, but when they hit the air magic flies into them. We always worked hard on the groove so our music wouldn't sound disparate. Cass used to say that we weren't about being 'clever bollocks', until Robbie (the drum virtuoso) proved him wrong when he wrote 'Fuck you jazz c**ts' out in Morse code and then played it for fun. I call that very clever bollocks!

Sylvia was always tuned into our playful energy. We did, however, finally drive her up the wall one night when we were being hyped-up, noisy, partying kids, playing snooker till four in the morning. She got so annoyed that she left and checked herself into a hotel because she was tired of getting no sleep. We had to send her flowers to say sorry and convince her to return to the studio.

At the beginning of our career the music press establishment loved us, with *NME* and *Melody Maker* running full-page reviews with front covers saying how wonderful we were. Steve Lamacq and Jo Whiley had championed 'Little Baby Swastikkka' on their famous Radio 1 show, *The Evening Session,* and because we listened to them religiously, this was heaven. After finishing the album, we were excited to join the inaugural *NME* Bratbus tour in January 1995, our first-ever tour. Dreamt up by *NME* editor Steve Sutherland as an alternative to the Brit Awards, the *NME* Carling Brat Awards championed new bands and, in a move to counter music industry London-centrism, they loaded us onto a Bratbus and drove us round Britain. On the Bratbus there was us, Veruca Salt – a grunge femme-rock band from Chicago fronted by singer Nina Gordon and guitarist Louise Post – the 60 Ft. Dolls, a Welsh rock trio who did pub-metal blues, and Macclesfield band Marion. We were supposed to create some anarchy. Oh, and journalists were on the bus too.

We were slightly older and definitely wiser than some of the other bands. The tour vibe was to create havoc, go mad, let off fire extinguishers and create column inches for the magazine. Every night was rowdy. As a result there were crates of free alcohol, but we couldn't even begin to get into that kind of trouble because we had a major problem: we realised we had to fire our drummer. From London to our first gig in Manchester, Robbie drank twenty-four beers. Just in that journey. For five hours he sat next to the bus driver, gulping down the free alcohol and stacking the empty beer cans into some weird installation. It was strange for me. I was a rocker and a clubber, so I'd seen some sights, but I'd never been this close to someone as desperate for alcohol in my life, and it was scary. Selfishly, I saw the future of my band seeping like vodka down his throat into the abyss. Straight off the bus we had a serious band meeting.

'You don't have to drink the tour bus dry in one day, mate. What's the rush? There's no sell-by date on it,' Cass said. We had no tools to deal with someone suffering that level of addiction. He was totally smashed before each gig but, to his credit, he never played a wrong beat, and that was always his defence.

Inside I knew it wasn't going to work. We were on our way up, we had a massive buzz around us, and we were on the metaphorical steam train, going full speed down the track. I admit I didn't have much in common with Robbie. He was Cass's friend, he was sweet, he had some crazy rock stories, and he was a talented drummer, but he was from a different world. He was always a worry. 'Where's Robbie?' people would ask. 'Is he drinking?' He was also super-precious about his drum kit. During gigs when he thought I was about to take a running jump onto the kit, he'd stand up and catch me before I landed – not very rock 'n' roll being caught like a baby mid-flight and carefully placed back on the floor!

The more Robbie drank, the less we did. We were trying to set an example, so we couldn't tell him to curb his ways then get loaded ourselves – not great when *NME* journalists are trying to get to know you. But even without Robbie's antics that was never our vibe. For us it was about Skunk Anansie being a killer live band, and that's the one thing we felt we had over everyone else. We knew we were different and unfamiliar, so we had to prove ourselves every single night. We couldn't get away with being rubbish because of a hangover; we knew we'd be treated differently. Other bands can do that, but to this day we've always felt we're only as good as our last gig. It's like I carry the weight of every black female-fronted band on my shoulders – if I mess up, they're not letting anyone else in. We did enjoy a few drinks, and we had our crazy moments where stuff got broken, but we weren't going to smash everything up just to get press. Somehow we knew it would backfire on us, and on me, and besides, I always felt bad for the low-paid cleaner who had to mop up rock vomit.

We were looking for allies. I loved Veruca Salt's music and watched them every night, but I thought they were a bit distant. They were the huge American band headlining the tour with their entourage and separate dressing rooms, so they didn't feel very approachable. I was still a little timid offstage in those days. It was our first tour, we didn't know tour etiquette, and we didn't know that we could probably just say hi and start chatting. But maybe they felt like us – they weren't getting drunk and trashing the place like the 60 Ft. Dolls. Maybe they thought, *Let's keep away from these English bands with their rotten teeth, bland food and drunken ways!* We did rock though, and played some great gigs on that Bratbus tour. The crowd were never sure at first, but the mosh-pit always arrived midway through our set and mayhem would follow, ensuring us fans for life – job done!

In March, our first proper single, 'Selling Jesus', was released and, despite zero radioplay, it did well. At the same time, our label mate Björk asked us to do a remix of her hit 'Army of Me'. We beefed it up with strange, dark riffs and a howling vocal from me. When the song went to Number 10 in the UK charts, she asked us to perform with her on *Top of the Pops*. We were ecstatic! *TOTP* was my favourite childhood show! It was a great afternoon. I shared a car to the TV studio in Elstree with Björk, and she told me why she had written the song – it was about her brother who was being negative and needed to sort himself out or feel her wrath. When it came to the performance, our duet provoked a barrage of complaints, with parents phoning the BBC to complain that I had scared their children! Björk loved us and we loved her. She was that rare combination of being completely down to earth but at the same time odd and otherworldly. And the way she said 'innit' at the end of every sentence like a Brixton girl used to make me chuckle.

At that point, things were harmonious with our label, One Little Indian, and Derek Birkett worked hard at launching our first album. I also got on with him as a person. One night when we were in the States, meeting American record labels, for some reason Derek and I ended up getting into a tequila battle, even though I was half his size. We were staying in a rented house with his wife and kids and, after they had gone to bed, the two of us carried on drinking. I downed half a bottle of tequila, and he told me afterwards that I insisted on going for a swim in the pool in the back garden. Derek told me I was absolutely paralytic. 'But I wasn't really worried,' he said, 'because I knew as soon as the air hit you, you'd just be out.' Apparently I went outside and just fell straight-legged onto the grass. Derek picked me up, carried me back inside, and I was literally sick for five days. I haven't drunk tequila since.

Even though we finished our debut album *Paranoid & Sunburnt* in 1994, it wasn't released until the summer of 1995. The delay drove me crazy! By the time the album was released, I hated it because we had become so much better as a band. We had done five tours of the UK and felt we were really smashing it live, so the record sounded naïve to my ears, and I viewed it with disdain for the next twenty years. Now, when I listen to it, I hear what other people hear – *Paranoid & Sunburnt* captured a freshness and magic that touring inevitably dissolves. It really sounded like us, in a room, rocking out. It was a new UK sound that was rooted in 1970s rock and punk but living smack-bang in the '90s. If we had recorded it a year later, I think it would still have been great, but in a different way.

To my mind, it also stands out because it was mixed by the great Andy Wallace. We were obsessed with every record he mixed or produced. He was our idol. How did lil' ole Skunk get to work with such an American legend? This was the man who had mixed Run DMC's *Raising Hell* and Nirvana's album *Nevermind*. Quite simply, Leigh did it. Years before, when she was starting out in the industry, working for the Rolling Stones' booking agents, Leigh had spotted Andy's home address on the office's Rolodex and had copied it down. When we got our first record deal, every time we had a gig she would send him a flyer, even though she knew he probably wouldn't come. This was a piece of genius foresight because he later told us how it had sparked his curiosity. 'I kept getting these red flyers from this English band that looked cool,' he said, so by the time we had an American record deal, he took the meeting. He wanted to be involved, so that was the beginning of a beautiful relationship!

The title *Paranoid & Sunburnt* was inspired by Black Sabbath tracks we loved: 'Paranoid' and 'Snowblind'. It was also a reference to our antics at our first-ever Glastonbury gig in June 1995. We were so excited to be asked to play the UK's biggest festival that year, but very nearly didn't make it onstage. Our slot was on the Thursday at 12 noon, but at 11.55 we were still arguing with security to let us backstage because our tour manager had got the wrong passes. Ace had been clever enough to arrive the night before, and was standing onstage waiting for us. Eventually we convinced them to let us through. We were the first band on that day and we ran onstage, played four of a planned six songs to a half-empty field and then came off. We spent the rest of the weekend having one crazy experience after another – camping in tepees, meeting cool strangers in the Green Fields (and being stupid enough to sip their drinks), walking for miles, losing each other, falling on tents, waking people up and getting chased, and watching the sunrise and sunset with topless people dancing in circles. *Paranoid & Sunburnt* seemed to sum up the whole mad experience. Ace and I performed an acoustic version of 'Charity' backstage for the BBC, and people said afterwards that was one of the high points of the TV coverage.

Four years later we returned as headliners but, before that happened, we were tried and tested to our limits.

NINE

YES, IT'S FUCKING POLITICAL

Yes it's fucking political,
Everything's political
Yes it's fucking satirical,
Everything's satirical

'Yes It's Fucking Political'

'Can you check my teeth alignment?'

An extra in a bandana and camouflage poked his head through the door of the trailer on the *Strange Days* film set. The make-up artist, who was painting a large white cross on my face, said, 'Are you serious?'

'Yeah, I had my teeth done recently and I wanna check the alignment.'

She didn't bother to answer.

It was a warm summer night in 1995, and Los Angeles Street in downtown LA had been cordoned off with military precision. At one end, cranes hovered over a futuristic stage and a giant video screen, while at the other, 150 extras put finishing touches to their make-up. A rag-tag mixture of bin-liner punks, drag queens and thrift-store freaks formed the moshing crowd for an imaginary 1999 New Year's Eve street party, and Skunk Anansie were the band onstage. We were going to be in a movie, a big one called *Strange Days*, a sci-fi techno thriller scripted by James Cameron and starring Ralph Fiennes as a virtual reality drug dealer, Juliette Lewis and Angela Bassett. At that point, director Kathryn Bigelow was emerging as a force in Hollywood, with films like *Point Break* and *Blue Steel* to her name.

Dave Massey, head of A&R at Epic, our label in the US, told us that when he sent a demo of 'Selling Jesus' to Kathryn she responded so positively to the song that they decided to reshoot a segment of the movie to fit in our band. By the time we arrived in LA, the song had been released and the New York shock jock Howard Stern was playing it on his WXRK radio show. He loved 'Selling Jesus', which honestly felt a little weird, but at the same time an absolutely massive deal, because his show had millions of listeners. 'Selling Jesus' became our route into the US market.

On the *Strange Days* set the crew began filming the party scene just after sunset. We'd never seen anything like it – a huge, proper Hollywood set with the whole street blocked off. 'Selling Jesus' thundered out from massive speakers, while we performed at full steam swathed in dry ice, and stage-divers launched into the mosh pit. I screamed as loudly and defiantly as possible: *They're selling Jesus again/They want your soul and your money, your blood and your votes* . . . We thought our first performance was brilliant, we were really pleased, but then they wanted to do another take, and then another and another.

We weren't actors, we had no idea we were supposed to save our energy, and it was unbelievably hard work. We literally played our heaviest, hardest song non-stop without a break for a full eight hours. I had a great relationship with Dr Martens, so for the movie I'd asked them to make me a pair of double-layered steel-toecap boots. I was testing them out but they were solid as a rock with no spring in them (they got it right in 2015 when they launched a softer version and called them Jaden). The crazy leather pants I was wearing were brand new, made by the legendary leatherman Stan Leather, who later created all of our guitar straps and many beautiful bespoke pieces for me. The leather was double layered, so the trousers were very tight with no give in them. My bottom half was totally rigid, so I was jumping around onstage like a pogo stick in a super-stiff outfit that felt like being stuck in concrete. If I performed in those leather pants and boots today, I'd have me back out in two minutes!

The only break we had was when a giant possum invaded the set. Possums may look sweet on TV, but this one resembled a tall, mutant rat with humongous front teeth! The extras ran screaming while the producer, a guy with 'SLEEP IS FOR SISSIES' emblazoned on the back of his T-shirt, yelled at everyone to keep quiet, and a security guard chased the animal back into the sewer. The extras on set started the shoot full of energy, but by the end they were very bedraggled, including two drag queens stomping wearily on two-foot-high platform boots. 'I'm flagging,' Cass said towards the end. 'And I've got a sore arse. A bouncer accidentally kicked me.'

I was knackered too. To this day I have never been that tired – it was just relentless. Although I was miming, I still had to sing so it looked good on camera, and at the end of each take I did a stage-dive into the crowd. I must have stage-dived 200 times during what was basically an eight-hour gig – it gave me new respect for actors. It took me weeks to get over the shoot, but I loved every sweat-dripping second of it. It was awesome! We thought the film would make us huge in America, so we were happy to do it and were prepared to work hard.

By June 1995, we could see that our relentless schedule was paying off when we won Best New British Band at the *Kerrang!* Awards. Blur and Oasis were the biggest bands in the UK at that point, due to fight for the Number 1 chart spot in what was to become the Battle of Britpop, but Phil Alexander, editor of *Kerrang!*, the UK's biggest-selling rock magazine, liked the fact that Skunk Anansie were offering something completely different from Britpop – super-heavy and tight, part classic rock, part futuristic – with a shaven-headed black woman singing political lyrics. He made a conscious decision that *Kerrang!* would work to develop our band and support us for the long term.

Earlier that year, things had come to a head with our drummer Robbie. We were touring on a budget, and Cass had become tired of sharing a room with Robbie because of the latter's drink problem. The situation became so bad that one night, at the Piccadilly Hotel in Manchester, where we were staying, Cass just slept in the bar. Eventually, Robbie left the band and joined German synth outfit Alphaville the very next day. I must confess it was a relief to see him go – it was him or Cass – but he was going be a nightmare to replace, and we needed a replacement fast.

We tried out a new dude called Louie, who was very sweet and great company, but we could tell the band dynamic wasn't right. His playing style was too different to our album. He grooved very well, but he had a floppy, more relaxed indie style. He was only with us for six weeks, but in that time we shot the *Strange Days* movie and music videos and did loads of press, so he became immortalised into Skunk history. We urgently needed someone else, because this was our moment; we were on the rocket. The stars were aligning and we were lifting off! But it had to be the right drummer. The chemistry, look and attitude needed to be just right or we would be screwed.

Then, one day, in walks Mr Mark Richardson, like a tall glass of water on a steaming-hot beach. At the time, Mark was in a bluesy rock band called B.L.O.W. Both his band and Skunk Anansie had been nominated for the same award by *Kerrang!* Two weeks before the *Kerrang!* Awards show, he had been drunk in a kebab shop in Andover and seen our 'I Can Dream' video on the portable TV there. It inspired him so much that he went to see us play, supporting brilliant Irish alt-metal band Therapy? at Nottingham Rock City. Mark told me later that as I ran on stage singing 'Selling Jesus', he turned to his friend and said, '*This* is the kind of band I want to be in!'

The following week at the *Kerrang!* Awards, I clocked Mark before he saw me – he was bloody tall and muscly with dyed, floppy blond hair and dolphin-blue eyes. I thought, *Bloody 'ell, that guy's hot!* He came straight up to me. 'Hi, Skin, I was at your gig last week. Your drummer's shit. I want to be your drummer.'

Beaming like a Cheshire cat on E, I knew we'd found our man. I told him, 'Actually, Louie is only temporary, but we are looking for someone permanent.'

Mark comes from Whitby, a small fishing town on the northeast coast of the UK. He had started off playing for the hard rock band Little Angels before forming B.L.O.W., and one of his biggest influences was John Bonham, the swaggering, dynamic drummer of Led Zeppelin. Mark describes his own drumming as 'very heavy, and supportive, not flashy. I play for the song.'

And it was those qualities we heard when he then came for an audition with Cass at Jumbo Studios in Willesden. He was solid as a rock. Drums are the foundation of a band – you depend on them, you need them to stand firm and hold you wherever you go. I know onstage that if I want to change anything, which I frequently do, I get Mark's attention first and then Cass and Ace will follow. In that first audition he just played what was necessary to make the song sound great, and I'd never heard anyone play that loud. He had a completely different style to Robbie, who was incredible but a little precious and fussy. Mark is a proper rock drummer: passionate, fun, with loads of ambition. Shortly after that, we called him late one night when we were recording a section of the soundtrack to *Strange Days*, and Louie couldn't get it right – not enough fire. Mark jumped in the car from Andover and came straight over, getting there at midnight and finishing at four in the morning. He nailed it and that was that.

Despite our rapidly growing audience, and the fact our videos were being played regularly on MTV, Derek Birkett at One Little Indian was always complaining that we cost the label too much money, and Leigh was often at loggerheads with him. This started after the release of our first album in September 1995, when we were building up to a Top 10 single with 'Weak', but Derek was reluctant to make a video. In the end, video production duo Hammer & Tongs (who later made videos for Blur and Pulp) shot it in the car park at Santa Monica airport in one morning in the middle of a US tour. MTV were keen to support us, so how could Derek justify not making a video? This skirmish was the first in a series of battles that started to undermine our relationship with One Little Indian. We felt we could never rest on our successes and that we had to keep fighting for a slice of the label's promotional budget.

We were also finding it difficult to break America because, in an industry that was still segregated along colour lines, there were so many hurdles to overcome. The first time we went to the US, to have meetings with labels, we flew business class. It just so happened that one of the people we were going to see was on the plane two seats away from us. He introduced himself, then, looking at me and Cass, said, 'When you get there, make sure I introduce you to the head of our urban music division.'

We said, 'Why?'

'Oh, he's a great guy.'

Cass and I looked at each other, like, *He has no idea what we do.* In the US we were always getting introduced to the head of the urban division, where they worked with black artists doing rap, hip-hop, soul, funk. Wanting to remain polite but make a point, we said, 'You realise we're a rock band?' In our heads we were thinking, *This isn't going to work.*

We ended up signing to Epic Records because they had diverse and original American bands on their roster, like Rage Against The Machine and Living Colour. It was never going to be easy to market Skunk Anansie; we were an odd combination for the American market. When signing us, they promised us the world – we met some good people, we got the top treatment, first-class flights, lunch on the executive floor. We had a lot of support – executive Harvey Leeds loved us, as did Richard

Griffiths, the Head of Promotion. Epic went on to fund eight US tours for us, but in reality America wasn't ready for a band like Skunk Anansie.

America wasn't going to accept a diverse rock act, we could feel it. There was a whole movement with the Black Rock Coalition, a collective founded in New York in 1985 to combat racial stereotyping in the music industry, but it was an uphill struggle for black rock musicians, and still is. After a while we felt that Epic gave up and we were in the record company undercurrent, watching bands in the jet stream shoot by. Everywhere we went, in every record shop in every town in the US, our album would be in the R&B section instead of rock, just because there were two black faces in the band. College radio support was vital for success and we had none. We would turn up at radio stations and DJs hadn't listened to the album and knew nothing about us. Howard Stern bloody loved us! I did interviews with Mr Shock Jock himself! But it's striking that the only radio play we could get was from a shock jock, because we were considered so alien.

America was a great shock in terms of the prejudice, particularly in the South. When we were on tour in 1996, we'd pull into a town every day searching for good food. Sometimes the tour bus would stop, we'd get out, look around, but then just get back on the bus and leave for the next town. Some places stank of racism; you could feel it burning your nostrils. I remember us stopping at a bar in Texas – a place that sold food with a pool table at the back. Cass and I decided to have a go, when a woman came up and started overtly flirting with him. Cass isn't stupid – he knows that game, so he ignored her. Still, she continued to come on really strong, and fifteen minutes later a huge cowboy came over and said, 'Ya'll talkin' to my woman?'

We just put the cues down and walked out. We were sitting ducks about to feel buckshot in a 'shoot first ask questions later' kinda place. We got straight back on the tour bus and drove to the next town.

At one point in Texas, in some small roadside town outside Austin, we stopped at a store looking for cigarettes, but it was full of Nazi regalia – swastikas, hoods, caps, helmets, T-shirts, *everything* had fascist insignia. Then out from the back came an Asian guy. We said, 'D'you realise the people who are buying this want you dead?'

He shrugged and answered, 'I'm taking their money, I don't really care.' It was so strange. As English kids, we had a false sense of America. We'd seen the stock images in Hollywood films of skyscrapers and yellow cabs and diverse cultures, but apart from cool cities like New York, LA, San Francisco and Chicago, everything else seemed like small-town Bible belt. We toured for months and played all of those little places. That's the *real* America, what became Trump's America. Every town we went to there'd be a strip with the same franchises – McDonald's, Wendy's, Taco Bell – and that was it, there was literally no other food available unless you cooked it yourself. America felt like an uphill struggle, that there was intrinsic resistance to a diverse band playing rock – playing 'their music'.

I did love touring America, though. The gigs were always packed, so we had loads of fun. We did eight tours there, supporting bands such as Rammstein and Henry Rollins, doing huge festivals with the likes of Slipknot and Sevendust. Our gigs attracted the freaks, and we loved that. The outsiders came out to play. We met so many kids gagging for something different.

There were gays, goths, black dread-headed rockers, Asian punks, drag queens, muscle boys all dressed in leather, and girls with multi-coloured hair years before the Brony revolution. We had some of the best nights of our lives hanging with those guys before we were forced back on the bus by our weary tour manager. Those little towns always had wicked and wonderful subcultures that our image and music spoke to – if everyone in your town thought you were weird, then a Skunk gig was the place for you to be yourself. It opened my eyes and changed how I viewed the world, because it was such a massive country with so many cultural extremes.

I appealed to an alternative crowd. We all know that sex sells – but I wasn't that kind of artist. I signed my first record deal when I was twenty-six. I was a grown woman, I had my politics down, I had my attitude and my band. I wasn't manipulable. I didn't get much negativity about being bisexual – by the mid-1990s people were cooler about gay sexuality – but at the same time it meant that I couldn't be marketed as the straight sexy rock chick.

My personal style began to be noticed in the fashion world. Not long after *Paranoid & Sunburnt* was released, the designer Alexander McQueen called me to a meeting to see his work. When I came to look at his clothes, I was surprised to find he wasn't there, and later discovered he was too shy to meet me. Apparently he kept calling his assistants, asking what I liked. I thought it weird that *he* was shy when I was so nervous myself, feeling well out of my depth. Clothes were important to me, but I knew very little about designer brands. Fashion works when it's organic and comfortable, and one style that suited me was McQueen's 'bumsters'. They were a stand-out piece, a real talking point, so-named because of their extremely low-cut waistline at the back. I wore a pair on the raucous Channel 4 show *TFI Friday*, and they were so low and tiny that every time I turned round the cameraman cut to something else because apparently my bum crevice was too racy for mainstream TV. Oh, how things have changed!

As we got bigger, so my interest in fashion grew, and I started to see the art in fashion instead of just clothes that cover my back. Style and music are interlinked, feeding off each other. I was becoming aware of how I could use fashion as a tool to enhance my stage show and my personal self-worth. Clothes directly influence my mood – if I get it right my confidence is boosted and I feel high on life with the audience in the palm of my hand. Get it wrong and I feel like a scruffy mouse that needs to crawl back into its tiny hole. I have to feel comfortable in my own skin, so what I wear has to be functional and suit my shape.

As a skinny teenager, I was self-conscious about my arms and never showed them because, to me, they looked like brown string hanging out of each armhole. But by my early twenties I was doing press-ups in the morning and before bed, so I had become lean instead of wafer thin. I went to Marks & Spencer and bought white T-shirts for age 3-4, three in a packet – what a bargain! When I put them on they became crop-tops above my belly button, and I'd wear them with big baggy trousers and trainers. It wasn't until I did my first photo shoot with the late Corinne Day, the iconic photographer who worked with Kate Moss, that I knew it was now okay to be skinny and appreciate my body shape.

In the early days, my clothes had to be inexpensive, and

I'd get them either from local Brixton shops I knew well or second-hand shops in Covent Garden masquerading as vintage, or Roman Road market. My style was part goth, part grunge, part yardie, with a lick of skinhead and a sprinkle of eau de punk. I never really wore sexy, girly clothes because I felt too exposed. When I was in Mama Wild, I tried to conform to the 'rock look' by wearing black leather jacket, spikes and skinny jeans, but by the time we started Skunk I realised there was no point trying to look like all the other dudes in bands. On me, the usual rock 'n' roll uniform would look boring and weird. So I began to experiment with my own style. Back then, a shaven-headed black girl was seen as quite radical and made some people uncomfortable, but I also realised the thing I'd been trying to run away from was what people liked about me the most – that I was uncompromising with my look. If you try to conform, I concluded, you're taking away your own power, putting your best asset away in a box, so instead I decided to accentuate and love my differences.

As the band got more attention, I started to be approached by designers, and I was able to choose pieces from their collections to wear in our videos or on TV. I liked Copperwheat Blundell's fitted trousers, for instance, and would wear them with beautiful see-through tops by Sulture, one on top of the other.

My relationship with McQueen – Lee for short – grew after we eventually got to meet each other and we became friends. In 1996, only four years after he graduated from St Martin's College of Art, he became Chief Designer of Givenchy, the luxury French fashion house owned by Louis Vuitton. I'd go to his shows in Paris, brilliantly dramatic events full of famous characters. But because we lived on the same street in Hackney I was lucky enough to see another side to him. On occasion we'd meet and do simple stuff with a small group of friends, which was always lovely. He used to giggle to me about the fact that he made the McQueen perfume exactly like a cheap aftershave he grew up with. He just loved the smell and it made him happy; he didn't care that it wasn't of the correct pedigree.

McQueen was one of the first designers to dress me. I remember a fashion shoot we did, when he was guest-editing *Harpers & Queen* magazine. I wore a leather jacket he'd made with a big, flouncy, sheer shirt underneath, cinched at the waist with a belt. McQueen styled me himself, and I put on the shirt and the jacket and knee-high boots, and was about to pull on some trousers when he looked at my bum and said, 'That's it, we're shooting. You've got to shoot her from behind, looking over the shoulder.'

After the shoot, he said, 'You can keep everything you've got on.' I was delighted! I still have all those pieces, and I love them. McQueen did all the tailoring himself, and knew how to cut things well, so before a shoot I might be wearing one of his designs and he would take the scissors and cut while I was there. I think he liked my personal style, and the fact that I didn't wear things that were super girly or super butch. But I could also wear something by him that was very feminine yet wouldn't make me feel silly.

I was devastated when he died in 2010, truly devastated. By then I had bought a house in Ibiza, and I found a tiny secret church at the top of a hill near San Jose. It's filled from floor to ceiling with precious mementos, photos and prayers from the living to people who have died. It's gorgeous, really beautiful and peaceful. I have two private pieces pinned up in there: one for Lee McQueen and one for Susan Okukenu, the friend who taught me it was alright to say no to men. I think they'd really like it there. McQueen was a naughty-as-hell genius, the *enfant terrible* of the fashion world, and he really didn't give a fuck. He was an East End boy, and he remained an East End boy to the end.

By spring 1996, we had released a hit debut album and four singles, including 'Weak', and were riding a wave. We had to keep up the momentum. To capitalise on this, Leigh said, 'You need another album out *now*.' So, right in the middle of touring and the summer festivals, we went back to Linford Manor. Garth Richardson, who had worked with Red Hot Chili Peppers and Rage Against The Machine, was our producer for our follow-up album, *Stoosh*. We thought up the name driving from one gig to the next, when Leigh declared, 'We need an album title right now or we'll miss the deadline.' (That album felt like it was just successions of crazy deadlines.) We all looked at Leigh and said, 'Let's name it after you.'

'Stoosh' is Jamaican patois for 'posh' and Leigh has always been so stoosh, with excellent taste. She has to have the right pair of shoes and the right handbag – she *is* fashion. We loved that about her. We would all be in our rough army togs, old tees, mash-up fashion (except Cass, who was also very stoosh), then she'd walk in and people would sit up straight, like someone announced, 'The management has entered the room!' There aren't many female managers, so I always felt her commanding presence was a great way to make sure people didn't mess with us. She knew her shit, you could tell by the cut of her coat.

The way we named the album, so quickly, rushing from one place to the next, sums up its energy – intense, highly pressured and not comfortable at all. Garth put us through our paces, and we made the record very rapidly. Most of the songs were written in nine days and recorded in five weeks onto two-inch tape. We had three studios running day and night. Ace had the graveyard shift, so he had to play rhythm parts through the night, putting sparkle on the melodies and solos.

Garth had a completely different style of recording to Sylvia Massy. She loved spontaneity and happy accidents whereas he was incredibly precise and wanted every note to be perfect. He would record everything and have his engineer calculate, with a tape measure, the distance between each snare or kick drum sound and take an average. Then the engineer would splice the master tape so that when you played it back it was absolutely rigid, perfectly in time.

This was before digital editing software like ProTools or Logic, so everything had to be edited by hand. When you listen to Rage Against The Machine, you can hear how tight it sounds, but Garth still managed to keep the fire and edge in the music. Editing like this wasn't a new idea, but the way Garth worked created a fresh take on it. It gave the music a pulsing energy that made it sound exciting. The downside was it blew your confidence out the window, because you had to do a million takes knowing you could never match that kind of perfection, which almost destroyed Mark. I had gone through the anxiety of multiple retakes on our debut album, so I could relate to what he was going through.

On 'Brazen (Weep)', for instance, Mark's drums were so heavily edited that the character and style of his playing sounded more like the editor than Mark; it lost all its beauty. I put my foot down, insisting that it be recorded again, and because we had no more physical space left in the studio, we set up the drums in the snooker room above and recorded it live. It was hard on Mark, because he hadn't actually toured with us yet – he so badly wanted to do a great job. His confidence was knocked but he played brilliantly, like a powerhouse, an engine. Recording that album was pure torture, but the result was that Garth knocked it out of the park and the record took us to another level.

The band was white-hot and doing well across Europe, and in the studio we were on fire. This brought us closer, solidifying our chemistry and sound. The breadth of our songs got us a lot of attention. I was still writing with Len, and we tended to write the slower/mid-tempo, melodic songs that were intricate stories of love and lust, like 'Secretly' or 'Hedonism'. With the band, I'd write louder, more shouty numbers to go with all their instrumentation; songs full of riffs or big chords like 'All I Want' or 'Twisted'. Then there were songs I wrote by myself at home, struggling to learn the guitar, which covered all styles. I took these to Len or the band – tracks like 'Weak', 'Selling Jesus' and 'I Can Dream'.

I love writing with other people, because it's more exciting. On my own it's easy to go round in circles, dragging myself down with insecurities about the quality of the song. If I'm collaborating with someone, we can ping-pong ideas back and forth. I can put a lyric out there and that will spark an idea that can spark a groove. Although there are times when great songs have come out of nowhere. I particularly remember 'I Can Dream' because it emerged one very painful evening when I was attempting to learn barre chords (a really hard thing to do on my wide-necked acoustic guitar).

Due to my limited guitar talent, the songs I wrote on my own were simple and easy to play, but what also made the track more complex was the weird bassline that Len wrote, underpinning the song and adding a delicious tension. Len came from a jazz background, and when we first started writing together he had to relearn the guitar in order to write rock music, so he would create complicated lines that sounded simple. 'Hedonism' starts with a complex, technical guitar hook that's reminiscent of a 1950s sax player. It took Ace a while to learn the hook line, because it's not very natural for a rocker, and that's what I believe separated us from the regular riffs beloved of other bands. Cass adored the complicated notes because it meant he could play creatively and not just sit on the root and fifth bassline.

Len did four European and three of the US tours with us. We'd write on the tour bus, in the hotel room or even backstage before the soundcheck. He had a little travelling writing system that he'd carry around and use for recording demo arrangements for songs in progress. 'Secretly' was written on the road, along with other songs like 'Follow Me Down' and 'Brazen (Weep)'.

One of the strongest, most defiant songs we wrote for *Stoosh* was 'Yes It's Fucking Political'. By that stage, we were constantly being criticised for being political, because half the songs on our debut album – from 'Little Baby Swastikkka' to 'Rise Up' – had strong messages about race, religion or sexual identity. Having a political voice never sat well with the mainstream music press, but our fans loved it because we had something to say. We were all working-class kids who had grown up in different parts of the country, but we'd had to deal with the same issues, and

My great grandmother Annie Louise Milton.

Grandad Bertie and my mother, Patricia Dyer.

Mum and Grandad Bertie's car, in Brixton, mid-1960s.

My dad, Kenneth Dyer, 1970s.

With my brothers Maurice and Beavon outside Grandad Bertie's house, 30 Effra Road, Brixton.

Me aged six.

With my brothers Maurice, Beavon and Nicholas at Trafalgar Square, late 1970s.

Me with my new flat-top haircut, aged
17, outside our house in Tulse Hill.

My final year photo at
Teesside University, 1989.

Singing with my vocal group at Sauda,
early 1990s.

Rick Lennox, our One Little Indian A&R, at
the Splash Club in 1994. © Skunk Anansie Collection

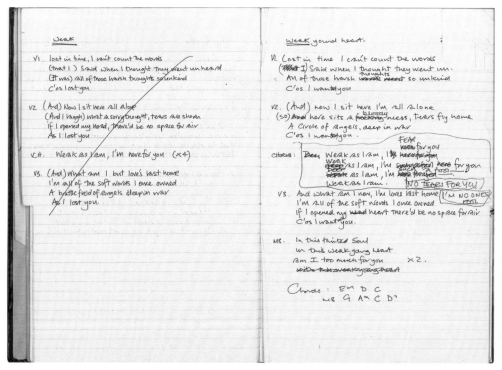

My handwritten lyrics to 'Weak'.

Skin winning best Fart

Me recording 'Paranoid & Sunburnt'.
© Skunk Anansie Collection

Getting in the zone at Linford Manor.
© Skunk Anansie Collection

With producer Sylvia Massy. She loved to shake it up . . . no idea was too crazy.
© Skunk Anansie Collection

In the bunker at Linford Manor. © Skunk Anansie Collection

It Takes Blood and Guts . . .

© Skunk Anansie Collection

Skunks in the studio, 1995. L-R: Ace, Leigh, Cass, Len Arran, Dave Wibberley, A&R at Chrysalis Publishing, plus me and Robbie France.

© Dave Wibberley

Poster for the first NME Bratbus tour in 1995.

© Skunk Anansie Collection

Early Skunk Anansie promo polaroid. © Michael Halsband

Mid-1990s, my Corrine Day shoot for *The Face* magazine. © Corinne Day

Demonstrating my live neck-biting technique . . . © Hayley Madden

With Björk in the garden at BBC Elstree Studios, 1995. © Jeff Simpson

With my co-author Lucy O'Brien and the band in Los Angeles, 1995. © Skunk Anansie Collection

A photo shoot for *Select* magazine.
© Simon Fowler

With Lenny Kravitz on the European leg of the *Circus* tour. © Skunk Anansie Collection

Crowd-surfing at the Concorde in Brighton, mid-1990s.
© Skunk Anansie Collection

Anton Corbijn
doing a shoot for the
Stoosh album cover.
© Skunk Anansie Collection

Me and Leigh
in a hotel on the
Stoosh tour.
© Skunk Anansie Collection

Us backstage with The
Stereophonics, 1996.
© Skunk Anansie Collection

The iconic Lemmy with Mark, Ace and me. © Skunk Anansie Collection

To one of the best bands I ever saw. Lemmy x

Posing with our platinum *Stoosh* records, Virgin Records, Germany. © Skunk Anansie Collection

Me and Ace with the Spice Girls at the BRIT Awards, 1997. © Skunk Anansie Collection

Nelson Mandela's 80th birthday party. L–R: Mandela, Graça Machel, Cass, me and Michael Jackson. © Pool / Getty Images

Chilling out with drinks, *Post Orgasmic Chill* tour, 1999. © Skunk Anansie Collection

Backstage with David Bowie and Beverley Knight, 1999. © Brian Rasic / Getty Images

Me and Ace, Roskilde Festival, 1999. © Skunk Anansie Collection

'The only time I'm truly competitive is when I'm onstage . . .'
© Rune Hellestad / Corbis / Getty Images

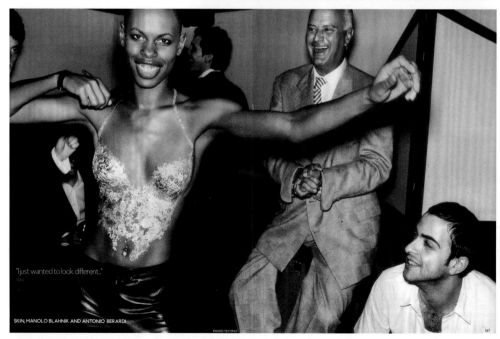

Wearing nothing but gold leaf paint; photo shoot for *Vogue* in 2000, with Manolo Blahnik behind me. © Mario Testino

With Grace Jones in 2003 (and the back of Maxine Clarke's head!) © Skunk Anansie Collection

Me and Ladyfag.
© Serichai Traipoom

Photo shoot for *Fake Chemical State* album, at
Manumission, Ibiza. © Derrick Santini

With the lovely stylist Kim Howells.

Keko Hainswheeler's praying mantis body piece for the 2009 *Smashes & Trashes* tour.
© India Fleming

With designer and close friend Liborio Capizzi. © Giovanni Montuori for Club Plastic

Live at Albert Hall, Manchester, 2016. © Melanie Smith

Me onstage as a fireball, *25Live@25* tour, 2019. © Melanie Smith

the songs reflected that. Many of our fans felt the same way as us, and had been on anti-apartheid, poll tax, Clause 28, or anti-Criminal Justice Bill marches. Len came from Hull, and remembered the Miners' Strike in the 1980s, seeing hundreds of unofficial trucks being given a police escort to cross picket lines.

One journalist complained that we were 'spoiling it for the listener', and a record label A&R we met before signing with One Little Indian told us radio stations wouldn't play political music because they want to remain impartial. But no one's impartial; everyone has a viewpoint because of their experiences, so therefore everything is political. We added 'Yes It's Fucking Political' to the 'keep politics out of music' debate because political songs are important and give people a voice. The great ones sum up the feelings of a generation, putting words to how people feel – songs like 'Strange Fruit' sung by Billie Holiday or The Special AKA's 'Free Nelson Mandela'. As a consequence, we have some incredible heartfelt music that might otherwise have been suppressed.

One day, we were doing a soundcheck at *TFI Friday*, and our hero Billy Bragg was on the next stage. *Negative are all your views/ So you can prop up your fake cool/A puppet all the same*, I sang. He'd heard our song and was a fan. After doing the soundcheck for his single 'Upfield', he turned to us and said, 'Yes, it's fucking political. Everything's political.' *Boom!*

Released in October 1996, the hard work we put into *Stoosh* was rewarded. It was Top 10 throughout Europe, yielding four hit singles. By then we had got into making surreal, filmic videos to bring out the darker emotions running through our songs. 'All I Want', the first single from *Stoosh*, was aided by a lurid video directed by Stephen Norrington. He had made his debut in 1994 with cyberpunk horror movie *Death Machine*, and later had a global box office hit with the Marvel comic-inspired film *Blade*. That was a mad day! The set had vertical flames shooting upwards and bombs exploding all around us; Stephen even blew up instruments, with pieces of guitar flying everywhere. He used our video shoot to try out loads of mad studio effects he wanted for his up-and-coming movies.

The video for the next single, 'Twisted', which followed two months later, is one of my all-time faves. We were in the middle of an Australian tour, so director Anton Beebe took us to Lake Eyre, a salt lake in the Australian outback. It was an otherworldly place, like being in a lunar landscape.

They sometimes raced jet cars to break the land speed record on the salt flats, but on the day we filmed, there was no one else around, and it was silent, baking hot and glaringly beautiful. I'd never seen so many bugs in my life! Everything was covered in all kinds of tiny creatures. We slept in tents and I tried to have a shower, but the metal shower shack housed so many ants and flies, I could barely see the cracked white tiles ... better to stay dirty.

We grew with each single release from *Stoosh*. It felt at times like we were on a train rushing down a mountain at full speed and all we could do was hold on tight. MTV gave us full backing; they loved playing these videos, especially the rocking ones. But it was our emotional, slower songs that got the most powerful response – people are softies at heart. We had the song 'Hedonism' in our back pocket as the third single, but One Little Indian weren't getting behind us, and Leigh and Derek had started to have shouting matches in the office.

'We're not making a third video,' said Derek.

'But we haven't gone with the best single yet,' argued Leigh.

'The album's not doing anything. The label is losing so much money,' he complained.

Leigh, exasperated, told him that after the next show he had to explain to us why he wouldn't make a video for 'Hedonism'.

Derek agreed, but when he showed up backstage at Southend Cliffs Pavilion, Leigh was ready with the accountant. He tried to tell us there wasn't enough money to make a third video, but our accountant disagreed, saying there was plenty. Despite that, he still refused.

As Leigh would say later, it was like watching someone shoot themselves in the foot. We were the label's biggest band, but she felt that because Derek was also managing Björk, she had the biggest slice of the promotional budget. Finally, after some lengthy negotiation it did go ahead.

Directed by style warrior Thomas Krygier, our video for 'Hedonism' was shot using CGI to create stark effects, which was new technology at the time. It featured same- and mixed-sex couples embracing and kissing, which became a big deal. It was groundbreaking, not just because of the CGI techniques, but also for its depiction of LGBT relationships. This got us into hot water with MTV, who refused to show it until we edited out the girls kissing. 'Hedonism' became a smash hit throughout Europe and our *Stoosh* album went on to sell three million copies.

After that, we wanted to get out of our record deal with One Little Indian. They had been reluctant to make videos for the two biggest songs of our career to date. They were proved wrong both times, so we were done. Then, for the next eighteen months, the label wouldn't let us go. I'd loved being on the label, but by then I didn't feel sad because although we'd started off with a great team who understood us, one by one those people left. One of those no longer there was our original A&R man, Rick Lennox, a genuine music lover who went to gigs all the time, who understood bands and who never came across to us like a cold businessman. We were gutted. While Leigh was trying to get us out of the deal, we spent the time touring. As Ace said, 'I packed my bag, and four years later I unpacked it. I didn't have a flat for four years, just a suitcase. It was the most liberating period of my life. To own nothing and live nowhere.'

We were like a pack of wolves, restlessly touring the world looking for our next kill.

TEN

HEDONISM

Just because you feel good
It doesn't make it right, oh no
Just because you feel good
Still want you here tonight

'Hedonism'

The only time I'm truly competitive is when I'm onstage. It's raw. The minute I hit the boards I want to be better than everybody else. When we play festivals, we get into our zone; we need to feel the music right in the middle of our chests, our chemistry spinning round us in circles so that we can be the best band of the day – the one that gets talked about when it's all over. That's my aim. We need to blow off whoever's before or after us, and if we're headlining, the aim is to show why we deserve it. I could be humble about it, but festivals are war – we learnt that the hard way. You're there to steal everyone else's fans. When you do your own gigs, you're preaching to the

converted and can be more relaxed, but at festivals you're stealing from all the other religions, aiming to crush everyone else
to smithereens. Of course, it doesn't always work out like that,
but that's the prayer I say to myself before every performance.

At school I was the sports captain three years in a row, I
did long jump, discus, javelin, 400 metres, 1,500 metres and
cross-country, which was my best sport. I was a long-distance
runner, and I now use that competitive spirit onstage. I make no
apologies for it. I approached performing like an athlete – two
hours of jumping, stage-diving, climbing, running around the
stage; it's relentless. You can't do those things unless you're fit,
so I constantly trained in order to do the best gig possible.

I remember doing a concert in Italy with Iggy Pop, in 1996.
I knew he was a legendary front man, so when I walked on
and saw him watching from the side of the stage, I made sure
we did one of the gigs of our lives. I pulled out all my tricks,
the crowd went ballistic, and when I walked off and saw his
face I knew we'd nailed it. *Follow that, Iggy!* I thought. His
answer was to go onstage and completely destroy us! He was
incredible, one of the best performances I've ever seen – going
crazy, throwing the mic stand around, doing his weird dancing – he was absolutely fucking phenomenal, and he totally
killed us with tune after tune. He was a GOD! He did the gig
of *his* life, and he's been doing it for decades. I thought we had
it in the bag, but he rose to the occasion and showed us how
it was done. That's what it's about, it's competition. We were
like, 'Touché!'

Some tours are pure hell, like the time we toured with
industrial post-punk band Killing Joke. The musicians – Jaz
Coleman, Youth (who later became a top producer), Geordie

Walker and Paul Ferguson – were all really nice and sweet as pie whenever we met them, which was rare because a lot of the time they were somewhere else getting mashed. This meant that behind their backs their crew took real pleasure in making our life on tour as miserable as possible. We decided to aim high and did some great gigs, which made them so crazy they just ramped up the sabotage.

Every night we seemed to have a brand-new problem to conquer. We would find that something else 'just broke'. They also started putting us on earlier and earlier, so that by the end of the tour we were going on stage *before* the doors opened! For the first half of every gig there'd be barely anyone in the venue, but, by the end, we had the crowd jumping. A lesson we learnt early on is that your tour manager represents you, and if a band's crew think they can mess with your tour manager, then they can mess with you. They terrorised our tour manager, even banging on her hotel bedroom door at four in the morning demanding to be let in, for God knows what.

Cass finally lost his temper the day they unplugged the sound during our set. Apparently a plug 'fell out' during the gig, but we knew that was impossible because those kinds of plugs are massive and have to be clipped in for safety reasons. They can't just 'fall out'; they have to be yanked out. Our sound died mid-song, and when Cass looked over he could see them giggling, so he took off his guitar and swung it at them. He'd had enough.

The crew scattered, the sound came back, and we played the rest of our set fuming. I doubt very much that Killing Joke knew what was going on, but you have to take responsibility for what your crew get up to, as they do it under your name.

All these experiences toughened us up. A lot of the

groundwork was laid in the early days of the band, being resourceful and putting up with discomfort. Leigh's parents Tom and Norma were huge supporters, and often we would pool our lowly resources with them to do small tours outside London. Leigh's dad was a hospital driver so he'd requisition an old ambulance, and we'd throw our gear in the back and follow him in a rented Ford Escort. Because I was the smallest I would be squashed in the middle seat between man-spreaders Mark and Cass, the cheese in a skunk sandwich.

As the tours grew bigger we learnt about backstage politics, and also how to do a memorable gig. We learnt a lot from Lenny Kravitz, for instance, when we supported him on his 1996 *Circus* tour in Europe. Lenny is a *born* '70s rock star. With his shades and long superstar dreadlocks, he's got the power to just walk onstage and drive you crazy. I made good friends with Lenny's amazing guitarist, Craig Ross, and the lovely drummer, Cindy Blackman. Every night during the gig, Lenny had a section where he would jam for ages and lose the audience. He didn't give two monkeys though; he knew he had the songs to win them back, so he just enjoyed himself.

I remember Lenny's tour because that broke us in Europe; it was the tour that changed everything. As we toured, we began to see a pattern. During song one, people would stand with their mouths wide open as if to say, 'What the *hell* is this?', but by song four the crowd would lose their minds, form a mosh-pit and stage-dive. From Lenny we learnt about sound and style. His band were always on fire, they could really groove, and they looked so chic doing it. Every night I would watch him, learning new moves, and the next day trying to be better than him. We tried and tried, and a couple of nights we definitely got close. When Lenny was having a bad gig we slaughtered him, but mostly he slaughtered us.

On our *Stoosh* tour, throughout 1996 and 1997, while Leigh was negotiating us out of the One Little Indian deal, we supported or played festivals with U2, David Bowie, Aerosmith and the Black Crowes, as well as with the aforementioned Henry Rollins and Rammstein, and we learnt all about stage etiquette. At one extreme, there was Bon Jovi. We did two stadium gigs with them, in Manchester and Glasgow, as part of their humongous *These Days* tour. They were top of the rock hierarchy and were treated like kings, while we were the peasants. We didn't see them, weren't allowed anywhere near them, and couldn't even use the same staircase or lift. It didn't feel good, so now, every time we tour, I always make a point of saying hello to the support band and making them feel welcome, because I never want them to feel like we did. If you've hired them, go and socialise, take a photo with them – it creates a positive vibe and everyone benefits.

We learnt that from touring with U2 on their 1997 PopMart tour in Europe – the one with the gigantic lemon mirror ball. Sometimes after a gig they would get on a plane and jet home to Ireland, and other times they'd invite us to their dressing room for drinks. They were super-fun and so classy, totally down to earth. The first night we came offstage, we found a bottle of wine in our dressing room and a note from the band saying, 'Welcome to the tour'. We were dumbfounded. What a lovely thing to do! We totally stole that move and have done it with all our support bands ever since, because their crew made us feel welcome. It was fascinating to see how Bono ruled his audience. He was a real ringmaster, in synergy with the rest of the band — they worked as a team and had great chemistry on stage.

David Bowie was the icing on the cake! We supported him one summer on a festival run, and he flew us in his private jet from the UK to Les Eurockéennes festival in Belfort, northern France. He invited us to listen to his show from the side of the stage. Usually, if you watch a gig from that position, the sound is bad because everyone wears ear-monitors, and there are no speakers, but he created a little area for his family where the sound was amazing. His wife Iman was there. I didn't know the zone was for his family only, so their security kicked me out until she stepped in and stopped them. She was so lovely to me — people forget that she's a powerhouse in her own right, and she was at a lot of those gigs. That day, Bowie showed us one of his tattoos, a Sanskrit prayer on the back of his calf. Then later, onstage, he sang 'Jean Genie' and segued into one of our songs, a naughty one called 'Milk Is My Sugar', because he said he liked the words . . .

Milk is my sugar
Sweet grovelling
Thy shall convert me
My favourite sin

Bowie was intent on taking his fans on a journey. I noticed this, and the more we toured, the more I realised you have to create your own rhythm for a gig. It's like a theatre performance, with a beginning, middle and end. We would start off fierce, then calm down, and then raise the energy again. You've got to remember that what you're doing is spiritual and soulful — not that it's religious, as such, but the connection between you and the audience is circular. You send out the energy and they give it back to you. It's like your performance wakes them up and gives them permission to lose their minds for a couple of hours, and they don't have to worry about anything else. People walk into a room with their nice clothes on, and they want to go a bit crazy but don't want to embarrass themselves. You've got to give them permission to freak out, and wake up the demon inside. Once you transmit that wild vibe into the audience, they lose it and don't care. I can feel the energy before I run onstage – sometimes the crowd feels like a giant keg of gunpowder and I am the match.

The lead singer plays an almost mystical role. I love to break the invisible wall between the stage and the audience, and come down offstage as fast as I can, even if it's just putting my foot on the stage barrier. By going into the crowd, that 'them and us' feeling is shattered, broken into a million beads of sweat. They get it – we're all in this together for the next two hours. You've got to do your part and I'll play my part. We're on the same level; we're equals. I'm not untouchable and, actually, you can put your hand on my shoulder, I'm standing right next to you. I need to be close to the audience because I remember what it was like to be a kid in a gig, moshing like mad to my favourite band. It's always the best spot in the venue, so when the singer comes offstage and goes into the mosh-pit, it lifts the gig to another level.

I've been stage-diving from our very first gig. But one of my proudest dives was in downtown LA at a Rage Against The Machine gig in 1995. To this day, it's the most violent gig I've ever been to. Men were beating each other to a pulp, and half of them were supposed to be the security! At the same time, I realised that the front two rows of the mosh-pit were full of women and none of them were getting hurt. There was an unspoken, gentlemanly rule where men were enjoying themselves hitting each other and moshing like crazy, but without harming the women, so I became desperate to get to the front row. Above the stage was a huge bull's head with a giant ring through its nose. My eyes were fixed on that prize. Guys were crowd-surfing and desperately trying to raise themselves up high enough at the last second to slap the ring before the death drop over the barrier, where security had no intention of catching you. The few who managed it became instant gig heroes. I had to do this! Cass picked me up and threw me with both hands into the middle of the mosh-pit madness and, minutes later, I slapped the bull's head and the place erupted. Zack, Rage's lead singer, smiled at me in admiration, and then screamed, *'Fuck youuuuu!'* into my face. Bliss!

I remember Courtney Love saying that sometimes when she was crowd-surfing she had been groped and assaulted and, as a woman, I was very wary of that happening to me, so I always crowd-surf on my back and wear clothes that make it harder for people to grope or grab me. The only place I will never stage-dive again is Russia. The last time we played in Moscow, I went for a crowd-surf and was assaulted throughout by men who tried to rip my clothes off, pinch my nipples and grab me between my legs. The crowd were so sexually aggressive towards me that when I returned to the stage I lost my temper and gave them a mouthful. Never again.

I was inspired by the way Courtney found a way to deal with the abuse by calling people out on stage. Offstage she could be formidable too. The first time I met her was after the MTV Awards one year, at a party in a hotel suite. I walked down the corridor past a room-service tray on the floor, which had a plate on it with a huge slice of cake topped with red-cherry sauce and whipped cream. I went into the party and, twenty minutes later, Courtney walked in with cake and whipped cream all over her face and hands. I said, 'Courtney, your face!' We went into the bathroom to wipe it all off. I thought it was hilarious that she had just seen the cake on the floor and demolished it.

The relentless touring was paying off, and our audiences were steadily growing throughout Europe, but by the time we hit the platinum 300k sales mark for *Stoosh*, reviewers were starting to turn. I felt worried, thinking, *We've put all this work into everything and it's all going to fall apart.* As an artist you have to grow a thick skin, but typically I could only hear the negative, not the positive feedback, and so I was missing the point, really – bands that become successful always get slagged off. That's what the British music press does.

Also, the bias was too obvious to ignore. It felt like the first line of every interview published would say, 'Six foot, bald, black bisexual Amazonian ...' First off, I'm nowhere near six foot, and I'm rather shy and polite in person. Black women – from Grace Jones to Mel B – are so often portrayed as intimidating creatures. Every time I met a music journalist, the reaction was, 'You're not scary at all.' The image the press had of me was that of a caricature: a really tall, aggressive and angry woman, anti-men and super political, stamping on everybody with my Dr Martens.

At the end of 1996 we had a hit with one of our darkest pop

songs, 'Twisted (Everyday Hurts)'. Because of its light, disco beat, people miss how menacing that song really is, with the lyrics 'Twisted ... everyday hurts ... a little more.' I love to do that in songs, creating a strange opposing mixture of music and lyrics, like salt and sweet caramel – it shouldn't be delicious but it is!

The lyrics of 'Twisted' were prescient. Slowly, slowly, my relationship with Maxine was disintegrating. I was always away on tour, and when I was at home I wasn't present. I was consumed with band business, leaving her neglected and lonely. Everything was happening so fast with the band, and we knew we had to take advantage of that. Unfortunately that led to Maxine and I breaking up. We were very civil about it – we went to a spa hotel in Bath for the weekend and amicably separated. It was sad, but we've always remained close and are great friends now.

There is no training for becoming famous. There's nothing that can prepare you for it. You just have to think on your feet and try to keep hold of your sanity and your friends. I returned home after months on tour, elated and full of stories, only to realise my friends had all moved on. This was long before social media or mobile phones, so nobody knew where I'd been, what I'd done or when I'd be home. To them I'd just disappeared. In those days, I knew all my friends' home numbers by heart, but phone calls from hotels were super-expensive. I'd send postcards every now and then, but most of the time it was really hard to send mail. My friends became pissed off and began to forget about me, so I learnt the hard way that friendships need to be worked on. I couldn't just assume they would still be there when I got back.

The bigger the band got the more I wanted to make an impact. We could see wonderful things happening to many bands around us. We hung out with Oasis and watched them go ballistic, dominating the charts with massive hit singles, and along with Echobelly, Suede and all those cool Britpop bands, we wanted that too. It's funny – you climb to the top of the mountain, and all you can think about is getting to the next peak.

ELEVEN

WE DON'T NEED WHO YOU ARE

Succulent white
Secrete revenge
God gives right
For you and your laws
You kill and dine
In cold sublime

'We Don't Need Who You Think You Are'

In October 1996, we toured Australia with the Sex Pistols. It was horrible. Back in the 1970s, Sid Vicious wore a swastika armband to be hateful and controversial. The Pistols were all about offending people – the more they could do that, the more successful they were. Nineteen-seventies punk was a different period, when people could get away with nihilistic shock and confrontation. But now we are more aware of how fascists will identify with whatever they can, and if they see someone in a cool band wearing Nazi regalia, they think they have a friend.

We had supported the Sex Pistols a few months earlier at Finsbury Park, on the third date of their *Filthy Lucre* reunion tour. We loved it. It was the Pistols FFS! *Never Mind the Bollocks* is one of the greatest records EVER made! Our agents got talking, and that was the catalyst for us playing with them in Australia. Initially it seemed hopeful. Especially for Ace, because someone from their crew had turned up at his hotel room with a bag full of weed to sell. Ace said yes!

'How much do you want?' the guy asked, opening a satchel brimming with top-grade leaves. Ace and our crew laughed in astonishment as their greedy eyes snatched up a $200 envelope each. It was *wayyy* too much to smoke, but they had a great first night strolling around Sydney completely zonked.

Once we started the tour, though, things went downhill. The Pistols had a huge human mountain of a security guard, who was also black. He took a fatherly role, coming over every night to warn me: 'Don't go into that corner because it's the Nazi League of Australia over there.' At every gig there were people *sieg-heil*ing and screaming racist obscenities at us. The Pistols had chosen Skunk Anansie as their tour support because they wanted to show their fans that they *weren't* fascists. But at the same time, Lydon never spoke out against the *sieg-heil*ing, not once, and never said anything to the audience. I felt his silence gave them permission. He was separate from the rest of the band, and I sensed they weren't the best of pals. We flew from one gig to the next, and Lydon would sit at the front of the plane while his band went to the back, and at each venue they had separate dressing rooms.

We got on really well with Steve Jones, Paul Cook and Glen Matlock, though. We had a laugh and a drink with them, and they would hang out in our dressing room. Steve Jones had the craziest unrepeatable stories. In contrast, Lydon scowled at everyone except me. In fact, he was extremely nice to me in a way that I didn't know how to take. He would come up and say, 'Hello. How are you? How are you doing today?' Meanwhile, at every gig, people were calling me a 'black bitch' or 'black bastard' and shouting at me to get off the stage, so it was a very strange juxtaposition of Lydon's extreme politeness and the gross insults from some fascist fans.

The audience was split between those who loved us and those who bitterly resented us. I could see some people were appalled by the behaviour of the racist fans – there were apologetic faces, sometimes there were arguments, sometimes people would just move away from them. For us, it was really hard work. I was trying to be strong and fronting it every night with a gutsy performance, but the racism was wearing me down. One of the last gigs we played was in Adelaide, where there was a very strong fascist contingent in the audience. There was a strange atmosphere – someone told us the whole town was built on an aboriginal burial ground. The indigenous Kaurna people had a sophisticated language and culture, but within a few decades of British settlement in the nineteenth century, that was destroyed. Even though Adelaide has worked a lot to revive that history, and is proud of its indigenous arts and music culture, when we were there in the '90s, it was going through a recession and was a bleak place.

The gig was tough, and it was a relief to get offstage and watch the Pistols. They were amazing live – their songs were amazing, their playing was amazing. On this particular night, I was standing next to the sound desk when a really tall skinhead came up to me. I was wearing a new Skunk Anansie beanie hat, one that I really liked. He pulled off my hat and threw it on the ground, laughing. I was in shock.

'What the fuck did you do that for?' I asked. He then chucked a full glass of beer over me and I was drenched. It was too much. We'd endured gigs full of racist abuse from their fans that no one seem to care about. We'd just had to suck it up and carry on, time after time, day after day. That night I finally lost it. I put my hand on his shoulder, jumped up and punched him right in his face. I hadn't punched anyone like that since I was fourteen years old.

He was clearly drunk. He staggered back and fell on the floor. His friends went ballistic, and I thought I was about to be attacked, so I legged it to the dressing room to tell the boys. Cass and Mark instantly jumped up enraged. We all came out from backstage and found the man in the reception area with five of his skinhead mates. Cass went up, tapped the guy on the shoulder and threw a pint of Jack Daniels and Coke right in his face. The two of them angrily squared up to each other, until our tour manager, Ivan Kushlik, said, 'They've called security on you, Cass.'

Even though the Pistols' fans had started the trouble, the venue security threw *us* out – all the band and our team. Classic racism, because although the skinhead had attacked me first, *we* were the black kids and therefore the problem. I wanted to leave the tour, but we were persuaded to finish because there were only two dates left. As Cass said, beneath a thin veneer of tolerance there was a vile undercurrent of racism and hatred. For me, that was our worst tour ever.

*

The early 1990s were landmark years in the fight against racism, particularly with the end of South African apartheid in 1994. The trade boycott and anti-apartheid movement meant that for years musicians refused to play there to segregated audiences. In the UK, we actively supported Artists Against Apartheid, and fought for the release of ANC leader Nelson Mandela, who had been held in captivity for twenty-seven years. When I was living in Brixton in 1984, the Special AKA song 'Free Nelson Mandela' became an anthem for music fans black and white. It was a symbol of the change that finally came about after South Africa, economically and culturally isolated, was forced to repeal its apartheid legislation and move to majority rule.

It was a volatile period for the country, and we were one of the first multiracial bands to tour South Africa after apartheid crumbled and Mandela was freed and sworn in as the first black president of the country in 1994. The year after our Sex Pistols tour, I went backpacking in South Africa for a month, hanging out with my long-time pal Yvonne, who introduced me to her group of friends. When I first landed in Johannesburg, I realised I looked like a tourist because of my edgy London strides. So I went into a local shop and bought the kind of clothes I saw black South Africans wearing. I left all my London clothes in the shop, exchanging them for a hoodie, a high-waisted, faded pair of ripped jeans, crop-tops, baseball caps that I wore backwards, and my very first and only pair of Spice Girl Buffaloes. I needed to blend in, guys! Certain parts of Johannesburg were still dangerous, so if I looked like a tourist I risked getting mugged. It worked a bit too well, because people would start talking to me in the clicking consonants of Xhosa (the most common black language in South Africa), without realising I was a black gal from Brixton, innit. And for the first time ever, my shaven head meant I fitted in perfectly!

I did experience some classic racism, but more from the older generation of Afrikaner whites. For example, when entering a shop, black people would hold a door open for you and strike up a conversation, but white people wouldn't; they would just glide through and let the door slam in your face, pretending they didn't see you. But the minute I opened my mouth, releasing the Queen's Brixton ('Excuse me?'), I was treated with more courtesy, because a British black accent trumped an African one. To them I was a tourist who needed to be treated correctly. White kids were much cooler and more aware. They were being raised in a new South Africa, and were trying to slowly redress the sins of their fathers and forefathers.

Soon after I arrived, I flew to Namibia to visit my old friend Tom Minney and his wife Bience, whom I'd known from St Matthew's Road. Back in 1989, they were part of the revolutionary anti-government core of Namibian exiles living in London, going on anti-apartheid demonstrations and campaigning for Namibian independence. Even though the United Nations was given direct responsibility over the territory in 1966, the former German colony was controlled by South Africa at the time, and the same apartheid rules governed Namibia until it gained independence in 1990. By the time I arrived, in 1997, the government had been overthrown and, shockingly, my friend Tom was running the stock exchange! To me, this seemed hilarious. I used to help them make political banners for marches, on our kitchen table at Number One, wearing sweats and drinking beer, and now they were all running the government! They had been part of a movement to end apartheid and now they were in power. It was strange to see them all in their suits, being so respectable and serious, but at the same time hugely inspiring to see they'd made it.

While I was there, Tom took a break from work and we went on a trip into the jungle, to the Naankuse Wildlife Sanctuary near Windhoek – a reserve for orphaned animals. We stayed in little tents by a water hole, and I was too scared to sleep at night because I could hear elephants and hippos tramping past our tents to get to the water. I was a city girl, and this was the first time I had been around wild animals.

One afternoon, we went to a field in part of the wildlife rescue centre that was full of hyaena cubs, tiny fuzzy creatures about the size of a cat. I thought they were cute, so I bent down to stroke one. She yapped at me and then another tried to bite me. 'Oh, bless,' I said, before realising that his little friends were circling around me. I began walking backwards, suddenly surrounded by eight or nine of them, snapping at my ankles one at a time as if in formation. You could see how they might easily kill a human. The guards at the reserve saw what was happening and ran over to me, shouting and beating the ground with sticks. I was terrified. One minute I was a friend; thirty seconds later I was dinner.

On day two, we went to a field where cheetahs with broken backs hauled themselves along on two paws. Apparently, the way small children move triggers something in a cheetah's brain. At one point, when Tom's three-year-old daughter ran across to play with the cheetahs, they started dragging themselves really fast towards her and he had to hastily scoop her up. These animals are deadly creatures, there's no messing around, and that's why I couldn't sleep that night, worrying about them outside my tent, waiting for me to fall asleep so they could eat me. As I say, I'm definitely an urbanite.

After Namibia, I went back to South Africa – first to Cape Town, where I went to a club that had ten rooms, a spaghetti junction of a place, with different music in each room. The people were super-friendly, mostly white and gay. From there I returned to Johannesburg, hanging out in an area called Yeoville, which was full of artists, musicians, students and political activists. Every night we went to a club in the centre of Yeoville, which again had many rooms, each one with a different crowd and playing a different type of groove. That was the first time I heard a sound called kwaito. My friends told me that in the early 1990s, a DJ had played a house record at the wrong speed and people went crazy, so he kept doing it, and that was how kwaito was born. Newfound freedom had given South African musicians easier access to genres like hip-hop and R&B, and an ability to freely express themselves. Kwaito became the expression of this new freedom, and many anti-apartheid chants were mixed into the lyrics of the kwaito songs. With its pulsing mix of mbaqanga (South African township music) and dance-hall, house and disco, kwaito was music for the generation that came of age after apartheid.

One the most amazing people I met was Thandiswa Mazwai, lead singer of the kwaito African pop band Bongo Maffin. We got on like a house on fire, still do, and she took me under her wing. In our favourite Yeoville club, I noticed the walls were lined with people standing up but asleep, and I asked her, 'Why are all these people asleep all around the edge of the club?' She told me that they lived in Soweto, but as it was too expensive, and took too long to get back to their own bed from

Johannesburg, they would just come to a club that was open all night and sit on the benches or sleep standing up, and then go to work in the morning. That way, they stayed in Johannesburg during the week and went home at the weekends. This was all part of the new South Africa.

At the end of my trip, I had a goodbye drink with all the friends I had met while I was there. I vividly recall sitting at the middle of a long, oval table. On one side were all my black friends, talking amongst themselves, while chatting on the other side were all my white friends, but at no point did they mingle. Apartheid has done so much deep, ingrained damage. I truly hope in the future that black South Africans will recover.

However, through Thandiswa I got to know a group of gay black girls who were whip-smart, witty and fun-loving, and who spoke different languages. It struck me that not only did they know the history of the UK and Britain's colonial connection with South Africa, they also knew the history of every European country that had had anything to do with apartheid. They had a fighting spirit, they were supporting their friends and starting urban community groups campaigning for better sanitation, medicine and housing. It was their time to push things forward, and they were doing it in such a positive way.

I was back home in the UK for only three weeks when Leigh called me up, saying, 'Guess where we're going on tour?' South Africa! Yeah! I get to see all my mates again! But it was so different when I went back that August with the band. Our promoters surrounded us with security, and there was a much less relaxed atmosphere. The driver who picked us up from the airport was lovely and sweet while we were talking to the agent and the record company, until we got to the hotel, which was a high-rise, high-security building in the centre of Johannesburg. A group of young black guys in hotel uniforms came running out to help us with our luggage, and the driver barked at them like they were dogs. He saw Cass and me as European blacks, and treated us the same as whites, but to him the local African blacks were like another species. We were shocked to our core, and realised how little had really changed.

Everyone instilled a fear into us because they seemed scared of black people and were terrified of us going anywhere without security. I knew that the centre of Johannesburg at that time was a dangerous place, but in other parts, like Yeoville, I was aware, but not afraid – I think it's about how you carry yourself. I knew from growing up in Brixton that it's important to look confident and strong, and to give the impression that you know where you're going. It's also important not to be flashy or just plain stupid.

Going back as a band was a real eye-opener, in contrast to my backpacking trip a few weeks earlier. One day, in that posh Johannesburg hotel, I happened to walk into the lift at the same time as an older white guy, and it was just the two of us in there. He didn't even turn around as he barked, 'Five!' into the air in front of him. Shocked, I realised that all he saw in his peripheral vision was a black person, and that's the way you talk to blacks. He was ordering me to press the button for his floor. Of course, I didn't, but it was a tiny reminder of the unimaginable racism black South Africans have had to live through. I was angry, but I also felt so very, very sad.

Talk to any credible old-school rocker and they will tell you the roots of rock come from black blues folk. They will list all the great blues players who lit a fire in their belly. And if your gods are Elvis or the Rolling Stones or the Beatles, a quick Google of their influences will lead you back to some old black dude sitting on a stoop, croaking through a blues ditty from heaven . . . or hell.

Despite that rich history, I've always been painfully aware that within the rock world, especially at festivals, I'm usually the only black front-person to grace the stage. So often, the only other black person I will see all day is our bass player Cass, and it's the same for him. I knew that if we didn't make a point of it, we'd be playing to a purely white audience in South Africa, and that was not acceptable to me. Leigh and I discussed it, letting the promoters know that we had to do black press and make sure black Africans knew they were welcome.

We joyfully ended up doing different types of promotion, going to township radio stations in Soweto and in black parts of the city. Even though for a long time it had been poor, unsupported and underfunded, and it took years before people got electricity and running water, Soweto was an amazing place. People had built their own houses out of breeze blocks, and they reused what could be fixed. There were geniuses who built radio stations and studios, finding the parts they needed, wiring them together and making great sounds. They made their own music and sold cassette tapes and CDs to everyone in the locality.

I discovered the best music while sitting in taxis, and when I heard a great track I would persuade the driver to sell me the CD, in the taxi. We went to four established pirate radio stations, and the DJ presenters were really interested in our story, curious to know what it was like being a black person in England. And because I'd been in the country earlier in the summer, I could talk about South African music and the clubs and bands I'd seen.

On the day of our gig at Johannesburg Arena, we invited some black kids backstage, and our lovely crew showed them how to set up the instruments, lights and speakers. Ace, Mark and Cass gave them mini demonstrations of their gear, then we let them stay and watch the soundcheck, giving them free tickets to the concert. It was a really fun, magical day. I adore working with kids who love music and want to learn; it's one of my favourite things to do.

As I walked onstage that night, I was so happy to see some black people rocking out all through the gig. I knew it was because of the township interviews, and because Cass and I were in the band that they felt our music was also for them.

We went on to play in Cape Town, and later Durban, performing to mixed crowds. South Africa had experienced generations of apartheid, so multiracial audiences at that point were still a new concept. I'm so glad we achieved that, because if you take the easy option, you're just perpetuating the old racist system. I remember chatting with bands like the Prodigy and the Smashing Pumpkins, after we got back to the UK, because they wanted to play there but felt nervous. I told them, 'No, you need to go because you need to put it onto the touring map. You just gotta make sure you let everyone know they're welcome.'

South African audiences had been starved of international music because of the cultural boycott, and starved of bands playing live. We showed them it could be done, and I like to think we helped to open the door, so that by the 2000s, South Africa became part of the global touring circuit.

Because of our concerts, we were invited to Nelson Mandela's eightieth birthday party. In July 1998, two thousand people assembled for a dinner in a huge marquee on the Gallagher Estate between Johannesburg and Pretoria. Mandela had got married the day before to his new wife, the Mozambican activist and politician Graça Machel. The dinner was full of stars and world dignitaries like anti-apartheid activist the Most Reverend Desmond Tutu, and artists like Miriam Makeba, Stevie Wonder and Nina Simone. After dinner, a few people were invited to come and shake Mandela's hand and have their picture taken with him. I remember Nina Simone, who was in a wheelchair, went up first. The next person I recognised was Stevie Wonder, followed by the film star Danny Glover. I turned to Cass and joked, 'Skunk Anansie', imitating the compère's voice, thinking no way would we be allowed to share the stage with these huge artists. We both cracked up so much we didn't hear our name being called out. They said it again: '*Skunk Anansie.*' We panicked. 'Shit, it's us!'

We went up and both shook Mandela's hand. He was very welcoming, and we had a quick conversation. We then found ourselves standing next to Danny Glover and Michael Jackson. After all the VIPs had been called, the South African children's choir stood in front of us, very excitedly taking tiny peeks at Jackson, then turning back and giggling with each other.

It was a real pinch-yourself moment. I just happened to be in the company of three of the most influential artists of my childhood: Michael Jackson, whom I used to watch as a child on TV when he was in the Jackson 5 (and whose poster, of himself as a child with a huge afro, was the only artist ever to have graced my bedroom wall); Nina Simone, whose four-track ten-inch

EP featuring 'Love Me or Leave Me' was the first record I ever bought; and Stevie Wonder, sitting in front of us at his keyboard. I had to smile to myself – *Songs in the Key of Life* taught me how to sing harmony. My voice was too high for lead vocals, so I used to sing along in a higher range, finding which notes worked with his.

I'd met Stevie many years ago at our very first TV appearance on a music show called *The White Room*, but he was with his handlers, so I couldn't really get further than blurting out something embarrassing like, 'HiStevieIReallyLoveYourWorkI'mSoExcitedToMeetYou!' This time I played it cool and joined in harmonising with Michael while Stevie played his megahit 'Happy Birthday'. A smiling Mandela danced a tiny jig.

The memory of that event has stayed with me. Back at the hotel I hung out with Nina Simone for the rest of the night, sipping cognac and some other insanely strong alcoholic drink she liked. We've all heard stories about her feistiness, and I don't think she was the easiest person in the world, but that night she decided she liked me and she was in a fabulous mood, so I got lucky. I told her that her record was the first one I'd ever bought, but I didn't hear it for a year because our turntable was in the front room and I wasn't allowed in there. She thought that was hilarious, giggling about black folks and their smart front rooms waiting for the Queen to come to tea!

The following Saturday, 25 July, there was a marathon twelve-hour birthday concert for Mandela at Johannesburg Stadium. We were proud to be sharing a bill with everyone from Stevie Wonder to soul singer Chaka Khan to South African stars like

Springbok Nude Girls and reggae king Lucky Dube. I hung out with Chaka Khan backstage, and she was magical. I owned loads of her records, including the early ones with Rufus. The concert was severely delayed, and started hours late. While other American artists as big as her would've had a fit, she wandered around backstage popping into everyone's dressing rooms, cracking jokes and keeping all our spirits up. It didn't matter what time we were supposed to play because we were hanging with Chaka! Finally it was her time to perform, and they let me watch from the side of the stage. She started singing 'Ain't Nobody', and within seconds she had dragged me onstage with her. I couldn't believe it: me singing with Chaka Khan, in South Africa, in front of Nelson Mandela! WOW! It was a long way from Venus Rising in Brixton, when 'Ain't Nobody' was a 1980s club anthem. Her band all wore ear-monitors and, with no speakers onstage, I couldn't hear a word, but what the heck, it didn't matter – I knew every word. It was a killer classic and I was having a great time.

When I look back, the absolute highlight was meeting Mandela himself. When I shook his hand, I felt like he was a very old soul, gentle and kind. I know absolutely nothing about reincarnation, but the only way to describe it is that it felt like this wasn't his first life. His energy was unique, unlike any person I'd ever met. He was comfortable, wise, settled and strong. Being in his company, celebrating his birthday, was one of the greatest honours of my life.

In the late 1990s, in between tours, I was able to support some charity and political projects I'd been interested in for a long time. I'd been involved in working with the campaign against Female

Genital Mutilation (FGM) since my college days, when I'd first heard about the ritual cutting of girls' genitalia through the charity FORWARD. I found it unbelievable that young girls, and sometimes babies, were having to go through this in the name of modesty and 'purity'. Our clitorises are at the core of our private, personal and mental wellbeing. It is the centre of our spiritual and sexual pleasure and power, and to destroy that is abhorrent. Even though FGM has been outlawed in most countries, the practice is still widespread. UNICEF estimated that in 2016, over 200 million women in thirty countries throughout Africa, Asia and the Middle East had undergone FGM, whether it was removal of the clitoris or the more extreme practice of infibulation, where both the clitoris and the labia are removed and the vulva is sewn up, with a small hole left for urine. During childbirth, these women have to be cut open to let the baby out, resulting in a dangerous situation for mother and child, with a high risk of infection and mental trauma after the birth.

I wanted to support the campaign, but through actions as well as philanthropy, so in 1999 I went to the Ivory Coast with campaigning journalist Angela Robson. She was coordinating anti-FGM work in Africa for Amnesty International, setting up a project at Korhogo, a remote region in the west of the country. She became a great liaison person and a good friend.

BMJ Global Health studies show that local sharing of information about the health risks for women and girls can make a huge difference, so I funded a conference for the chiefs, the hospital nurses and women doing the cutting. Leigh came along, as she was also deeply interested in the campaign.

We arrived in the Ivory Coast but our transport didn't. With no driver we had to adapt, so Angela found a taxi and we rode for twenty-four hours in a rickety car deep into the bush. We then spent five days in Korhogo, on the border with Liberia. It was one of the remotest regions of Africa I've been to, and it was very humbling.

We were invited to a ceremony where girls aged 13-15 years old had undergone FGM, and had just spent two weeks in the bush learning cooking skills and how to be young women. FGM was considered part of this rite of passage. They were beautifully dressed but totally stunned. It was a sad intro. Then the conference started, and this was the first time the chiefs, cutters and hospital nurses had ever been in the same room together, discussing in detail what cutting involved. Everybody began to understand that cutters are not evil women (which is how they are portrayed in the West); they were doing it to protect the girls from rejection by the village. The chiefs were shocked to hear from the nurses about how cutting is done with dirty razors, with no anaesthetic. The girls experience searing pain, then later, infection and disease, when the menstrual blood can't leave the body.

I felt really sad for everybody involved. When the nurses explained the long-term dangers of FGM, one of the cutters was horrified – she thought that what she was doing was an act of love. The women were doing it because they were afraid of how ostracised their girls would be. The villages are small, and girls needed the protection of the community for food, shelter and work. It was obvious that many of the women didn't want to do it anymore, but only the male chiefs had the power to stop it.

Everyone's stories had a real impact, and the chiefs were open to listening, so everyone could speak freely. Some men came forward to talk about their experiences with their partners who had been cut. They talked about all the pain and distress it caused. I was so moved by the speeches; it became clear that they were all caught in a circle of trying to do the right thing out of love, but in the end they were causing nothing but pain and distress by continuing this outdated practice.

After the conference, a female choir stood up, singing and clapping and playing drums. This was a bit of beautiful light relief after the traumas of the day, so I jumped up and sang with them. They would sing a line and I'd repeat it, like a call and response, two different styles of singing melded into one. The conference was the start of important conversations between the male chiefs and the cutters in that area. It made me truly believe that it is so important in the anti-FGM campaign for people to share information and connect the dots, as this leads to real possibility for change.

Afterwards, we drove back through the capital of Yamoussoukro, but on our way we stopped to visit a massive cathedral in the middle of the jungle – the huge Basilica of Our Lady of Peace, which is bigger even than the Vatican. It was built in 1990 and is 518 feet high, with enough room for 18,000 worshippers. The Ivory Coast President, Félix Houphouët-Boigny, wanted to memorialise himself by building the biggest church in the world, and he made sure to put himself with the apostles in the stained-glass windows. What an ego! His death in 1993 had left the country unstable, and by the early 2000s the Ivory Coast imploded into civil war. This made it harder for Amnesty to go back and monitor campaign work in that area, but figures for West Africa as a whole show there is some progress. In 1996, 74 per cent of women there had undergone FGM, for instance, but by 2017 that number had decreased to 25 per cent.

After my trip, I became a patron of the FORWARD charity, and we were pleased to have their information stalls at our gigs. Many people don't want to get involved, arguing from an anthropological viewpoint that it's an African cultural practice. Even MPs will say, 'It's an African issue.' As if Britain never gets involved with the laws of other countries! I think if the custom was to cut off a man's penis, those MPs would be more bothered.

The practice was made illegal in the UK in the 1980s, and finally, twenty years after my trip to the Ivory Coast, there was a landmark case in February 2019, when the mother of a three-year-old girl in Walthamstow, east London, was the first person to be found guilty of FGM and prosecuted. In some small way, I hoped that conference I did back in 1999, and the information I shared later at gigs, became part of that change in awareness.

TWELVE

ORGASMIC CHILL

I awake
From blood-thick dreams
Washing blame from my knees
Softly done, so secretly
I'm awake
As Charlie sleeps

'Charlie Big Potato'

'They'd rather split up than release another record through One Little Indian,' Leigh told Derek. 'It's over, so you might as well let us go.' Those eighteen months of negotiations – from early 1997 to the summer of 1998 – were long and protracted, because he wanted to keep us. All the major labels were interested in buying us out of the contract, and, in 1998, Virgin won.

I remember the moment when Leigh said, 'Where do you want to record the next album? You can record anywhere you like, you have the money.' Anywhere? Whoa! We must be doing okay. We'd sold millions of records by then, but it didn't feel like it because in those days it took years for publishing royalties from radioplay to come through – for us, the average at the time was about four years after record release.

Because we were on tour nine months of the year, we were in a giant Skunk Anansie touring bubble, so we didn't have a strong connection to the real world. If we found an English newspaper we'd devour it, even though it was usually a tabloid like the *Daily Mirror* or *The Sun*. When we were on tour back then, we'd smash a gig, go to bed and wake up in the next town with no clue that the previous city was doing frenzied back-flips about our band. The excitement was always behind us. This was early days of the internet, so there was no social media, no smartphones and no information, and we had no idea we were that famous until we stopped touring and went back home and would be recognised in the street.

We finally had the money to pay for our favourite producer, Andy Wallace, with whom we'd kept in touch ever since he mixed our debut album *Paranoid & Sunburnt*. We were so excited. In the summer of 1998, we recorded *Post Orgasmic Chill* at Bearsville Studio in Woodstock, upstate New York, one of those studios that has so much history. Bearsville was opened in 1970 by Albert Grossman, the legendary manager/producer of artists like Bob Dylan, Janis Joplin, The Band, and folk acts Odetta and Peter, Paul & Mary. Built as a rehearsal space and studio for his bands, during the 1970s it evolved into a hip, rural community for musicians. Its remote location made it a tranquil place where bands could retreat and focus solely on their music. You'd walk down the corridor and the walls were lined with classics, like *Wave* by the Patti Smith Group, *Trash* by Alice Cooper, the Isley Brothers' *Funky Family* and REM's *Automatic for the People*, along with albums by the Pretenders and Todd Rundgren.

For the first two weeks, we were with Andy at his house in the countryside, doing rehearsals and pre-production, choosing songs and arrangements for the album. Not only was his house immaculate, Andy was a car collector and had a big garage outside that housed his vintage car collection. We loved being in Woodstock – it was a small town with just one bar and a really good cycle shop, so we had these beautiful custom bikes built, and we blissed out riding around town on our days off.

We were in Bearsville Studio for six weeks, and the vibe was fantastic. Andy knew exactly how to set things up so that everyone was happy playing live together in the studio. We took our time recording the album, editing in overdubs and recording the additional parts afterwards. He's one of those producers who know how to make a band feel comfortable.

Cass called him 'the man, the general', and Ace said he was like the 'Santa Claus of rock'. He helped Mark get his drum tracks right, particularly in 'Charlie Big Potato', which has a tricky, complicated rhythm. We kept having to record different takes, and after Take 12, Mark hit a mental wall because he was so frustrated he couldn't get the middle section right. The session had gone well up to that point, but he was starting to feel pressure, having had a nightmare recording our second album *Stoosh*. But instead of adding to the stress, Andy said, 'Take the rest of the day off. We'll carry on tomorrow.'

Mark didn't need the rest of the day; he just needed to know that the producer was on his side. He walked outside for an hour and sat in the middle of the woods, in a quiet, beautiful place.

After some fresh air and a cup of tea, he came back, did two more takes and it was in the bag.

The songs on the album reflected our lives at the time. There's a line in 'On My Hotel TV' – *How dare I have a view and a Versace tattoo* – which reminds me of the day Italian designer Gianni Versace died. It was 15 July 1997, and we had been in rehearsals on the Spanish Steps in Rome, because we were due to play there live during the Versace fashion show. We'd arrived the night before and had dinner with his sister, Donatella, who was genial and charming. She wore a ring with a yellow diamond the size of a golf ball! I couldn't believe it was real. We both laughed and she let me try it on. I had a fitting for the dress I was going to wear – an amazing cream Versace dress with lots of lace and a long chain down the back. I had performed at Fashion Rocks with McQueen, but at that point the Versace party was the most glamorous fashion event we had been involved in.

At dinner she said, 'In the morning I want you to go to every Versace shop in Rome and take whatever you want. I'm going to arrange a van.' We're working-class kids; we didn't know whether to take her suggestion seriously, and we certainly didn't want to appear greedy.

'No, seriously,' she said, 'I want you to take what you want.'

We ended up with a vanload of cool clothes, and went back to the hotel laden with bags, but when we got to the lobby everybody was crying, including the hotel staff and the concierge. Someone said, 'Gianni Versace has been shot.' We were so shocked. We'd looked forward to meeting him that day – we'd heard so much about his creativity, exuberance and zest for life. Donatella and her team just disappeared, and the mood plummeted from one of happiness and excitement to utter desolation. Versace was a legendary figure in the fashion industry, and so the whole of Italy went into mourning. Our show, of course, was cancelled straight away, and all we could do was sit in the hotel room watching the news. His death was devastating.

'On My Hotel TV' captured the monotony of my life when we were touring non-stop. I was even staying in hotels in London because I'd bought a wreck of a house in Maida Vale that needed complete refurbishment. In total, I spent three years living in hotel rooms and rentals and on friends' sofas. I lost so much stuff in those years, moving around constantly, that it changed how I look after my things, and I learnt to carry around a lot less stuff. Now my attachment to possessions had lessened, and I like to travel light. If I had to move to another country and take nothing but a suitcase, I'd be fine.

In other tracks on *Post Orgasmic Chill*, I was also reflecting on our experience of South Africa, the grinding racism and the white flight that affected the country post-apartheid. Black Africans had finally achieved political representation, but people from the powerful white elite took much of South Africa's wealth with them when they left. The song 'We Don't Need Who You Think You Are' was inspired by the systematic racism and abuse of apartheid. I sang in a way that was deliberately clipped and succinct, like the way that white man in the lift had barked at me: 'Five!' We made the track sound brutally compressed and crisp as I sang:

> *Starve the minds and drain the face*
> *Segregate shit nigga race*
> *Cry for credible debate*

But now them blackies legislate
So leave for anglo-aussie shores
There you'll find your heaven . . .

But much of the album is about the darkness and complexity of human relationships. The song 'Good Things Don't Always Come To You' is about the unfairness of a world where good people are continually hurt and bad people thrive; karma doesn't seem to touch them. For 'Lately' we wrote some big chordal guitar sounds to symbolise the sharply defined disappointment of a relationship that peters out, while 'Secretly' was inspired by some close friends of mine detailing the consequences of having an affair. It's rare that one song is about a single situation; usually I have some words about an idea or experience and I snatch the rest from things I overhear. Songs don't have to be completely true; they are stories or snippets of memories, so I allow myself some poetic licence.

Although the recording for *Post Orgasmic Chill* was going well, we got some frightening news. Leigh became very ill and had to go into hospital. She was diagnosed with a brain tumour. We always say there are five people in our band – we've been through so much together – so the thought of her not being there was unimaginable. We were scared, and for a while things were very hairy. Leigh doesn't like to tell us if she's worried until she has to, and she carries a lot of stress. But despite my fears, I felt certain that she was going to be fine – maybe it was blind faith. She was the bedrock of the band; she had to be okay. Luckily the operation went well, but she lost her hearing permanently in one ear, which is terrifying for someone in the music industry. She had to work hard to regain her balance.

Leigh spent some time with her parents in Wiltshire, recovering after the operation, and then, as soon as she could, she was back in the office working again. We were worried because she came back too quickly, even though she didn't like to show any vulnerability, and kept saying, 'I'm fine.' But I knew she was under a lot of stress, and I was glad later when she took some time off for a proper rest and recovery. Leigh felt terribly responsible because she had just negotiated us a big new record deal, and there was pressure on us to have a hit album. Virgin Records had put a lot of faith in us and we were a huge priority for the label.

In March 1999, we released 'Charlie Big Potato' as the lead single, but BBC Radio 1 felt it was too heavy for daytime play. It was crucial to have Radio 1 airplay at that point, because the station had a large audience throughout the UK, and was the main conduit into the charts. Now, we open or close a lot of gigs with that song because it's such a massive fan favourite, but then it was counter to a lot of pop sounds at the time.

By 1999, Britpop had been superseded by Britney Spears and the Spice Girls and a slew of pop bands in their wake – Steps, B*Witched, Boyzone, NSYNC. The sardonic songwriting of Britpop had been replaced by softer groups like Kula Shaker or Travis, so our 'Charlie Big Potato', with its compulsive, unforgiving riffs, was at odds with the UK singles chart.

In truth, we weren't really a singles band. Our albums used to go into the charts and just sit there in the Top 40 for months on end. People wanted to buy the album and be taken on a journey, so Radio 1 was always a little tricky. MTV was much more important for us – they loved our videos, which were broadcast on heavy rotation. This made a huge difference, especially across Europe. We went from making videos for £30,000 with One Little Indian to having a £150,000 budget with Virgin. At the time, that was considered normal for a band of our size. Missy Elliot was making videos for a million apiece, and the Fugees' video for their hit 'Ready or Not' cost £1.3 million and was filmed in a submarine! Video budgets were through the roof because MTV was such an important ally for selling records. This was before the days of digital streaming, when people actually bought records and CDs, so the music industry was awash with money. Back then, Virgin Records employed over twenty full-time staff – they had three people just for booking flights! Ten years later, they had three overworked people running the whole label.

In 1999, Leigh won Manager of the Year at the Music Managers Forum Awards, which was brilliant! The MMF is a huge global organisation, so this was a great accolade. When she went to collect the award, the room was full of men and just a handful of women. Leigh achieved so much for us, but continually encountered obstacles as a female rock manager. Men in record company A&R or marketing often preferred to do business with male managers, and in meetings would quietly shut Leigh out. There was an assumption that men know more, but Leigh didn't let that affect her confidence. When negotiating a deal for us, her main focus was to get artistic independence and tour support. She had secured a big enough advance from Virgin for the record label to be nervous about us not doing well, which meant we were a priority on the label.

From the moment we released our first album on One Little Indian, other managers circled around trying to poach us – all men who'd yet to break an artist – but we didn't trust them. Leigh cared deeply about us in a way no one else could because they hadn't been on the journey with us.

I'll admit that Skunk Anansie is a strange band. We've discovered along the way that the usual tricks other bands use don't work for us, so we've always had to think outside the box. In the US, for instance, we were regularly approached by dubious characters with perfect, neon-white teeth. We had this private joke: when we saw one coming, we'd catch each other's eye, then slowly put our sunglasses on at the same time, or fake a migraine – private jokes that set us off into fits of giggles. Maybe Leigh had never solely managed a band at an international level, but I'd never been in a band at that level either, and we were all growing together. From the beginning the plans were always long term; we wanted to be involved in music for the rest of our lives. I've seen managers do big deals, take their percentage, then do very little else. We were always confident that Leigh would never do that.

'Secretly' was released in May 1999 and became a hit in the UK and throughout Europe, and Leigh had the pleasant problem of not being able to release a third single from the album because they couldn't get 'Secretly' off radio playlists! The video was directed by Italian film-maker Giuseppe Capotondi, and the song was on the soundtrack of American teen drama *Cruel Intentions*, an adaptation of the novel *Les Liaisons Dangereuses*, but set in 1990s New York City instead of eighteenth-century France. While our video was played on rotation on MTV, we toured enormous festivals that summer of 1999 – playing to 90,000 people at Spodek in Poland, 96,000 at Roskilde in Denmark and 150,000 at Germany's mega Rock am Ring. Leigh likened us to a conquering army.

Headlining Glastonbury Festival in 1999 on the final Sunday night of the decade was our pinnacle. As everyone knows only too well, the Glastonbury rain and mud can be as legendary as the bands. But that year, when we came on after Lenny Kravitz's set, the clouds parted and the sun came streaming through. I stood on the Pyramid Stage, looking at a 120,000-strong crowd stretching all the way back to the tents in the distance. In 1995, we had missed the beginning of our slot, running late onto the *NME* Stage at midday; we had been the first band on, we performed four songs, and that was it, done.

Four years later, we were back, headlining the Sunday night with a seventeen-piece orchestra and playing to a huge crowd. The set is featured in the BBC documentary *Glastonbury's Greatest Headliners*, but back then, there was grumbling in the music press that our 'stadium punk' wasn't right for headlining the festival. In the late 1990s, Britpop bands had dominated the Pyramid Stage for some years, and even though we were a hugely successful band by this point, we still felt we had to prove ourselves worthy. Part of the reason I think there have been so few POC headliners at Glastonbury is because diehard fans and sections of the press and music industry think only rock or indie bands deserve the slot. We were rock through and through, but to some people, having a black front woman and a groove to our sound meant we weren't rock 'enough'. Festival organiser Michael Eavis did something special when he gave us a seat at the table, letting it be known to all that Glastonbury would have a more diverse future. He was ready to take a risk and withstand the backlash. His daughter Emily followed suit in 2008, when she put Jay Z in the top spot.

We were on form and ready to give everyone the gig of their lives. Our set the previous day – on a speedway racetrack at the Hurricane Festival in Germany – had been one of our best to date. I remember thinking afterwards, *If we play like that in Glastonbury, it'll go off!* To get himself psyched up, Mark got our make-up artist to put Maori-style warpaint on his face as if he was going into battle. He said to her, 'I need something on my face that says, "Fuck off, the lot of you."' She then put Maori tattoos on his face. Nowadays that might be considered appropriation, but to Mark, an ex-rugby player, it came from a place of love, and it was meant to give him strength in the face of adversity.

A young designer called Cathryn Roberts put together something very special for the day. She'd already made a load of my crazy looks, but for Glastonbury she went all out, designing a suit made out of *ole-skool* cassette tape, to reflect the light. It was shiny and mad and had the desired effect – I was like a lightning bolt across the stage.

On that tour we had a huge stage set made out of 30 square-inch mirrored tiles. Each section could be independently controlled, so we could create a lot of drama depending on how the lights hit them. This was important, because our songs are quite varied, and it gave us a simple way to instantly change the mood from soaring riff-tastic overtures, to intimate, delicate lullabies. The show was like a drunken argument: one minute you'd be jumping for joy; the next minute you'd be on the receiving end of a creative bitch slap.

We launched into 'Charlie Big Potato' and, from the first second, it went *off*. People were screaming, singing, dancing and waving flags. As I sang, I climbed onto Mark's bass drum and leapt off, running towards the front of the stage and the crowd. By then, Mark had a special contraption made called 'the Skin protector', which was a metal bridge that went over the bass drum and bolted onto the drum riser, so I couldn't crack his kick drum when I used it as a trampoline. I was performing at full steam, turned up to Number 11 and taking no prisoners.

We were all feeding off each other and the audience – the energy was electric. I jumped down to the crowd barrier and the fans reached for me. I was to discover that cassette tape is not the strongest of materials, so the fans were able to tear off pieces of my outfit. Song by song it began to disintegrate, leaving streams of tape all over the stage and in the hands of the front row. I didn't care; it added to the joy and unpredictability of the show and became a whole new look.

As I climbed back onstage, I could see people jumping up and down all the way to the horizon. Mark looked like a northern Incredible Hulk smashing his fists into the drum kit. We had to screw it into the floor every night to stop it crumbling to pieces under his assault. I could see Cass was loving every second, spinning around, ruling the stage, dreadlocks flying behind him. Ace, on my right, attacked his guitar in that deranged way that sent the crowd ballistic.

We all looked on top form. I had no idea that Ace was in intense pain with seven prolapsed discs in his back from constant touring. He had to have steroid injections every day and lie on ice packs after each show. During the gig, he was wracked with nerves, not wanting to play a wrong note. To the outside world he was on top of the world, but on the inside he was thinking, *Don't fuck up, don't make a mistake!* I almost feel bad for clambouring all over him now!

We sang 'Hedonism', and when we got to the chorus, the crowd sang back in unison at the top of their voices: *Just because it feels good/Doesn't make it right!* I saw Michael Eavis at the side of the stage. His wife Jean had died earlier that year, and the whole country mourned with him, so I dedicated 'You'll Follow Me Down' to her, and blew him a kiss. I gazed at a stunning sea of lighters while the light reflected off what was left of my outfit and it looked like I was on fire.

We were the last band to play on the Pyramid Stage that century. It was an incredible experience, but it also felt like the end of something at the same time. We were interviewed by Radio 1's Jo Whiley as soon as we got offstage, and I remember feeling so happy it was almost like I was floating. She asked us, 'What are you going to do now?'

We laughed, saying, 'We've got the string players with us and we're going to get drunk all the way back to London.' We were as good as our word. Sitting on the bus later, drinking wine and celebrating, I thought, *Is it ever going to be as good as this moment again?*

THIRTEEN

FOLLOW ME DOWN

You see the drinks stay sipped
Cos we've lost our grip
Too exhausted to rebel

'Burnt Like You'

That summer, after Glastonbury, our song 'Lately' became a hit. The video that we made to go with the song was directed by Howard Greenhalgh, as an homage to his award-winning 1994 video for Soundgarden's 'Black Hole Sun'. In it, I played a comet burning out on a collision course with Earth, singing: *Sometimes all the moments that we savoured for the last/Get crushed . . . from pressures we have had.* The image symbolised what the song was about – a burnt-out relationship where the people involved don't talk anymore, and that was an apt description of where we were as a band.

We had been running on adrenaline for six full-on years, and it had finally caught up with us. Glastonbury was the peak of our early career, and I remember feeling very strongly: *Wow, the only way now is down.* It had to be; no band only goes up. We never argued, we weren't upset with each other; we had just lost our chemistry. No one really seemed to care as much as they should. The one thing that Skunk Anansie have as a band is great chemistry, and that vital energy began to dissipate. If we'd written an album at that point, it wouldn't have been a good one, because we weren't a gang anymore. We were touring and recording constantly, barely going home, which meant we were not connected to real life or family and friends who could have individually kept us sane. Personally, I was starting to fade. I had an inner exhaustion that sleep couldn't cure. I ended up not wanting to get onstage. It's not rock-by-numbers – you have to *feel* it.

Touring is basically repetition; what makes it stimulating are the different venues, different fans, different countries you experience on the road. We had a massive production, which made it difficult to change the setlist, but I could usually get myself into the right vibe when I was onstage. There were occasional moments in the late '90s when I ran onstage not feeling much in the beginning, but at some point during the set the adrenaline would kick in and I'd be in the zone. But in the months after Glastonbury, I did three gigs in a row where I felt absolutely nothing. I was going through the motions almost like pantomime, and felt dead inside.

I remember feeling very separate from the rest of the band and the tour crew. I'd walk into a room and the crew would stop chatting and joking, suddenly on their best behaviour, and sometimes I'd hear them warn each other that I was coming. How did I get cast as the big bad boss, the band police, the

Massa? Over the years, we've learnt the hard way how one or two bad eggs can destroy the vibe of a whole tour. Negativity can be as infectious as positivity. Some people stay on the road too long and no longer know how to enjoy a moment unless they're doing something crazy or sleazy. Others consolidate their position with band members by being the one to get them anything they want.

Being on tour in the US supporting other groups was a real eye-opener. We saw crew members from other bands spot the pretty girls during the gig and invite them backstage for the price of a blow-job or a grope. That was not our vibe at all, and Cass, Mark and Ace were forever having to 'redirect' young girls out of trouble. Girls would get kicked off the other bands' tour buses in the middle of nowhere for not being obliging enough, so we'd take them to the next town and drop them off at a hotel or a train station. I remember Cass picking two girls up, one under each arm, from the centre of a crowd that was coercing them to strip and make out with each other. Cass has never lost that protective instinct over women, and is always the first person to step in when he sees a woman being mistreated. Once the girls were on our bus, they burst into tears. Cass had to seize Polaroids from the bus driver, who had taken pictures of them naked and put them in a huge folder. It was gross.

The touring was definitely taking its toll. Cass wanted to be at home with his young son and was finding the heavy schedule hard and emotionally draining. Mark is the sweetest, loveliest guy, but his behaviour had started to become erratic. We'd hear banging, then see him trash his hotel room, or get drunk and do crazy shit. One time, we were travelling down a European motorway at full speed on our tour bus, and Mark decided to climb out onto the roof through the emergency hatch at the rear of the bus, run across the top, then jump back in through a hatch at the front! At the time we were all in on it, laughing and being stupid, thinking it was just another crazy rock story to tell about Mark. But when we thought about it afterwards we realised how horribly wrong that could have gone. He told me later that his mental health was in a terrible state at the time, and he was really unwell. We're now much more aware of how mental issues can affect people, but in those days we knew nothing. In fact, bad behaviour was actively encouraged. I can't count the number of times an interview has started with, 'Oh, tell me, what is the craziest thing you've ever done?'

People would say to him, 'For God's sake, pull yourself together.' Or 'Man up!' Comments that, unsurprisingly, he found really unhelpful. Mark had always liked a drink, but during that 120-date *Post Orgasmic Chill* tour he became addicted to alcohol, drinking a lot just to get onstage, and then after the gig he would share half a bottle of vodka with the sound guy. The whole tour for Mark became a cycle of waking up every morning with guilt and self-hatred, vowing to stay sober, and then by the afternoon he'd be hitting the vodka again.

One night, after the tour, he called me up drunk, and I was vexed, thinking, *Why is that wanker calling me at four in the bloody morning?* I didn't quite get it. We're a rock band, and not a bunch of innocents, but I didn't put two and two together. Now it'd be obvious to me when someone close to me is showing addictive behaviour, but back then I couldn't see the signs. A few days after that, I called him up and told him, 'You need to sort your life out, otherwise there is no future in this band.' The only thing that got through to him was, 'You're going to lose your job.' He says he was defined by his job – the only thing he knew how to be was the drummer of Skunk Anansie. He said to me later that phone call ricocheted around his brain like a bullet.

After that conversation, Mark drove to Scarborough, to his parents' house, and Leigh helped him find a guy on Harley Street who told him to go to Alcoholics Anonymous. It took him three years to recover and stay sober. The help available for mental health and addiction was still very poor at the time, and that's why he vowed to try to do something about it. It took a long time but he set up the charity Music Support in 2015 with addiction treatment expert Johan Sorensen, manager Matt Thomas and tour manager Andy Franks, because he never wanted anyone else to have the same difficulty finding recovery.

That summer, the band rallied for a short while because we had a special treat in store. We were due to perform at a huge concert with the operatic tenor Luciano Pavarotti in his home town of Modena, Italy. On 6 June 2000, his Pavarotti & Friends concert for Cambodia and Tibet was televised worldwide, with proceeds from the concert going to children's charities in those countries. The Dalai Lama opened the event. We were appearing with George Michael, Eurythmics, Tracy Chapman, Enrique Iglesias, Mónica Naranjo from Spain and the Brazilian star Caetano Veloso.

I went ahead a few days early because Pavarotti had invited me to his house to hang out with him and his wife Nicoletta Mantovani, with whom I was already friends. He had a beautiful place in the Italian hills near Modena. We stood by the swimming pool while he decided to give me a singing lesson. We played around with some breathing techniques, and then it was time to eat. He sat on a big chair near a huge stove in his tiny kitchen while he cooked, telling me the secrets of making a good *vongole*. He was a massive guy, and would stand there with his apron on, drinking wine. For Italians, good balsamic vinegar is prized like rare wine, and he gave me a bottle of sixty-year-old vintage as a present. I still have it in my cupboard, and treasure it as my Pavarotti memory.

I stayed at the top of a lovely hotel nearby. It was meant to be George Michael's suite. I was only supposed to be there for three nights then move to another room, but they were too embarrassed to ask me to move, so I stayed there the whole time. George was genuinely a beautiful spirit, bright and fun, really easy to chat to, and so was his sister. The band had arrived by then and all the musicians hung out together. We ate breakfast with Annie Lennox, who was drop dead androgynous gorg, and stayed up all night becoming friends with Tracy Chapman. We drank wine on my roof terrace until daylight, watching the sun come up and light a terracotta heaven. Everyone had a genuine energy, and it was Pavarotti who set the tone for our hotel stay and the concert. It's a very Italian thing to create a relaxed family vibe – to eat, chat and drink wine. That harmoniousness helped us to recharge our energy and prepared us well for the concert.

I sang 'You'll Follow Me Down' with Pavarotti, performing a mixture of rock ballad and long operatic notes, accompanied by the band, who were all suited and booted for the occasion. I sang verses in English, and then Pavarotti sang some verses in Italian, and then we joined together in Italian for the chorus. It was my first foray into singing in Italian, but now, after years of studying the language, *ora sto molto meglio!*

Afterwards, all the artists were taken to a room backstage to meet the Dalai Lama and have our photo taken with him. The Dalai Lama smiled with an open face and shiny eyes. He felt like a very old soul, much like Nelson Mandela. It was clear he was used to meeting a lot of people very quickly – he has this handshake where he shakes your hand and then slightly pushes you away, moving you on so he can concentrate on the next person. *Very chic*, I thought, shake and push . . . I made a mental note of it.

My friend Richelle's brother was very ill at the time. She's a Buddhist, so I wanted to ask the Dalai Lama to bless a ring I'd bought with me to give to her. He paused, looked me gently in the eye and blessed the ring, closing his eyes and quietly saying a prayer. The next time I saw Richelle I gave it to her. When she put it on, she exclaimed, 'Wow, I feel energy shooting up my arm!' She wore the ring for a long time after her brother died and gave it back to me a few years later – it's something I really treasure.

Although the Pavarotti & Friends concert was special, the atmosphere in the band continued to be strained, so we decided to finally take some time off. I had been exploring different styles of music, and was chuffed to be invited to collaborate on a track with Maxim from the Prodigy's solo album, *Hell's Kitchen*. There are a lot of parallels with us and the Prodigy. We were both in-ya-face with our own weird mash-up styles. The Prodigy played raucous electronic music, but with a live band, and we played rock with touches of metal and electronic. Like them, we really went for it onstage, and shared the same edginess and madness in our music.

They sampled 'Selling Jesus' for their track 'Serial Thrilla' on their 1997 album, *Fat of the Land*, a song that sounds brilliantly riff-driven and deranged. We often played the same festivals in the late 1990s, and one of the best live performances I've ever witnessed was the Prodigy performing 'Firestarter' at the Strange Noise Festival in Germany in 1996, watching thousands and thousands of people in a field *completely* losing their shit.

We were a mutual admiration society – Mark got on really well with their lead singer, Keith Flint. They had the same love of motorbikes and rode together occasionally. Keith was always lovely to me. He was such a powerful front man, one of the best, and I was gutted to learn of his death in 2019, which was a deep shock. I was also friendly with Maxim, their MC and lyricist. Whenever we bumped into each other on tour, we'd always try and hang for the rest of the night. So I was delighted when Maxim contacted me and said he was doing a solo album and asked if I wanted to record a track with him. I went over to his place in the countryside near Peterborough, and we spent a day working on 'Carmen Queasy'. It was a magical house with a huge playroom attached to his studio, so ideal for creative work.

Maxim had sent me the music beforehand, and that inspired me to rap/sing a melody. I had a story in my head that involved a tumble of words like old-school 1970s rap, or loping '90s jazz rappers like the Pharcyde. I thought about how, during my career, people have given me advice about what I need to do in order to sell records, and I created this sardonic character, Carmen Queasy, who sings: *So now you're telling me it's so damn easy/Try to see yourself as Carmen Queasy/'Cos money-making is a wonderful thing.* I wrote dozens of words and phrases, and Maxim took them, restructuring them and creating a chorus that had a dark vibe and swing to it. I'm a singer, he's a rapper, so we found a happy medium and it felt very collaborative, with him focusing on how we could get the story across.

We shot a video for the song, which was directed by David Slade, who soon afterwards made a name for himself making off-kilter videos for space-rock superstars Muse. Maxim and I were both dressed in black, looking like sinister, futuristic vampires. I wore a slinky Alexander McQueen suit with cut-outs that showed lots of flesh, and my make-up artist Gina Kane stuck long white feathers to my lower eyelids. During filming I fluttered my eyes and didn't feel them, because they were literally as light as a feather. The song had a hook line that really stuck in your head, and it's still the one collaboration I get asked about wherever I go.

In 2000, I recorded another solo track, but this time with a heavy metal hero. Tony Iommi had asked me to work with him on a track called 'Meat' for his album *Iommi*, which featured everyone from Dave Grohl to Henry Rollins, Ian Astbury and Ozzy Osborne. I got Ace to play, to make it double the fun. I knew how much of a Sabbath megafan he was, so I wanted to share the love. I mean . . . it was Tony Iommi!

Tony is such a legend – his unique, almost drone-like style of playing on early Black Sabbath records was the soundtrack to many of our pre-gig warm- ups. We recorded his track in an old church in east London, suggesting different parts and a grinding '70s rock beast of a chorus, and Tony kept saying, 'Love it, do it! Love it, do it!' We then went out for an Indian meal round the corner, and he told us hilarious story after crazy story about him and Ozzy, so we could barely eat for laughing. Afterwards, Tony sent parcels to me and Ace. Mine was a small wooden coffin with a Sabbath-style gold cross inside, handmade with my name engraved on it. That cross is now one of my favourite possessions. In 2019, I bumped into him at the *Kerrang!* Awards and he gave me an earful for not wearing it enough!

I liked experimenting with new sounds, and started thinking about doing a solo album, working on song ideas with Len. I was unsure about Skunk Anansie, and was becoming more and more focused on the idea of making my own record. I started work on it, and sent Leigh a demo of 'Burnt Like You'. Leigh listened to it alone in her flat, to the lyrics:

> *I can't watch the same mistake*
> *Waiting for the boys to turn out straight*
> *No I can't run the same dog race*
> *And get burnt like you*
>
> *You're swollen in the gut*
> *From all those last nights*
> *Still swinging vodka punches*
> *That don't land right*

She told me later, 'I sat and cried my eyes out for a whole after-noon because I knew the band was over.'

Time apart from the band still hadn't fixed the tensions between us, and everything felt wrong. I didn't want to do it anymore. I wanted to move on. We barely saw each other, we had no songwriting time scheduled, we were utterly exhausted inside and out, and the friendships were starting to strain. After seven years of playing in Skunk non-stop, I think the deep tiredness I felt distorted my thinking. Leigh was also exhausted from managing the band, and was in need of some time to properly recuperate after her brain operation, and it wasn't fun for her like it had been in the early days.

It felt like it was all over and done, and things looked a lot worse than they actually were. Yes, we had some serious issues to deal with; we should have been able to ride through them but we didn't. Ultimately, I knew we weren't in a position to make great music. At that point, if we had just stayed on the track we were on, I thought that would destroy us.

In April 2001, Leigh organised a meeting with our lawyer in his London office to discuss the future of the band, and that's when I said to them, 'You know what, I'm done with this.' I was angry, because I felt like I had been steering the band for a long time and taking a lot of the responsibility. Ace said, 'Well, why don't we just have a break for a couple of years?' But I had decided I was done. I didn't hate them – I just felt like I was the glue trying to hold everything together. That's very difficult for one person to do. In hindsight, splitting up Skunk Anansie was a mistake. I should have just taken a break rather than ending it. It would have been better for us to sit down and have a blow-out, but we didn't know how to do that; we didn't have that level of maturity.

I needed some time. I wanted to make a different kind of music – something quieter, gentler and more electronic – and those kinds of songs weren't going to work with Skunk Anansie, because the DNA of Skunk is *rock*.

The guys reacted in different ways. Ace says that the music business is a powerful force for breaking people; that the problem is long touring, which can be physically and mentally tough. Lead singers tend to live an accelerated lifestyle that can be fragile, unrelenting, unchartered and unreliable. Ace liked touring and didn't want to stop. He told me later that after the band ended people didn't care about him anymore. They would say, 'Yeah, I'll put you on the guest list', and just not bother. That's a hard bump. But he took it in his stride. 'I'm the same person I was before this started,' he said. Ace has always had that self-belief.

Cass says that when he stepped away from it, he understood the value of the band. 'There's never going to be another Skunk Anansie in my life,' he said. 'I'm never going to have the vibe that I had with that band onstage.' Afterwards, he played with bluesy rock guitarist Gary Moore, and did session work, but he described it as soul destroying. 'Playing with another band felt like going back to the sports shop,' he said, which was where he'd first worked.

Mark was more anxious than the others. He told me, 'I did nothing for a year. I didn't want to start anything from scratch. Not being in Skunk Anansie gave me a huge shock. If the band doesn't exist, then who the fuck am I?' He said he lacked a strong sense of self then, that he was defined by his job. And me? I didn't feel happy at all. I basically just wanted to change everything. I wanted to get out of London and get out of England, because it felt sad being an ex-member of a band. I wanted to go and live in Barcelona and learn Spanish, but at that time, Leigh was dating a guy in the south of France, and she said, 'Why don't you come and check this area out?'

I moved there and took a long break from performing, focusing instead on writing new songs. Len would come over and we'd write for weeks on end. I lived in a top-floor flat next to an Irish bar, and one night I went down to have a drink to get a break from songwriting. There was a big crowd of people there, because it was somebody's birthday. They were really fun, and they became my posse for a while. It was a relief to meet them because it can be hard to make real friends in new places.

In my new home I was able to focus on writing my songs, and working on my solo album felt like going back to where I had started. Songwriting is a way of expressing all kinds of pain, but I don't think it makes it hurt any less. But I think time is the only real healer – the songs are just a product of the pain. It wasn't only Mark who kept things hidden. I had my secrets too. I was recovering from a personal break-up at the same time as getting over the break-up of the band.

BOOK THREE

THE TROUBLE WITH ME

FOURTEEN

FLESHWOUNDS

Some would say it's madness to split up your band at the height of their success, and for Skin it was a deliberate madness. Casting herself off without a safety net was a way to test herself, force herself to move forward, turning away from thundering rock riffs to explore and articulate her inner world. She wanted to find her power as a solo songwriter/producer, and she was in good company.

She was inspired by a number of women who had made the journey from being lead singer of a rock band to solo artist. Gwen Stefani was one – the platinum-blonde icon who in 2003 left Californian new-wave ska band No Doubt to record her solo debut *Love. Angel. Music. Baby.* Inspired by music she listened to in the 1980s, *L.A.M.B.* combined autobiographical songwriting with synth-pop and cheerleading electro, and after its release in 2004 sent Stefani stratospheric.

Leaving a successful rock band wasn't always easy, however. Shirley Manson, lead singer with post-grunge alt-rock group Garbage, branched out on her own in 2006 to make, as she put it, 'a quiet, very dark, non-radio-friendly record'. Her record label Geffen weren't impressed. What they had in mind was turning Manson into the next Annie Lennox, singing international pop hits, but she wasn't interested in 'writing nursery rhymes for the masses' and her solo work was put on hiatus.

And one of the most inspiring female artists for Skin was her former One Little Indian label-mate Björk, who left Icelandic post-punk band the Sugarcubes in the early 1990s to create sensual art pop. Skin, too, was itching to record music with electronic textures. With her solo album, *Fleshwounds*, Skin delved deep into her psyche, plucking out fragments of the jazz standards that comforted her as a child, and combining them with the savage guitar tunings of an electronic blues. Some say Skin made a mistake, a left turn. But it was a journey that led her to the source of her strength as a lyricist and musician. It was frightening for her to leave behind what had sustained her, but she needed to try something new. She needed to go forward, not back.

I have to admit that *Fleshwounds* was a break-up album. I hadn't done one before, and I haven't done one since, but I guess you always end up doing at least one in your career, don't you? At the same time as the band was splitting up, I was going through the break-up of a relationship with someone I was into. It was far from a perfect situation in that I was openly bisexual and she didn't identify as queer, so I resisted getting involved. Then, after a few months of being friends, we slowly evolved into something deeper. At first it was good, but then it became strangely one-sided, as I realised that after my initial resistance,

I liked her *wayyy* more than she liked me. Being in a closeted relationship meant that we couldn't be open, and that put extra pressure on it. We saw each other for about a year, which wasn't that long, but it was long enough to break my heart. Having to hide our feelings was stifling and claustrophobic, going against everything I felt and thought about who I should be. In my career, I'd been out from Day One, and here I was not out anymore – it almost felt like being in a kind of prison.

So, after all the positive things that I had come to believe about myself, like being open and political about my sexuality, I suddenly found myself having to be guarded about my life. I tried to get round it by convincing myself I was just being economical with the truth, but you get yourself into trouble pretending to be single when you're not.

That whole time I felt like I was standing on quicksand and sinking fast. Our relationship wasn't solid. It reminded me of my first girlfriend, Sabrina, in the way I gave everything; that's what you're supposed to do, right? I don't play games in a relation-ship – I want everyone to be happy and that sometimes means I'm too much of a pleaser. Our relationship eventually dissolved, and I channelled some of those feelings into a solo album.

I wrote the songs for *Fleshwounds* in a home-made studio with Len Arran in the south of France, and that reminded me of the early days, working with just guitar, vocals and some simple beats. I loved the simplification of the songwriting process; the way I could concentrate on the words, the emotion, and telling the story, reflecting on the intensity of love, hate and the ambi-guities in between. I'm a terrible guitarist, and I'm even worse on bass or drums, which forced me to keep things simple and work on what I'm good at – writing songs and singing.

In my design years my talent was translating what I saw in my head onto paper. Perspective drawings, mood boards, that's what I loved doing the most. With songs it's the same approach. I can take images from my head and transmit them through words to the audience, so they can feel what I feel and see what I see. With song lyrics I connect to how I feel, then find the precise words to describe that. They need to be my words because only I can express them in that way, and that's how I convey my emotions to others.

For that reason, the song 'The Trouble With Me' has one of my favourite lyrical lines: *The trouble with me, is my troubles with you*. It's about that eureka moment you have in a relationship when it dawns on you that your relationship is basically screwed, but in a way that's empowering. That song marks the point when I stopped blaming myself, stopped thinking things would change. In writing this album, I walked through the different emotional stages of heartbreak: when you're bargaining, when you're angry, when you realise you're going to have to let someone go. I tried to keep the lyrics spare, with no platitudes, no clichés. That's where the poetry is, in portraying the experience.

This reflection on the end of a relationship starts with 'Faithfulness', tentatively *Watching as my ego breaks your fall*. Then the denial of 'Don't Let Me Down' – *You've grown so cold/ Why have you frozen now?*, followed by the dishevelled rage of 'Trashed'. That song became the lead single on the album, and the video features me trudging through the streets all night through downtown LA.

Shooting the video was hell. It was filmed over two nights with a crew who were completely obsessed with getting footage of me walking and then speeding it up, over and over and over again. I wore a see-through T-shirt under my Hedi Slimane Dior suit and was freezing cold. Leigh and I were asking each other, 'What's wrong with these people?' Then, right at the end of the shoot, somebody offered me drugs and I wanted to kick myself. Duh, that was why they did everything over and over again! It was a terrible experience, and I was exhausted beyond belief but, in a strange way, the video conveys the meaning of that song and the relentlessness of grief when it hits.

In the song, 'You've Made your Bed', I love the line, *I'm a one-night stand/Screwed the whole damn year/Your cheeky face came streaked with tears*. For me, it captures the moment after a relationship ends when you realise where you went wrong. Writing that song enabled me to see the situation with new strength and clarity – that I had dragged it out. Idiot! I hadn't wanted to get into a relationship with her, because I knew that it wasn't going to work. It should have been just a bit of fun, a one-night stand. In my head, part of me was screaming, 'Don't do this!', but the other part of me was maybe attracted to the challenge.

The beautiful trumpet on the track was played by Mike Figgis, director of *Leaving Las Vegas*. I'd written music with him for his films *Timecode* and *Hotel*, so he very kindly returned the favour. He's a wonderful musician. His notes are like wispy traces over the grainy percussive loop, symbolising affection fading out.

Relationships are hard, all of them, but you have to make your own mistakes and deal with your own dramas. The only way to learn is through experience. We don't put enough emphasis on the value of failure and how overcoming it is character-building, and how pain can be a useful tool because, without it, you'll never know happiness. Anger is also a powerful tool that gives you the energy to move on, but you have to let it fade otherwise it will consume and poison your thinking. That's what 'Til Morning', one of my favourite songs on the album, is about.

Take these sore eyes/I've no use for them, I sing. I love the way the melody has tinges of 1940s-style jazz phrasing, ending the album harking back to where I started, which was singing jazz. At thirty-five years old, I was coming full circle. With *Fleshwounds*, each song is part of an emotional journey, as if I'm awake through the night reflecting on all my relationships, and the last song, 'Til Morning', with its long, echoey trumpet solo, signals the dawn, the light coming in and a new understanding.

I recorded *Fleshwounds* in Belgium, with the very talented darkwave electronic producer David Kosten, who had worked with artists such as Chris Martin, the Flaming Lips' Wayne Coyne and, later, Bat For Lashes. I felt his production style really suited the songs I'd written, which were dark, twisted, and downtempo.

David was a perfectionist, so the first thing he did was travel around Europe at our expense to find the perfect studio. That's what happens when you sign big record deals – people spend all your money for you! I had a wonderful team of musicians. I was honoured to work with Gail Ann Dorsey, a great artist whom I'd met at festivals when she played with David Bowie, and who played bass on my record. I had bought both of her solo albums, *The Corporate World* and *Rude Blue*, when I was younger, and had listened to them in my university bedroom. Ben Christophers and Jacob Golden, both supremely talented guitarist/songwriters, also played on the album, along with Richard Jupp, the now ex-drummer from Elbow. He had a unique, loping style with no showy fills or unnecessary riffs, which worked really well. I also flew to Toronto and spent time there writing with Craig Ross, who plays guitar and produces Lenny Kravitz. Together we wrote 'Listen To Yourself', and he was also kind enough to add his skill to 'The Trouble With Me', which, to my mind, put it in another league.

We recorded in a high-tech studio near Antwerp, and halfway through the session something happened that affected the whole atmosphere and ended up influencing the record itself.

The studio was residential, and I had a bedroom upstairs. On 11 September we were recording in the main studio when someone ran in and said a plane had just flown into the Twin Towers in New York. We dashed to look at the TV in the sitting-room area and were mesmerised by footage of a plane flying into the North Tower of the World Trade Center. 'What's going on?' I said, feeling utterly shocked. I was staring at the screen when, five minutes later, I saw a second plane, United Airlines flight 175, crash into the South Tower, sending plumes of fire and smoke into the blue sky. Everyone – David, the musicians, the engineer, the cook – we all stopped what we were doing and didn't do any more work that day, all glued to the news. Repeated shots of the planes going into the Twin Towers were played over and over again, adding to a real sense of impending doom. Later that evening, at 11.20pm Belgian time, we saw the Twin Towers finally collapse to the ground and got the chills.

Fleshwounds was a dark album, and 9/11 added to the sense of doom. Everyone felt a little afraid, like, *What the hell is going to happen now?* That seeped through to the sadness of the record. In some ways those songs are about the dark feelings of a break-up and rejection, but in a wider sense they also reflect the sadness of human nature – look at the things we do to each other.

After the recording session in Belgium, I came away with beautiful music, but no obviously commercial singles. Somehow the pop sound was lost to a more stripped-down sense of uber-cool beauty – whereas I wanted and needed both. Bono once gave me an excellent piece of advice: make sure your album has two pop radio singles to sell it and after that you can be as arty-farty as you like.

We booked a separate songwriting session with Robbie Williams's producer Guy Chambers. He already had ideas, and was working on a track called 'Golden', that was sweet and cute. It was too cute, though, and it wasn't really me – it needed a dark underbelly. I had a very strong premonition that if I didn't come up with something better right then I was not going to get enough out of the session. I had three days to work with one of the greatest songwriters in England, and his time and my money would be wasted. The only way it was going to be my style was if I wrote some great lyrics. I felt the pressure build in my head. He had a mezzanine in the studio, so I went upstairs with a pen and paper and came down ten minutes later with the verses and chorus of 'Lost'.

'What about this song?' I asked, then I sang it to him.

Guy looked at the verse and chorus, then looked at me and said, 'That's better.'

I wrote the words, he did the music, and when we were about to lay down the drums, he said, 'Let's record it at seventy-six BPM (beats per minute).'

'Why that tempo?' I asked.

He said it was the same tempo as 'Angels', Robbie Williams's enormous 1997 hit single.

'Oh,' I said. 'That's the magic tempo then.' We giggled.

I love that track and the lyrics: '*What was I waiting for/Waiting for the bubble to burst/Over your stagnant pauses . . .*' I love the video for it as well, depicting the aftermath of a romance, with its shots of trashed flats, dirty beds and heartbroken people. It was like ten different lo-fi versions of Tracy Emin's *My Bed*.

'Trashed' and 'Faithfulness' were remixed and given a heightened sense of pop drama by my lovely friend, the film composer Marius de Vries, whom I'd known for years. Björk introduced us in the '90s, and we hit it off and have always loved each other's company. We had loads of fun in the studio putting the pop back into those songs.

After recording the album, the first person I played it to was my friend the actress Saffron Burrows, while she sat on the floor, legs folded, in my house in Maida Vale. 'What are you going to call it?' she asked.

'I've no idea.'

'What about *Fleshwounds*, because each song is like a cut, a flesh wound. You might end up with a little scar but you'll survive.'

I loved that. I knew what she meant – we're both streetwise. At heart she's still a lanky kid from Dalston, and I can always hear the 'norf' London in her voice. I have many physical scars from childhood, games or crazy moments onstage, but I also have scars unseen. It was the perfect title.

After the album was finished I became embroiled in record company politics. EMI and Virgin were changing. Ken Berry, co-founder of Virgin Records with Richard Branson, was always very supportive of me as an artist, but in 2001 he had left his job as CEO of EMI International. Leigh knew that Skunk Anansie fan Mark Collen was heading up Chrysalis, so it made sense to move sideways, to another label, where I would get the support I needed for my solo project. While I was recording the album, Leigh negotiated my move to Chrysalis, but just before the signing celebration dinner, Mark rang to say a new executive was taking over, a very successful A&R man from Parlophone, whose big calling card was Radiohead. In the early days of Skunk Anansie, Leigh had been to see this guy with a demo of 'I Can Dream'. He played it a quarter of the way through before turning off the cassette and giving it back, saying, 'This isn't for me.' So, Leigh and I knew we were in trouble.

I was a priority when I signed with Chrysalis, but from the moment the man took over as CEO the atmosphere soured. Suddenly I had to jump through hoops. The label made me go to media training, as if I were an eighteen-year-old pop novice. The trainer looked at me after five minutes and said, 'Why are you here?' I had no idea. It was a waste of everyone's time so he sent me home. We could never do anything right. We set up a meeting about the album cover with the incredible photographer Nick Knight, my friend and genius designer Alexander McQueen, and uber-stylist Katy England, but the CEO sent along some record company dude who was flippant and rude about all of our ideas and I felt totally embarrassed. It felt like sabotage! So we flew down to Spain and shot a great photo session for the album cover. The label rejected it wholesale. £24,000 down the drain!

Finally, Leigh and I had a meeting with him where we played him *Fleshwounds*. He said I should change my voice, as there was a tone in it he didn't like, and gave no further explanation. If I had a horrible voice people wouldn't want to hear it, and I wouldn't have sold records. As an artist you have to be able to wade through criticism and work out what is constructive feedback and what just simply ... a kicking. When someone says they don't like your songs, or your music or attitude, that's okay, because that's just personal taste, but when someone — especially the CEO of your record label — tells you they don't like your *voice*, that's a lot more personal. You can't change your voice; you know you're screwed. It means you're done. Enjoy the ride home.

Being a solo artist can be the loneliest place in the world. It takes massive ambition and drive because you need to constantly push your own agenda in a way that can seem quite narcissistic. You need to ensure the record company makes you a priority, getting record sales, radioplay and media coverage. Touring with Robbie Williams taught me that, and that's not a diss on him — that's just what you need to make it. I did two tours with him when he was right at his peak, around 2004, and we were playing stadiums to crowds of 60,000 people. He was super-sweet to me, and would pop into my dressing room and chat. He stood up for me in Moscow when a club refused to let me in because I was black (they actually said that to my face), coming to the door to let rip at the bouncers. But on a professional level, I could see how single-minded he was. As a solo artist you need to drive yourself as fast and as hard as you can, because everything's on your shoulders. I hated the fact that, as a solo singer, you can rarely get an honest opinion because everyone wants to keep their job, and nobody dares upset you. I'm very collaborative, I like to work with people, and I missed that sense of being in a band when you're all in it together. I'd found a great bunch of session guys, but it took a long time to get the sound right. It didn't feel like being in a proper band, where everyone has an equal say, and being the boss making all the musical decisions was for me a huge learning curve.

The one thing that kept hitting me in the face time and time again was that no one was better than the three guys I had started with in my own band. I felt sad and found it very draining. When I went solo, I grew my hair, which prompted Leigh to ask me, 'Why are you unhappy?' I've only grown my hair when I don't want to be myself, so growing my hair became a way of me running away from myself. When you have hair, you can shape it in different styles and have different looks, but when you're shaven-headed you have one core identity and it reflects a clear self-confidence. I guess it was also that I associated being shaven with Skunk Anansie, and I had run away from Skunk Anansie.

FIFTEEN

JUST LET THE SUN

That's where I'm going to
Someplace that's far from you
I'm movin' on

'Movin''

Fleshwounds did well despite the lack of support from Chrysalis Records, selling over 500,000 copies in a changing market where the internet was just beginning to have a major impact on CD sales. But I was dropped by the label in 2004, a year after its release. I was delighted to be dropped because then it meant I was completely free to make music but with no huge debt to pay back. For this I have eternal respect for the Chrysalis executive, as he could have kept me on the label but put me on a shelf and left me there to rot. Many artists have found themselves in that position – most famously Prince, who became a symbol in his battle with Sony – but I was free! We drank a lot of champagne that night.

Leigh then negotiated me a deal with V2 for the second album, one where I had much more creative control. As an artist, from the moment you sign to a record company you are an investment that needs to be protected, and also manipulated, so it can be a constant battle to assert control over your image and your music. It's hard enough maintaining control over the course of one album release, let alone a career – so, after *Fleshwounds*, I learnt how to stand up for myself in the studio. That driving energy is captured on my second solo album, *Fake Chemical State*.

As I developed my solo career and toured with my band, my confidence grew and I began to co-produce my own music. I had come a long way from the frightened girl who stepped up to the mic at Linford Manor in 1994. One thing I learnt very early on is: don't shy away from the technical side. I recall one session in Skunk's early days, when I had ideas about the sonics and production of a song, but the engineer kept saying, 'You can't do that.' Eventually I asked why, and he replied in a patronising drawl: 'It's too complicated to explain.' So, from that day on, I have always asked questions about how the gear works. I watched and listened to everything, absorbing as much knowledge and information as I could, so that I'd never have to hear those words again. You need to have the right words to communicate your ideas properly. There's no point asking an engineer to make something sound 'nice' – it's too vague. Better to say, can you compress the vocal, EQ the harshness out of it but add some air, then add a touch of reverb to sweeten it? *Boom!* The engineer knows exactly what you want. Knowing how the gear works gave me more power and creative control in the studio, so I could capture the sounds and feelings I imagined, rather than what the engineer wanted.

When I started work on my second solo album, I was in a more positive frame of mind. I'd been on tour for a few years since going solo and I was enjoying it. The songs I wrote reflected my life on the road, and also in my new hangout in Ibiza, where I'd bought a cottage in the early 2000s. It was a charming little 200-year-old finca set in a sunlit valley on the border of a great forest. As soon as I saw it, I knew it was going to be my home away from home. My friend Angela Robson and her daughter Isobel were my first visitors after I bought it. Isobel loved being lost in the woods so much she called it 'the secret forest', and that became 'El Bosque Secreto', the perfect name for my house.

Ibiza is a magical place, a spiritual island steeped in good vibes. Since rave culture hit in the 1980s, it's become a mecca for dance music, a place with great beaches and incredible DJs, but still unpopulated enough for you to get lost in nature. *Fake Chemical State* is influenced by my times in Ibiza, and also harks back to my early raving days in London. For the album cover, we went to my favourite Ibiza club, Manumission. The club co-founder Mike McKay, and his partner Claire, ruled Ibiza with their fantastical shows and cutting-edge DJs, so to capture that gritty energy, photographer Derrick Santini shot me in Manumission's dark, over-painted backstage corridors, wearing lace tops and rock T-shirts styled by my friend Analiese Dean.

Sitting on top of the hill, beside the main road from Ibiza Town to San Antonio, Manumission grew into the largest club on the planet, sometimes attracting a 9,000-strong crowd of ravers. I went to Manumission from the late 1990s, when it was a wild place, going there with freaks and friends and dancing for hours. In a symbolic sense, my new album was about me finding my freedom as an independent artist again, and being happy – Ibiza is my happy place.

My first solo album, *Fleshwounds*, sounded low, sparse, spacious, whereas the follow-up, *Fake Chemical State*, expressed the hedonistic fun of Ibiza and myself reborn. By then I'd been playing with my musicians for a couple of years, so the songs for my second album had a back-to-basics energy that was lighter in mood and groovier.

'Just Let the Sun', for instance, was fuelled by a night of pounding four-to-the-floor beats then going home watching the sun come up, ready to write music. I loved that juxtaposition of experiences, of living on an island of dance culture and writing an indie rock album. I'm a raver with a rock soul; I've always loved both genres. The title track was inspired by being on the streets of the Old Town, watching parades of insane characters in super-sexy outfits. I loved the queer club-kids who would dress up and influence the scene; everybody was accepted, no one was rejected. The best club nights were the ones with an eclectic mix of people. As legendary club promoter Peter Gatien says in his book, *The Club King*, 'A club needs at least thirty per cent gay people in the crowd for it to be good. Gay people bring an energy and wildness to the party that gives everyone else permission to be free.'

Fake Chemical State also has some soulful tracks, like 'Purple', a song I wrote with Gary Clark, who after his stint in the Scottish pop band Danny Wilson became a successful songwriter for artists like Lloyd Cole, Skye, and Liz Phair. He put a lot of work into our collaboration, a song about submitting to the pain of love. It became a big hit in Italy and, with the chiming guitar of my guitarist Elliot King, and a ghostly, dark undertow, it's probably my most popular solo song. The video, however, was another kind of pain, because I had to perform in freezing cold water in an old warehouse under the arches near the London Dungeon. The production crew flooded the place with hoses, and stood there in Welly boots filming me while I was made to flounder in the water. I got really sick afterwards. I know water is a strong way of signifying emotion, but I just looked like a wet, purple lagoon monster, drowning in my own shit video.

Some of the songs on the album had a difficult birth, like 'Nothing But', recorded in a session with Linda Perry, the prolific songwriter/producer, whose mega-hits included Christina Aguilera's 'Beautiful', Gwen Stefani's 'What You Waiting For?' and 'Get the Party Started' by Pink. So I went to LA full of anticipation, because I'd been casual friends with Linda for years. We understood each other. Sadly, she had split up with her girlfriend the day before I arrived, and seemed distracted and unhappy. My guitarist Elliot came with me, all ready to work with his beautiful guitar ideas. When we walked into her studio in Burbank, forty-five minutes outside LA, we were stunned. It was impressive, with around fifty amazing vintage guitars in the live room. Elliot and I exchanged glances – what Linda didn't know is that he is a left-handed guitarist, so he couldn't play any of them. Ouch! That did not help the vibes.

Linda and I butted heads a little during recording, a dynamic I like because it can be creative. For instance, she wanted to record the whole drum kit punk style, with only two overhead microphones, none on the kick or snare drums. I'd been in a band a long time, and knew it would be hell to mix because all the sound would be recorded through all of the mics, and you'd never be able to separate the pieces of drum kit afterwards.

Luckily, I won that argument after the session drummer agreed with me – they were very good friends, so he knew how to win her round.

I walked in with thirty ideas for songs and we were there for two weeks, but we recorded just two songs, one of which, 'Nothing But', I'd written completely. To Linda's absolute credit, she didn't take publishing royalties on it. Most producers would have done so in those circumstances, but Linda didn't and I respected her for that. A hitmaker is a difficult position to be in – hit songs are actually hard to achieve; they rarely fall into your lap. There is a pop formula, but that's no guarantee of success, because as well as a great track you need a good team and a whole load of luck on your side. After working, Linda and I still managed to have fun. She's a real character, and I like that, so we got on – one night, she took me to her favourite club and we had a riot of a time.

'Nothing But' – the song I recorded with Linda that ended up on my album – is about seeing your ex going off with a new person and having to grit your teeth and smile through it, something I've been through. Why try to reclaim someone when a relationship has finished? Maturity means being happy for someone when you're not in love with them anymore. By contrast, 'Take Me On' is a temper tantrum for attention, with M.I.A-style agit-pop, cheeky lyrics and layered guitars. It was recorded with my friends Marlene Kuntz, an uber-cool, edgy Italian band referred to as the 'Sonic Youth of Italy'. I'd previously collaborated with them in 2000, on 'La Canzone Che Scivo Per Te' ('The Song I Write For You'), which was a massive hit in Italy.

Writing the songs was a liberating experience, but when it

came to recording them, I totally clashed with Gordon Rafael, the producer of *Fake Chemical State*. He had done great work with New York garage-rock band the Strokes, and I thought the songs would sound powerful with his kind of production. Gordon gave great chat. I felt he understood the songs and my vibe. He had a studio around the corner from my flat in east London that was brilliantly rough and ready, and I loved the way he produced my voice, creating a gorgeous sound through a set of beautiful vintage Neve pre-amplifiers. But he also had an old-school American rock attitude, declaring, 'Nobody can play to a click; we're just gonna throw things down and jam.'

I wanted the songs to sound tight and punchy, with no wandering tempos, whereas he wanted them to be more languid. I was going for a focused, clean, garage style, so I kept having to say, 'No, let's do it again.' He said he was keen to capture the moment, but sometimes I felt he just captured an average performance, and I wasn't used to that. I knew my musicians were just warming up and had a lot more to give.

I'd recorded a demo I loved for 'Alone In My Room', but Rafael's production made the track sound long and drawn out, with none of the prickly English punk energy I wanted. There is nothing more frustrating than trying to get a song to sound as good as the original demo. It's a producer's nightmare! Afterwards, I had the demo mastered myself, and that went on the record instead of his version. When *Fake Chemical State* was finished, Gordon called me up and went ballistic, swearing down the phone. I was so shocked I couldn't even speak. I wasn't used to that kind of tongue-lashing from a professional producer. I hadn't seen that side of him.

'I went to play this to my friends,' he said, 'and all of a sudden

this horrible thing starts up and I think, *What the fuck is that?*'
He was annoyed because I had put my demo on the album –
but that was my prerogative as the executive producer, and it
was *my* album. I don't think he would have spoken like that to
a male artist. He called up later to apologise, but the damage to
our working relationship was done.

Fake Chemical State is a sexually ambiguous record that has
an aura of flitting from one romantic adventure to the next.
Around the time I wrote it, I was living in Ibiza and had a
boyfriend – a very sweet guy who was gorgeous to look at,
super-fit, metrosexual and well-groomed. Everything was fun
in the beginning. For a while it was oddly liberating because,
with a straight boy, I could walk down the road holding hands
and didn't have to worry about public displays of affection,
whereas with a woman you need to stay on alert and be aware of
what's happening around you to avoid homophobic harassment.

At the same time, I found the affair confusing because it
brought out my girly side a little too much. I wore floaty dresses
and heels for the first time in ages, but it felt strange, like I was
repressing part of myself. I remember visiting my friend Sasha
Moon at her clothes shop. She looked at me, saying, 'What the
fuck are you wearing?'

I looked down at the frills in horror. 'You know what, you're
right.' The dress was tossed and I bought a whole new outfit.
Shortly after, I shed the boyfriend as well. He was a great guy
but he brought out an inner frill in me I'd rather never see again.

I'm not particularly girly, I'm happiest being in the middle,
and it's so strange to have a career where I'm constantly being
asked by journalists about my sexuality. In the 1990s and early

2000s, there was still pressure to put yourself in sexual categories, like lesbian, bisexual and straight. How wonderful it is that sexuality is now seen as fluid, and if I'm forced to define myself, queer is the flag I'd wave – it's what I've always been and I guess always will be.

After the relationship with the metrosexual man ended, I was back on tour. *Fake Chemical State* was released in spring 2006, and I travelled to Italy, where I sang to a million-strong crowd at the 1 May Labour Day concert in Rome. That was a wild one. Before I went onstage people kept saying, 'It's a million people', and what they meant was 'Don't fuck up!' I couldn't actually see a million people; there were about a hundred thousand in front of me, and the rest were watching me on massive screens in other squares, also full of people. For gigs that big, your performance changes – you're reliant on the camera, lights and your voice, and you need to sing really well. It's good to play to the camera, so the cameraperson catches you at the right moment. It's a more considered, thought-out performance than a regular live gig.

When the tour finished, I started branching out into new areas of music, saying yes to things that were nothing to do with singing. The rise of the internet was redefining roles and turning everything upside down, with the boundaries between actors, DJs and musicians shifting and changing. Mr C, for instance, from indie rave band the Shamen, had a wicked club night in Ibiza. Björk went from indie rock to electronic pop to creating events that were a mixture of music, visual art and cutting-edge technology. I began saying yes to DJing, and played house and tech-house sets in clubs everywhere from Switzerland to Italy, LA and London.

I'd been interested in DJing ever since I was a seventeen-year-old student playing my vinyl collection at college parties. After Skunk Anansie started, the band took over everything, and I didn't DJ for a long time but I kept being asked, probably because I was always on the dancefloor! In 1999, I had a massive millennium New Year's Eve party at my house in Maida Vale, and instead of renting DJ equipment, I bought my own. My friend, and excellent DJ, Smokin' Jo taught me how use all the gear, and from then on my love for the decks was reignited. By 2008, I started taking it more seriously, with a complete overhaul of my set-up, which meant getting into new technology and software. I started doing more and more DJ nights, but it took me a while before I fully grasped it and felt like I could rock a room.

Having spent a lot of time in recording studios, I had a considerable advantage, as I already understood how the technology worked. But still, DJing is something you need to love doing, because it's complicated, frustrating and, well ... long. Developing a style is the trickiest part, as within electronic music there are many different tiny musical spheres, so it takes a long time to hear the subtle shading between them, and some of the nuances are slight but vital. There is a magical, spiritual side to understanding the flow of energy in a room, knowing which track to play next, nurturing a crowd and taking them on a journey with you. There's no fast way to becoming a good DJ – it takes a ton of gigs, with lots of embarrassing mistakes along the way.

My love of dance culture went back to the end of the 1980s, with warehouse acid parties and raves. Then, when Skunk Anansie was on tour in the 1990s, I loved sampling the New

York nightlife. We played famous rock venues like CBGBs, but our favourite was Squeezebox at Don Hill's in SoHo. It was *MAD!* One night we played a short thirty-minute set alongside drag queen punk bands before everything turned into a full-on party. I remember seeing cult film director John Waters at the back of the club surrounded by gorgeous boys, while I danced in front of the DJ booth trying to get the attention of Miss Guy, who had the face of Debbie Harry and the body of a New York Doll. I had a massive crush on them but was totally wasting my time there! Body and Soul in Tribeca on a Sunday afternoon was electric, with funky soul music and brilliant dancers, while Twilo was hot, a huge warehouse club in Manhattan with an incredible sound system. It's lovely to note that our coolest hit in America is actually a remix of 'Weak' by Junior Vasquez, who was resident DJ at Sound Factory. We're known in New York more for that one track than anything else. I remember going to legendary drag queen Lady Bunny's Wigstock festival in New York at the end of the '90s. As we arrived, the DJ played the 'Weak' remix and everyone went crazy. I was shook!

It was through clubbing that I met the female artist I've been compared to the most – Grace Jones. Until I saw her perform live I had always been a little irritated with the constant comparisons, thinking it was so reductive to compare the two of us just because we're both outspoken black female performers. After a Skunk Anansie gig in the '90s, some friends took me to the Tunnel club, and we arrived just before her set. From the second Grace hit the stage I was transfixed. Raw, theatrical and dynamic with killer songs, she blew my head apart! She was in-ya-face, and unpredictable – quite simply one of the best performers in the world. After the Tunnel gig, we sneaked backstage. I got myself introduced and I've hung out with her many times ever since.

Offstage Grace is playful, motherly, and wants everyone to be happy, ready to share oysters and champagne. One of my fondest memories is when I was (happily) kidnapped by her for two days. We were at an Alexander McQueen show in Paris in 2006, the one where Kate Moss appeared as a ghostly hologram. Afterwards, I went out for dinner and clubbing with Grace and her friend, the actress Sarah Douglas, before coming back to the Hotel George V, where she was staying in a luxury suite that even had a room especially for her furs. We all danced and chatted until morning, and she was working on some new material, so she played us some demos before I crashed out on the sofa. I was meant to be checking out from my hotel later that day and, unbeknownst to me, Grace called Leigh and said with great charm, 'Good morning, this is Grace Jones. I'm kidnapping Skin – could you possibly pack her suitcase and send it over?' Grace and I then spent two days hanging out, having saunas, going to her son Paolo's brilliant comedy gig, seeing exhibitions and shows. It was a lovely spontaneous adventure.

For me, Grace is the ultimate artist. I love how she brings different art forms into her world – from music to fashion to photography – and makes them her own. She's the benchmark for everyone who followed, from Madonna to Lady Gaga, changing the narrative of what's possible for a female artist.

When we started out in the 1990s, rock music was post-grunge anti-fashion and anti-sponsorship. It was cool to have a track in a movie but not cool for it to be featured in a car advert. There was a much stronger division between the aesthetics of rock and pop. As a rock singer you needed to look good, but it had to look like a bit of an accident, like clothes you picked off the floor that morning just happened to look amazing. Pop was the opposite. Madonna showed us how it's done in Gaultier cone-bras, while rap stars had massive logos slapped all over their streetwear, but none of that really worked for me. By the 2000s, grunge was dead, the rock scene had changed and, as a solo artist, I could experiment more with designer looks. I loved the Tokyo fashion label Comme des Garçons, and I once splurged on a trip to Paris and bought an entire rail of Hedi Slimane 'skinny suits' at Dior. I'd mix them up with yardie string vests from Brixton in Jamaican-flag colours, or tiny lace Victorian blouses, loads of neckwear and a smoky eye.

DJing opened up a whole new world for me musically when Hanover-based DJ/producers Timo Maas and Martin Buttrich invited me to collaborate with them. It started with just a single track. Timo was a big name in trance music ever since his remix of Azzido Da Bass's single, 'Dooms Night'. He had worked with a range of singers, including Kelis and Tori Amos, and approached me in 2007. I wrote the lyrics and melodies to 'Love Someone Else' and recorded it in New York with Martin and my friend, DJ and producer Loco Dice, who was hanging out with us, offering encouragement and good vibes. When Timo heard it, he loved the track so much, he said, 'Let's do an album.'

Excited by this new adventure, I went to Hanover, northern Germany, the following February, rented an apartment for a month and worked every day, mainly with Martin. I felt on fire that month, working on tracks with twisted lyrics and beautiful, menacing melodies. Great lyrics seemed to fall out of thin air, while Martin constructed the grooves. He created icy, glacial beats that brought out a different side to my voice – a sound that was intimate, husky and soft. Much of my songwriting is autobiographical, but for this project I explored a cast of characters: some hard and haughty, some voracious and lustful, and some pitiful, who represented people I'd met in my life – like a madame in leather who, in the early days of Skunk Anansie, came up to me after a gig and offered me £1,000 to be a dominatrix at her sex club. Or an elegant woman I knew who took pleasure in casting off a lover. Or another who seemed addicted to abandonment. It was a passionate album, sounding like a mix of '80s-style synth-pop and dark soul, and the songs were inspired by my surroundings.

Hanover in winter is a bleak place with a big red-light district, which lends the town a sexually deviant undertow. During the Second World War, Allied planes destroyed 90 per cent of the city centre in bombing raids over Germany. As if haunted by its past, the whole town had an eerie atmosphere.

One day I went to the famous Herrenhausen Gardens, which were owned by the Hanoverian royal dynasty. In the summer they're glorious, but because it was winter everything had been cut down and it felt barren, with the bombed ruins of the palace adding to the spookiness. I was also inspired by the dense forest opposite where I was staying: the trees grew so straight, tall and close together that there was little room for sunlight, and I tried to capture its spooky aura in my music. Another day I went for a drink in a bar in the red-light district in Raschplatz, and got chatting to a sweet, gorgeous guy who only slept with prostitutes. That intrigued me – why did he want it so easy? He also inspired another wicked character for my songs.

There's a dark beauty to the album that I love, from the spare opening track 'Moment' to the powerful 'Ending For Us'. I was super happy with it, and Timo and Martin were about to release it, but then fell out over allocation of music publishing royalties, and Timo left the project. I guess they'd had some underlying issues with each other that this album brought out. The album was shelved as a result. I was very hurt by the experience. I felt I'd written some of the best material of my career, and it seemed they put it on the shelf to gather dust.

The whole experience truly rocked me. It was the first time in my life that music I had made and was really proud of never saw the light of day. Eight years later I re-did 'Love Someone Else' – the first song we'd finished – for the Skunk Anansie album *Anarchytecture* (with a very different arrangement). As for the rest of the tracks, I nagged Martin for years to do something with them but it never happened. I don't think I'll ever get over that. It also deeply changed my approach to working with DJs after seeing how fast they move on to new projects.

After my experience in Hanover, I began working on my next solo record, but events soon took over. Cass had been subtly nudging everyone to put the band back together, and Skunk Anansie fans had started a Facebook petition asking us to reform. As it reached 100,000 signatures, the idea that I had been resisting for seven years started to feel like a positive move. Slowly, slowly, in 2008, we began to put the band back together.

BOOK FOUR

WONDERLUSTRE

SIXTEEN

STILL A FREAK

Skunk Anansie re-entered the fray at a time of crisis for the music industry. File sharing and the digital download revolution meant a dramatic decline in revenue for music, so bands and artists recouped their losses via live touring. A host of bands reformed in 2008–9 – from thrash-metallers Seventh Angel, to skate-punks Blink 182, to Jane's Addiction, My Bloody Valentine and Britpop kings Blur. New artists no longer considered a major record deal an important part of their business plan, and bands like the Arctic Monkeys and Enter Shikari emerged as a force thanks to the internet with their cohort of fans acting like unofficial street teams.

This was the new music world Skunk Anansie were relaunching themselves into, a world where pop and rock were more polarised than ever, with pop divas like Lady Gaga and Katy Perry at one extreme, and the newly reformed Rage Against The Machine at the other. The latter scored a Christmas Number 1 in 2009 with the reissue of their early '90s protest song 'Killing in the Name', demonstrating the power fans now had in the reconfigured music industry. Skunk Anansie's reputation as a phenomenal live band, plus the diligent support of their fans, meant that it was an ideal time to reunite. And in a scene dominated by polished pop super-divas, Skin stood out as a unique female warrior.

There's a scene in the animated film *Wreck It Ralph* where all the mini Ralph characters coalesce to become a huge, punching fist, and for me that's what social media is — thousands of tiny people who join together and form a new shape. Before social media, it was harder to see fans come together as a galvanising force, but by 2008, the internet had radically changed the music industry and brought our fans much closer to us. Thanks to the fan petition, people started finding old *Top of the Pops* footage and posting it on Facebook. That gave me a nice, warm feeling, but there were a lot of bands reforming and I was wary of being part of that nostalgia movement.

I hadn't seen Ace for a while, but I met up with him again during that summer of 2008 at the *Kerrang!* Awards. I was pre-senting an award and he was DJing and organising the aftershow party, and it was at that party that we started chatting. A week later I texted him, inviting him to a club night I was doing in a pub in east London. He came down while I was DJing and we got drunk together, and after a few hours hanging out, I asked, 'So, what are you doing?'

'I'm teaching at the moment,' he said.

I thought that was a waste of his talent. 'You're not a teacher, you're a rock guitarist,' I blurted out. He agreed with me, and a seed that had been planted in my mind by Leigh and Cass began to grow.

Cass had been niggling at me for years to reform the band, spending a lot of time behind the scenes calling Ace and Mark and trying to convince me with his cheeky smile that our reunion was inevitable. He's always been a constant friend, describing himself as my support, my wingman, my number one soldier. Sometimes I have to rein in his protectiveness, though, and tell him I'm a grown woman and can look after myself. He can behave like an overbearing older brother, but that's the way he shows his love.

Leigh mentioned getting back together a couple of times, but I danced around the conversation for a while because I wasn't sure. I thought, *Let's see the vibe when we meet.* I felt that if we could write great new material then the band reunion would be worth doing; without that it would be like flogging a dead horse trying to revive distant memories. In any case, Leigh called the guys and we all met up at my house. At first it was weird, because we hadn't hung out all together in years, but after ten minutes we were laughing and cracking jokes as if we'd never been apart.

The reunion was the start of a very long, slow, gradual road. At first, we got together in a rehearsal space in London. We were about to run through some old songs when I said, 'Let's write something new.' I was eager to see if we still had it. We were rusty as fuck, my voice was weak and thin, unused to the power of Skunk songs, but it was electric, the chemistry was still there. 'Because of You' became our first song as a newly reformed band,

Then, in August 2008, two Skunk Anansie megafans invited us to sing at their wedding on the African island of Lamu, off the coast of Kenya. The island had no cars on it, and people got around by riding on donkeys. We thought, if we do the gig, it's also an opportunity to spend some serious time together without distractions, and we could treat it as a therapy session, a time to talk and catch up with our personal lives, good and bad.

The wedding was riotous – we performed on a small stage at the top of the swimming pool and all the guests pogoed around the sides. We were still rusty, but it didn't matter because playing the gig was pure joy. As a finale, we jumped into the pool fully clothed, along with the wedding couple and all the guests. We drank and DJed until dawn, when Maasai tribesmen working at the hotel appeared, escorting us back to our villa.

The rest of the week we relaxed, went sailing to watch the sunset, ate together every day, played music, talked and drank good rum. We came to the conclusion that we needed to look after our band. Sometimes you can fix the major breakages by simply talking about what you've learnt. To quote one of Ace's 'pearls' of wisdom: 'It's like breaking a leg, it hurts, I can walk again, but I've no desire to break the other leg!' There were a few raw, honest moments. In the time apart, I'd seen Cass a lot, because we were friends before we formed Skunk Anansie, and as Mark rehearsed with Feeder in the room next to mine, we were always bumping into each other, and he had played on some of my solo tracks.

The only person I had to clear some air with was Ace, whom I hadn't seen much since the split. I heard via Lemmy that Ace had thrown some shade my way, blaming me solely for splitting up the band. I hadn't taken it seriously because I knew Ace didn't mean it, but I did have a go at him. That was as tense as it got – then it was too hot to argue, as I had to drink my rum before the ice melted! So, there was no big falling-out, no one had a beef with anybody, and no one had done something unforgivable, like shagging someone else's wife. It had been more a disintegration than a break-up. Having cleared the air, we returned to London, and at our first songwriting session after getting back together we wrote ten songs.

We decided to do a secret show to test the waters, and arranged a gig at the Splash Club under the pseudonym SCAM (an acronym formed by the first letter of each of our names). The secret got out, and after the announcement the gig sold out within a few minutes, so we announced a second date, and that sold out too. It wouldn't have happened without the fans. When we played the secret Splash Club gigs in April 2009, it was a joy, like finding your way back home again.

The place was tiny, but it went off like it did when we played our first gig back in 1994. There's still magic left in that venue, born out of the blood of many bruised guitar fingers and the sweat of a thousand bands. Even a newly installed air-conditioning system did not disturb the total eruption of full force Skunk Anansie! Backstage it was the cramped shithole we remembered, and we could barely fit all our equipment on stage, but that tiny gig was pure joy – the perfect place to relaunch a fresh-faced Skunk with a brand-new stinky attitude. Cass said afterwards it was the best feeling in the world.

We released our Greatest Hits collection, *Smashes & Trashes*, named after all the hits and all the new songs we intended to trash new venues with, and fulfilling a long overdue part of our old One Little Indian contract. It incorporated three new tracks that came out of our reunion: 'Tear the Place Up', a victorious alt-metal track that announced our return with the words: *I still attend the church of the loose . . . I'm still a freak*; the heart-wrenching

'Squander'; and the explosive drama of 'Because of You'. When we first got back together, everyone was very well behaved, but I was cautious, thinking, *Let's wait and see.*

You definitely marry your band. When you get together it's like walking down the aisle with them, and the first few years are like the rosy honeymoon period. You go into the studio and the albums you record together become the babies that you have to look after. So, even if there's a divorce, you still have connections and an ongoing relationship because of the music you've made together. The reunion forced us to work things out. Seven years apart gave us a decent amount of time to look back and reflect on our band dynamic and what we had achieved. My perspective had changed – I was much less stressed and better at living in the moment. I'd been through a lot of challenges as a solo artist, I was better at problem solving and I had lost my fear of the unknown. Everything had gone so well, and we enjoyed putting together the live album so much that we decided to continue and go on tour. This would be unknown territory; we didn't know if the magic would be the same.

The person I had worried about the most in the band was Mark. He had been through so much, and it had taken him a while to get sober and to stay sober, but when he did, it was the most beautiful turnaround. In 2002, after the tragic suicide of Feeder's drummer Jon Lee, their vocalist Grant Nicholas rang Mark and said, 'We're going to carry on. Will you do it?' We had all known Jon well, as we used to play together a lot at the Splash Club in our unsigned days when we were called Mama Wild and they were called Real. Feeder later supported Skunk Anansie on tour. Mark was reluctant at first, uneasy about taking on his dead friend's role, but eventually he said yes, and he played with Feeder for the next seven years. Jon's death had a major impact on Mark, making him realise, *That could have been me.* He and Jon had been close friends, and the latter was always there to chat to, as were Stuart Cable from Stereophonics and Ash Soan from Del Amitri, a small group of British rock drummers who emerged in the 1990s. But by 2010, Michael Lee, the original Little Angels drummer, Jon from Feeder and Stuart Cable were all dead, and Mark still feels grateful that he survived.

Now Mark is one of the people I love most on the planet. He went from behaving like the typical demented drummer the first time round to becoming one of the most solid people I know. There is no other drummer for Skunk Anansie; he is irreplaceable. I don't want to be in one of those bands that has rotating members. If one of us was replaced, the sound and energy would change – what makes Skunk Anansie work is the four of us. It's all of us or nothing.

During our time apart, Ace released a solo album, *Still Hungry*, in 2003, on his own label, Ace Sounds, with guest vocalists including Lemmy, Shingai Shoniwa from Noisettes and Skye from Morcheeba. That kickstarted his production career with artists like Icelandic rock band Dicta, Your Army and punk-ska outfit Sonic Boom Six. He's always been a great archivist and custodian of Skunk Anansie. When we reformed, he still had the key to the lock-up in Music Bank, a storage facility and rehearsal studios in Bermondsey, south London. He went into the storage area next to the studios, and it was like a period in musical history had been frozen in time. As he walked around, Ace could see cages full of flight cases and equipment, each one labelled with a different band name, from Placebo to Led Zeppelin to Black Sabbath. Oasis's cage was impressive because it contained 200 of Noel Gallagher's guitars. Eventually Ace found our lock-up packed with our amplifiers, stage backdrops, mirrors, radio packs and microphones just where we had left them.

We dusted off our equipment and, after a scrub-up, we went on the road as if the intervening seven years had never happened. Ace was so excited. He has always been the brain of the band; all he's ever wanted to do was play guitar onstage, it's that simple for him, and I love him for that. He just gets so much joy out of it, and still plays for an hour every day come rain or shine.

For the new *Smashes & Trashes* tracks, we went into Livingston Studios in north London with the producer Chris Sheldon, who had worked with bands like Foo Fighters and Garbage, and cut it together really fast. The stand-out track was 'Tear the Place Up', which, with its rolling riffs, stamping rhythm and my stuttering vocals, had the same energy as the early days but tighter, so we released it as a single. It was free, but the only way you could get hold of it was by recommending five other people to the band's email list, and then you got your download. Within a few days there had been 5,000 downloaded.

We decided to make the video for it in the Old Truman Brewery in London's Brick Lane, and shot it in a day. It was given a punky vibe by a new young director called Adam Powell, who had worked with UK hardcore and metal bands like Gallows and Bring Me The Horizon. That single kickstarted *Smashes & Trashes*, and our Greatest Hits tour in Europe throughout 2009. Releasing a new record and playing a sell-out tour was a good way to start Skunk Anansie Part Two, but what I really loved was our second and third new singles: 'Because of You' and

'Squander'. In my view they were better than a lot of our songs from the '90s, and have never left our gig setlist. Working on my solo albums had given me fresh confidence in my writing, and I couldn't wait to develop that in the new Skunk.

SEVENTEEN

I WANT YOU FOR A LIFETIME

You want me now
But that's not enough
'Cos I want you for a lifetime.
You say it loud but you talk too much
I still want you for a lifetime today.

'Talk Too Much'

The year 2008 was pivotal, not just for Skunk Anansie but also for me personally. It was the year I met my partner Lady – known as Ladyfag – at a Fashion Week party in New York for the designers Dsquared2. I was hanging out with my 'Italian 'usband', the designer Liborio Capizzi. I remember getting out of a lift on the rooftop, scanning the scene, and I saw her, bang in the centre of the dancefloor. *Who is that?* I thought. *She's drop-dead gorgeous and chic as hell!* She wore a dazzling outfit and had beautiful dark hair. Up to that point, I'd rarely chatted anyone up. I was scared of being rejected, so I always let people approach me. But on this occasion, I worked my way round the room to where she was standing.

'Hello,' I said. 'Would you like a drink? Would you like some champagne?'

'It's all free here, let me get you one,' Lady replied.

We got chatting and she invited me to her birthday party the next day, which was taking place in an infamous gay nightclub called Mr Black. Many years later she told me that when I curled my fingers around the champagne glass and smiled at her, she thought, *I think I'm going to be serving this woman champagne for very a long time.*

Lady didn't know I was in a band until one of her friends told her at the end of the night.

'Are you a singer?' she asked.

I was tipsy and mischievous and couldn't resist saying, 'Yes, well, I have sold five million records.' Unsurprisingly my attempt to impress was met with a giant New York eye-roll ... but we still ended up leaving together in a yellow cab. If you ask Lady how she spends her days, she'll answer, 'I throw parties.' Probably the understatement of the century, as her 'parties' are some of the craziest in New York, including legendary after-parties for some of the biggest fashion brands in the world. We dated for a few months, but in the end we went in different directions. Lady was busy starting up her career, while I was at a different stage in my life. We liked each other a lot, and wanted to be together, but didn't properly communicate that to each other, lighting a torch that never went out.

I had been happily single but was feeling the need to settle down. I was forty-two years old and felt I couldn't keep floating round the world. As the singer of a rock band, you can live out of a suitcase and be an eternal child, behaving like a 25-year-old for the rest of your life, and male musicians are particularly prone to that. I was drifting, searching for a reason to put down roots. I loved being in Ibiza – I found it a nice place to write. Len and I had done sessions there, and I wrote 'Purple' with Gary Clarke in my Ibizan finca – but apart from its dazzling dance culture, there isn't much else to thrill your brain cells, and I didn't want to base myself there. In 2009, I met Christiana, a fundraiser and environmental activist. We met while I was DJing at a wedding in Venice. A few months later we started dating, eventually living together at her house in Malibu with her six-year-old daughter, and later, in 2012, we relocated to England.

It felt like the beginning of a hugely creative phase with the band. After our Greatest Hits tour for *Smashes & Trashes*, we worked on *Wonderlustre*, an album that took us in a new musical direction, with a mellow, cinematic sound. When we dream up album titles, I like combining concepts, so *Wonderlustre* was a play on the words 'wander' and 'wonder', evoking the sense of us as musicians wandering the planet and reuniting elated after a long break.

We co-produced it with Chris Sheldon, going into Livingston Studios with the bare bones of songs we played and recorded live, before Ace and I wove in melodies and sonic effects after-wards. After the band reunion, we were more hands-on in the studio, because as musicians we knew how to capture the sounds we wanted and were confident with recording. *Wonderlustre* felt like an effortless album, but if it had been difficult we might have thought twice about getting back together.

We had all learnt something while we were apart, and we applied that in the mix. After finding my indie vocal sound on

Fake Chemical State, and recording those electronic tracks with Martin Buttrich, I wanted to use the full range of my voice in different ways – whether it was the soulful, funky tone of 'The Sweetest Thing' or the Black Sabbath-style snarl of 'It Doesn't Matter'. Ace, too, was creating more open melodic sounds with his guitar. It was like we were reconfiguring ourselves as a band. There was still some of our sardonic observations – 'Your God Loves Only You', for example, was written about someone very close to me who had no time for other religions because his was 'the best'. The idea that God has chosen only one religion, leaving no space for others, seemed to be a very man-made concept – *You're sweatin', shakin', 'cos your god loves only you*. It leaves no room for tolerance and respect towards religions that are different.

One of my favourite tracks was the lead single, 'My Ugly Boy', a song inspired by an ex-lover who was very handsome but who had a very naughty, wicked character. Making the video was tough but fun because we shot it in an old multi-storey car park in Belgrade for twenty-three hours non-stop. I drove a vintage BMW, playing a character imagining her unfaithful boyfriend on the car's backseat with other women and, overwhelmed by frustration, she keeps crashing the car. Even though filming took ages, the crew never complained; they just smoked and enjoyed the experience while I drove the car in circles, wearing towering Natacha Marro pink heels. I had to kiss my 'ugly boy' for hours. He was weirdly sexy though, so it wasn't that hard! Directed by film-maker Paul Street, it's one of my favourite ever Skunk videos, destructive and erotic, with overtones of Walter Hill's *The Driver* and J. G. Ballard's *Crash*.

Songwriting is a potent way to process emotion, and I had

so many crazy stories to tell. 'Over the Love', for instance, was inspired by a brief relationship I had with an ex-lover who turned out to be paying for her ex-girlfriend to have IVF so they could have a baby – all this behind my back. That was quite shocking. I couldn't believe that, even in my forties, with all my life experience, I did not see that coming!

> *You pretend the spell has broken*
> *Goods were spoilt from the start*
> *No complaints I release my claim on your heart.*

With songs like 'My Love Will Fall' and 'Feeling the Itch' I was trying to get to the centre of conflicting emotions like vulnerability, lust and power, and to describe how they collide in a relationship. Sometimes a song is like a puzzle, a lyrical Rubik's cube you're trying to solve, and sometimes it just surfaces, clear and spare and whole. The final track on the album, 'I Will Stay But You Should Leave', has that quality. By then we had toured so many countries, absorbing different pop traditions, and threaded through this quietly forceful song are echoes of French chanson and dark Italian pop balladry.

Wonderlustre was released on V2 Beneluxe in September 2010, went to Number 1 in Italy and was in the Top 10 throughout Europe. Skunk Anansie were by now a familiar band, but our sound was new, and at that point radioplay was still important to us. So, to avoid being labelled a heritage act, we decided to get our tracks remixed. We had always done dance remixes of our singles, but this time we needed extra pop instrumentation, so we paired up with Jeremy Wheatley, who has mixed records by artists as varied as Goldfrapp and Corinne Bailey Rae.

Wheatley gave *Wonderlustre* its cinematic sheen, and he has been our favourite mixer ever since.

By then, iTunes download culture meant we could be more flexible with singles, so rather than release one song for the whole of Europe, we could promote different tracks in different countries. Belgium, for instance, loved the panoramic rock of 'Over the Love', while Italy went for the salty, grinding sound of 'My Ugly Boy'. Italy was our stronghold and has the craziest fans. The first time we went there, in the mid-90s, was as part of a whistle-stop press tour where we would be in a different country every day, and you'd be lucky if the record company threw a sandwich at you. In Italy, however, they stopped and gave us lunch – a proper sit-down meal. For an hour! We couldn't believe it. As we selected loads of antipasti at a full buffet, we made a pact to be big in Italy. In the 1990s, we were a strange band for the Italians to take on – being a black, shaven-headed woman singing rock was not the obvious route to success there. They hadn't heard anything like us, but Sandor Mallasz and Gilberto Barantani – two guys in the promotion department of Virgin Records Italia – championed us and *worked it*. Getting radioplay was difficult at first, but they were determined and kept asking us to come back. It took a solid year, but we broke and we broke BIG. Italians are passionate about words, and take lyrics very seriously. That's what's special about many European countries. Once they fall in love with you – Italy, Germany, France, Portugal – they are very loyal and keep you in their hearts forever.

As a consequence, I was asked to accept the International Female award as a solo artist for Italy's Cavalchina Awards, which are held during the Cavalchina Ball, an eighteenth-century

Venetian tradition celebrating artistic talent. In Italy they love to do things in a way that is ridiculously dramatic, so at eleven o'clock one evening in March 2011, at the height of *Carnevale* season, I rode into Teatro La Fenice in Venice on a white stallion in full *Carnevale* dress, designed by my great friend Liborio Capizzi. It was a nod to that iconic 1977 photograph of Bianca Jagger sitting on a white horse in New York's Studio 54 nightclub. Wearing a black corseted Marie Antoinette-style dress and mask, I sat on this really tall, slightly edgy horse and slowly made my way through the stalls to the stage. It was a moment that, even for me, was fantastically off the scale.

EIGHTEEN

BLACK TRAFFIC

Well it feels like trouble
When their words ring dull
As my face sweats fever
Idle tongues suck gold
As summer kills the sun
We're halfway gone . . .

'Our Summer Kills the Sun'

The eighteenth of August 2011 was a boiling-hot day. We were
due to play Pukkelpop Festival in Belgium, and were so excited.
But by the end of the day, a freak tornado had blasted through
the site killing five people and leaving us shell-shocked. Earlier
that afternoon, the weather had been so fine that I got a touch
of sunstroke on my bare, shaven head. We had to do an interview standing outside, so I searched around for a hat while the
journalist remarked, 'They said there's a storm coming later.'
We looked up into a cloudless clear blue sky and laughed. 'Can't
see that happening.'

At around 5.30pm, clouds had started gathering, and there was a close atmosphere. Usually I have to sleep if I have sunstroke, but there was no time, so I was a little stressed about the gig, hoping that adrenaline would kick in and snap me out of it. When we went onstage at 6pm, the sky was still fairly clear, but by the second song there were banks of cloud building up. By the third song the clouds were dark grey, then by the fourth it started raining. The rain was accompanied by thunder and lightning, and then came the hailstones – as Cass said later, they were 'big fuckers that dented my guitar'.

When it rains at a festival, we normally stay onstage while the crowd go mad and abandon themselves to the elements. People were taking off their shirts and dancing, and I shouted gleefully, 'I don't give a fuck about the rain!' By the sixth song the wind got up, and it got stronger and stronger until branches were breaking off trees and flying across the field like arrows. Cass looked down at his pedal board and it was full of water. I was determined to carry on, declaring through the mic, 'We're not gonna let a little rain stop us.'

We were performing in horizontal rain, and had just one more song to do. Suddenly I was aware that the guitar tech was onstage, standing next to me, but I was in my gig zone, thinking, *Why is he standing like that, onstage?* Then a sudden gust of wind came under my feet, scooped me in the air and I fell down. A crew member ran over and picked me up, carried me down the stairs and literally threw me into a Portakabin backstage, slamming the door behind him. He fell down next to me while I was lying there star-shaped on the floor, completely sodden. We looked at each other as if to say, 'What the hell just happened?'

I lay there for a minute. Where was the rest of the band? There were three people cowering in the corner, and the crew member who'd saved me was soaked through and out of breath. The whole Portakabin was rocking while unidentifiable flying objects crashed and banged against the side. I was in shock, incredulous that I hadn't finished a gig. That never happens. We fully intended to finish it. We've done gigs in all weathers – snow, sleet, rain, it doesn't matter. You stay onstage and you bring the audience with you. But the violence of this storm defeated us.

After ten minutes, the storm died down and I went outside. Everything was trashed. Trees had been uprooted by the wind, tents had been shredded and the whole backstage area was wrecked. I clambered over bits of metal scaffolding and branches and torn canvas, and found my way to the Skunk Anansie Portakabin, where Leigh was sitting with the rest of the band, wide-eyed and stunned. Ace said they had run for their lives, and he'd had to grab hold of Leigh because she was literally flying through the air. The picture he painted of him standing tall like Popeye, with Leigh's feet waving horizontally in the air like a battered flag, and that made us laugh. As we sat there, a long line of fire engines and ambulances began snaking their way into the festival.

'Is everyone okay?' I asked. 'I hope no one got hurt.' We were happy to be okay, cracking jokes in the sheer relief of the moment. Our default position is taking the piss. Then a crew member came in to say the main tent had collapsed and people had died. That changed the whole atmosphere and hit us hard. Festivals were about pure joy and hedonism; this was not supposed to happen.

We had to get out to make way for the fire engines, so we pulled together everything we had, threw it into our two trucks and drove on to our next festival, which was in the mountains near Bern, in Switzerland. We were due to play on the same stage as Blur and the Chemical Brothers, but had no idea if our gear would work. We listened to the radio overnight, hearing Hilde Claes, the mayor of Hasselt, say that Pukkelpop was cancelled, with 60,000 festivalgoers sent home. A hundred and forty people were injured, some of them critically, and five people were dead. We were heartbroken.

When we arrived at Gampel Festival, our gear was unloaded out of the trucks but it was still full of rainwater and completely soaked. We were feeling intensely sad and shocked after the deaths at Pukkelpop, thinking about those kids who went to enjoy music, love and life but never came home.

Our equipment was ruined. We didn't know if we could go onstage, and thought it was all over. But then the most beautiful thing happened: every crew member from every other band brought all their towels and blankets, anything they could find, and stretched them out in the field backstage. Then they all proceeded to dismantle our entire production – lights, speakers, amplifiers, instruments, flight cases, amps – they even took the valves out of the guitar. All of our gear was spread out to dry. It took up a whole field behind the stage.

It was a clear sunny day, so everything gradually dried out. Then, all of those wonderful, beautiful human beings put our stuff back together again, and we did the gig. It was one of those moments when people pulled together and helped us, so that we could carry on and play in memory of everyone who had died. We could not have played without them, and it's one of the most special memories of all my years of touring. It makes me emotional just thinking about it. Reminds you of how much love there is in our rock community.

This marked the beginning of a more challenging period for all of us. The following January, our first drummer, Robbie France, died of a ruptured aorta. Even though we hadn't seen him much since he had left Skunk Anansie back in 1995 and joined the band Alphaville, it was very sad to hear about his death. After touring with them, he had moved to Spain, where he ran his own label, produced Spanish alt-rock bands, taught drumming and had written a novel. He was only fifty-three years old when he died. He was a beautiful, sweet guy. Robbie's contribution to the beginning of our band was enormous – his playing on our debut album was phenomenal and lives on forever.

By the time we recorded our fifth studio album, in spring 2012, we were a touring band again. We toured *Wonderlustre* for two years and our new album *Black Traffic* was the product of being on the road, influenced by political tensions in the countries we passed through. The title reflected on money and corruption, particularly money laundered through black markets like drug trafficking and prostitution. It felt like things were changing, and not for the better. The track 'This Is Not a Game', for instance, was inspired by the Occupy movement, protesting in eighty-two countries across the globe. In 2007, a US congressional report stated that the top 1 per cent of earners owned 43 per cent of the nation's wealth, and that since 1979 their income had risen by 275 per cent. Then, in 2008, the stock market crash exposed the way money is moved around the world through stocks and subprime loans that benefitted only a wealthy few. I was thinking about financial traders gambling with people's money, while people with 100 per cent mortgages lost their homes. The Occupy movement built a campaign against this financial inequity with its slogan: 'We are the 99 per cent'.

By 2011, thousands of protestors in cities across the world went on mass demonstrations, organised sit-ins, roadblocks and encampments, calling for banking reform and an end to tax evasion by wealthy corporations. 'This Is Not a Game' reflects that anger. It's a difficult song to sing, because I have to belt it out full and hard right at the top of my range, but in some ways that's what gives the track its intense energy.

The song 'I Believed In You' takes on the idea of the superhero politician, and the myth that they can singlehandedly save the world. I was thinking about the weight of expectation placed on President Barack Obama after he was elected in 2008. The fact that America elected its first black president was wonderful, it gave us all deep joy and a sense of hope, but two years later in the mid-term elections the Democratic Party lost sixty-three seats and control of the House of Representatives, and Republicans blocked Obama's efforts at every turn, including his plans for affordable health care and gun control. The song captures people's anger in the sarcastic lines: *I believed in you/Well I was wrong/I believed you'd make me better/I was wrong* – but it is unrealistic to expect our politicians to be superheroes. They face the challenge of a growing and increasingly belligerent and obstructionist radical right who did everything in their power to stop great ideas being executed simply because they came from Obama.

There were some lighter, more mischievous moments, like 'I Will Break You', with its deviant metal funk and muscular riffs. *I can be anything for you,* I sing. *No need to whistle 'cos I carry all the tools/I've all the weapons and I follow no one's rules.* In this song, the tools and weapons are sexual swagger and attitude. I like wordplay and double entendre in song – like Lee Dorsey's 1960s soul hit, 'Ride Your Pony', with the naughty words, 'Now shoot, shoot!' That song is played on mainstream radio, and older people understand the double meaning. I love singing our suggestive songs with a lip twist.

Observing relationships is also a rich source of songwriting material. The punky track, 'Sad Sad Sad', for instance, is about that one friend who can be in a room with brilliant men but still manages to find the absolute idiot who will treat her like shit. We've all had times like that, when we are repeatedly attracted to the wrong people, convinced the results will be different every time. 'Spit You Out', meanwhile, is about someone I knew who was trying to get away from a moody lover. It was a collaboration with a brilliant French electro-rock band called Shaka Ponk, who have a similar energy to us, fusing dirty guitar riffs and beats. I liked the way the grainy vocals of their lead singers, Frah and Sam, worked with mine.

We recorded some great songs, but there's a feeling of exasperation that permeates *Black Traffic*. Sounding loud, heavy and industrial, it's honestly my least favourite Skunk Anansie record. In 2012, our music tastes were changing, and there was a tussle between me and the boys. I was aware of how music was in flux, and told them that we had to evolve or we would plateau like we'd seen happen to so many of our peers. At that point, we still wanted to be on radio playlists – always a difficult task for us. I argued that we had to experiment in order to keep fresh and stay relevant, so we tried to develop a more electronic sound. For

Black Traffic we recorded many of our vocal, guitar and drum parts separately, so that even though we had some dynamic songs, it lost a lot of warmth, and to me it sounded loud and stiff – an album pieced together like a jigsaw of musical edits. I didn't want us to co-produce anymore, and was keen to work with a producer who had an overview and a casting vote when it came to a mix. This was a time when I felt I was fighting to be heard, not just in the studio, but also in my personal life and my relationships. That sense of distraction was true, both for me and Cass, whose father died around this time. As he said later, his head 'wasn't in the game'.

This was a period of big change in my life. In 2011, Christiana and I had entered into a domestic partnership in San Francisco (recognised in the UK as a civil union) and in August 2012 we had a wedding in Italy. It was a frenetic, busy summer, with so much going on, including the Olympic Games in London, where the whole of the city was transformed into a sporting paradise and my flat became a great vantage point for me to see the new Queen Elizabeth Olympic Park.

A month after the wedding, *Black Traffic* was released, and we did a twenty-date tour throughout Europe. It was fun playing those songs live, but as a band we had the urge to do something completely different. I'd DJed a few times at an acoustic festival in Switzerland called Zermatt Unplugged, and they were itching to have the whole band come back and perform. It was a massive undertaking that included a complete dissection of all our songs – too much work for one gig, so we decided to make it worthwhile. We curated a delicately woven set of our most loved songs with a string section, which we played at London's

Cadogan Hall in Chelsea. Then we thought, *Let's record it! Why not film it?* And *An Acoustic Skunk Anansie* was born.

This was our first gig with Mark's wife Erika Footman as backing vocalist/keyboardist. At that point, I was a bit lonely being the only woman on tour, so it was lovely to have Erika onstage and backstage to banter with. She is a strong singer, and an artist in her own right; her individuality onstage is important, she's not trying to be anyone but herself, and I think having her with us does something wonderful to the whole band vibe. It's rare to find someone who everybody adores, so she's been on tour with us ever since. We invited Skunk Anansie fans and all our friends to the acoustic set at Cadogan Hall, and afterwards had a celebration in Soho. At that point, I was living in the English countryside, near Petersfield in Hampshire, with Christiana and her daughter and our animals. I was living a quieter life but also popping up to London to reconnect with my friends.

Towards the end of that year I was in a reflective mood. Rearranging our songs for an acoustic set made me think about key moments we had experienced as a band, like playing at Nelson Mandela's birthday concert in the 1990s. When Mandela died on 5 December 2013, I thought a lot about meeting him and the energy he gave us. It was sad that he died, but he had lived a very long life and had been through so much. He emerged a man not soured by experience but someone who tried his absolute best to bring his people some power and some dignity, without anger, death or retribution. I'm glad he spent his later years in happiness at home with his family. But the damage apartheid did was so heinous and deep, I feel it will take many more decades to heal.

By the end of 2013, Christiana and I had moved back to

London, and our relationship was becoming very strained. Those closest to me know that I grow my hair when I'm not happy. I had stopped shaving my head for a few years, because I wanted a change, and at this point I had short, spiky hair. Then, a while after the *Acoustic Skunk Anansie* gig, I had a disastrous trip to a local barber who had no idea what to do with black hair. I was in a playful mood, and I said to Cass, 'I'm thinking of cutting my hair.'

'I'll cut it,' he said, and before I could change my mind, he got the clippers and shaved my head straight down the middle. I looked at him, incredulous.

'You'll have to shave it all off now,' he said. 'I want Skin back.' That little shit was right.

Christiana and I broke up in early 2015, and when I met with the band a few days afterwards to write songs for our next album, Cass knew something was wrong. Cass says I think I can disguise my experiences by putting them in little stories about friends or fictional characters, but he sees the truth of my life buried in the lyrics. He's been around me long enough to decipher the burial technique.

'I'm usually the first man in,' he said. 'I knew something was up as soon as it was up.' Cass is always listening to the words and phrases I use in my songs, and sometimes that gives him a clue about my real feelings. As my mum would say, his ears are too big!

Christiana and I had been drifting apart for a while. Even though the band was going well, my personal life was falling apart. I had been touring and she was always away at climate change conferences, so a lot of the time we were leading separate lives. Also, I didn't have the same depth of feeling as I had in the early days. I loved being a stepmother to her daughter, however, and one of the saddest things about the split was not being able to get up and cook scrambled eggs for her every morning while chatting about the latest book she was devouring, or going for walks with our dachshund Nutella – she *adored* that dog. I'd previously been nervous around dogs, but she introduced me to what wonderful creatures they are.

NINETEEN

X FACTOR

Stacey's got a brand new girl
She likes to play with sugar
'Til it makes sweet pearls
She likes to taste the danger
Makes her feel complete

'Love Someone Else'

Lemmy and I kept talking about working together. Then he started to get sick, so we said, 'OK, now, we need to do this.' We planned to meet up in Cass's studio to start working on ideas, but he had to cancel a couple of times, then finally he texted me the day I broke up with Christiana. I said, 'You know, Lemmy, I can't. I can't work for the next few weeks because my relationship has just ended and I have so much to sort out.'

He texted me straight back: 'I know exactly how you feel. I'm really here for you. Whenever you wanna talk, just let me know. I'm around.'

I really treasure that message from Lemmy. It was so lovely of him to say that, and I knew he meant every word. He had this tough, 'don't fuck with me' reputation – which he deserved, he was the real deal – but he was also always sensitive and super sweet. That was the last time I was in touch with him before he died in December 2015.

Lemmy had a great quote for everything. In 1997, me and the band all voted for Tony Blair, when he became Prime Minister of 'Cool Britannia', and Lemmy was quietly sceptical, saying he wasn't convinced. After Blair teamed up with Republican president George W. Bush to send troops into Iraq six years later, Lemmy turned to us and said, 'See, I told you, he was just another smiley cunt.'

I was awed by the fact that Lemmy loved our music, especially the slow songs. He would often come and watch at the side of the stage, which would spur me on to be better – some of my best gigs were because Lemmy was watching. We planned to write a song together for his solo album, because he wanted to do something completely different, something softer, gentle and moody. So many times we ended up in the Rainbow Bar in LA, drinking JD and playing pool with his mates instead of making music.

After the split, I threw myself into work projects, and I acted in my first film, playing a doctor in a sci-fi thriller called *Andron*, which starred Danny Glover, Alec Baldwin and Michelle Ryan from *EastEnders*. We shot most of it in a deep, underground quarry in Malta that was beautifully decrepit and dank. Quite like the reviews on Rotten Tomatoes! But better received three years later was my second film, *Ulysses: A Dark Odyssey*, a modern version of Homer's classic tale starring Udo Kier, Italian actor Andrea Zirio and, again, Danny Glover. In the movie I played a blind seer who could see the future and the past. I was in make-up for five hours being transformed into a slightly comical *Live and Let Die*-style witch.

The year 2015 was a good one for me musically. I explored the dark electronic female energy of the dancefloor with Nicole Moudaber, the world-renowned Lebanese/British DJ and producer. We met one day on a flight to the UK, and she asked me to sing on one of her records. I loved the fact that rather than just chop up my voice and fly it into a techno track, she wanted to write songs and develop lyrics together. I have the soul of a raver, so we bonded in the studio and I was able to match words with her beats on 'Don't Talk To Me I'm Dancing', one of the club tracks we recorded for an EP. It's about the many times my ear has been covered in spittle by someone determined to talk to me on the dancefloor, even though you can't hear a bloody word! She took our musical chemistry and created an elegant, exotic soundscape with the EP *Breed*. One of my favourite tracks was 'These Walls Are Made of Water', which captures a trance-like feeling of happiness and connection. The *Breed* EP was big in Ibiza that summer of 2015, and was shortlisted for a Grammy award.

Feeling renewed, I jumped into projects I'd previously said no to, such as being a judge on the Italian version of *X Factor*. I met the show producers and thought, *This is going to be heaven* and *hell, a brand-new crazy challenge!* I was DJing that year with Nicole at Miami Music Week, a huge electronic music event, and because I was staying in the city for three weeks, I started learning Italian with a tutor. Six weeks before filming started,

I was studying Italian ten hours a day with the lovely language teacher Giacamo. I found learning the accent strangely easy, because it's a bit like singing. Every language has its own melody, rhythm and phrasing, but Italian lends itself perfectly to sung music, opera in particular. My problem was remembering what I learnt. I'm used to memorising lyrics, but I hadn't studied anything but music since I left Teesside University. As soon as I thought I had the phrases safely stored in my brain, I'd feel them slowly leaking out! It's one thing learning the basics of a new language, but quite another being proficient enough to be cool, quick and funny and have an argument in that language. I'd wake up every single morning in a cold sweat, thinking, *What the fuck have I agreed to?*

But I was lucky, because spontaneous drama would happen that allowed me to show my personality. Like when the audience pointed out someone who was desperate to get on the stage and sing. I just invited her on stage and she performed – the first time that had ever happened on an *X Factor* show. It was so unusual that people thought it was fixed. Also, for some reason, the audience liked the way I said '*attaca*'. Every time I said it, there'd be a ripple of giggles throughout the crowd. I was trying to say that the singer should just go for it, but in Italy that word is aggressive, like a command used to order a dog to attack! The word became my catchphrase, and Italians still love to shout it to me in the street.

Running from September to December 2015, *X Factor Italia* season nine featured on the judging panel: me, singer/songwriter Mika, the Italian rock legend Elio, and young Italian rapper Fedez. I was looking forward to having the opportunity to mentor younger artists, but didn't have as much time as I'd have liked. Mika's schedule was chock-full, because he was also doing the French version of *The Voice*. I've never seen somebody fill up their week as much as him, and he had a backbreaking schedule that made it difficult to spend more time with his acts. Because all judges must have equal mentoring time, that meant we had less time with ours.

I enjoyed being on a panel with my fellow judges, yet we were all so different. Mika is a gifted musician and singer of crafted pop songs, with music that floats on a pink cloud of candyfloss; he's a real Disney Prince Charming. The rapper Fedez, meanwhile, was a millennial, social media-obsessed youth, and he knew it. He had fun with that. He had a brilliant knowledge of pop and cared about his artists, picking good tracks for them. I really liked that about him – that he worked hard for his team. Elio played the Tom Jones role, the older judge on the panel with an historical and technical knowledge of music. Influenced by experimental artist Frank Zappa, he wore a weird wig and a T-shirt with a cryptic message every episode, and was hilariously charming to work with because he totally took the piss but at the same time was very wise.

X Factor was a huge challenge. I must admit learning Italian at the same time as doing the show was one of the hardest things I've ever done, but I'm proud of myself for doing it, even though the stress it caused was off the scale. I have a deep love affair with Italy, but I don't view the country through rose-tinted glasses. Like Germany and Spain, there is a legacy of fascism that lingers from as far back as the Second World War, which rears its ugly head with the way the question of immigration is used by government as a political tool. In the UK there is an extreme right-wing element with the same fear of being 'overrun' by immigrants, which resulted in Brexit. You cannot travel the world and imagine that a place is perfect simply because the food is good and the wine plentiful. I am not blind to that, but I still love Italy in the same way that I love England and Jamaica, New York and South Africa. I love them, warts and all.

That year, I had a ridiculously heavy workload, partly because the month before filming started on *X Factor*, Leigh insisted we record another album, to be released at the same time as the show was broadcast. Any spare minute I had during our recording sessions at RAK studio in St John's Wood, I would go to a room upstairs to learn Italian with Giacomo. But despite the crazy schedule, our sixth studio album turned out to be one of our strongest yet. We had given the reins to Mr Tom Dalgety, a fun, irreverent, no-nonsense rock producer who had worked with a long list of incredible bands, including Mercury Prize nominees Royal Blood. We wanted to create a brave new world for our album, one where anarchy had a structure – how can one work without the other? – so we collided the words anarchy and architecture in the title *Anarchytecture*.

After the fall-out from the 2008 financial crash, there had to be a new political game plan, because disruption alone just alienates people. Belief in politicians or political parties had eroded, but what do you replace it with? We explored this theme on the track 'We Are the Flames', singing, *Watching all the puppeteers parade in evil news/Then they say we are all right . . . we are the price you pay, for feeling your desires.* As we worked on the song, I felt a crackling energy between us, and it was as if we had locked into a new groove. *Ah,* I thought, *we have arrived.*

Cass said recording the album was like emerging from the end of a tunnel. He'd had a difficult time after his father died in 2010, and for him *Anarchytecture* felt like a kind of rebirth and marked a new beginning. Reforming a band is just the beginning of a journey, and staying together can be a challenge. Each of us had to be honest with ourselves about why we were doing it, and for me it wasn't just about the music but about the person I become when I'm onstage with the band – Skunk Anansie was where I found my identity and my strength.

Rediscovering my friendship with Ace after we reformed was an important part of developing the band, because we work so closely together in the studio. It's so important to get the guitar melody and hooks working with my vocal lines, creating a soundscape for the vocals to rest on. We're always thinking about communicating an emotion. Once we have something that works, we experiment with textures and ideas. I grew up in a black world filled with soul and reggae music, a world where Bob Marley and Stevie Wonder were kings. But Ace grew up in middle England, where Motörhead and Black Sabbath were his heroes. He's on beat one, I'm on beat two, and because we're open to hearing things in different places, that sometimes creates wicked, weird, warped musical ideas. I love that. There have been days all four of us hear a riff in four different places in the groove – that's when magic happens!

With Skunk Anansie, you have to get out of your comfort zone. One of the strongest tracks we wrote was 'Victim', a taut tune driven by Cass's deep bass notes. I love singing this live because it has a dark swinging rhythm that gets deeper the further you go into the song: *I'm a victim of your love/I'm addiction you're the drug.*

Love isn't always a wonderful, beautiful energy. Sometimes it can suck the life out of you, making you feel like a victim in need of a fix, and that's not a good feeling. I felt that in my very first relationship, when I was utterly hooked on Sabrina. I felt out of control. Music is one of the ways in which I can free myself from that kind of psychological torment. It's also a way of confronting my fears, like the track 'That Sinking Feeling', where I sing, *Can't fight this feeling that is coming on the second wave/I get up, I get down . . . it's gonna be a fight today.*

I'm lucky – I've never experienced suicidal thoughts, but I have thought a lot about death, especially drowning. I'm the world's worst swimmer, still dreadful even after taking many swimming lessons. Drowning is therefore one of my deepest fears, and it's there as a metaphor in a number of my lyrics.

I have nearly drowned twice. The first time was while scuba diving on holiday in Tobago in the 1990s with my then girl-friend Maxine. That weird undersea world fascinates me, but while we were diving my equipment failed a few metres down, and I started breathing in water. I realised I would drown if I panicked, so I calmly tried to get my instructor's attention. At first maybe a bit too calmly, because he gave me a 'wait a second' glance, so after a few more, shall we say, persuasive hand gestures, he got the gist and took me back to the surface. I was lucky then, but the second time was much worse.

In 2006, in Ibiza, I went swimming off a headland called Sa Punta, near Talamanca Bay, on the south-east coast. There's a spot where you can jump off the side of the rock into deep water, and the diving points are marked at two, five and ten metres high. That day I was by myself, and jumped off the five-metre spot, climbed back up and then jumped off again. The weather suddenly changed, so it went from being a bright sunny day to stormy rain in what felt like seconds, and I got washed out to where there was an undertow. It felt like someone had grabbed hold of my ankles and was pulling me down.

I tried to swim up to the surface but kept being dragged under. When I came up a third time, I thought, *I've got no more strength*, but just at that moment a guy saw me and jumped in after me. Although he was a really strong swimmer, we both got drawn down by the undertow, and every time he tried to push me onto land, a wave would wash me back into the sea. I was getting badly scratched on the sharp rocks, and was starting to feel weak, so by the third time I knew that if I couldn't hold onto the rock I would die. In my head I was shouting to myself to hold on and, thankfully, the man pushed me far enough that I managed to scramble to safety before collapsing. He carried me off the rocks and up the beach and pumped the water out of my lungs, saving my life. It was only then I realised he was completely naked!

I very nearly died. Unsurprisingly I became friends with my saviour, and we were bonded by the experience. Now, if I think about death, I always think of drowning because that was the closest I came to dying. It felt like there was something invisible holding onto my feet, my lungs filling with water and making me splutter. That day I said over and over in my mind: *Don't panic, don't panic*, and I believe that's why I survived. That is something I've learnt to do in other realms of my life, whether it was escaping my abusive boyfriend Tony, back when I was a teenager, or confronting the fear and sadness I felt after the band broke up.

Drowning has become a recurring theme and symbol in my music, portraying situations where I fail. Sometimes I fail in relationships, and sometimes I mess up when I try to support family or friends and let people down without meaning to, so I'm always trying to make things better. One thing that I was able to put right was my relationship with Lady, the one who nearly got away. We had a very strong connection and we had many friends in common, so I was never able to truly forget her; champagne never quite tasted the same.

I summoned up some courage, put my feelings in a letter and waited for a reply that never came. Meanwhile, in the spring of 2015, our mutual friend Liborio took me to a dinner Lady was hosting. I noticed the air was on the chilly side, but after the triple combination of some Dom Pérignon, a gift of a McQueen ring and a heart to heart with Lady, the air cleared and a seed was planted. We took our time. On New Year's Day 2017, she invited me to join her with some friends in Marrakech. I was actually on my way to India, so I took a lovely detour, and that was the beginning of our real relationship. 'Promise me we won't ever be boring,' I asked her. We both knew it was serious, and the beginning of something good.

TWENTY

CLIT ROCK

Try and step into my life
Step into a life where you hold
Nothing but your fire.

'What You Do For Love'

It tickles me that a funny, off-the-cuff comment I made has
become a thing. I was being interviewed in the early days by
NME, and the journalist asked me what I thought of Britpop.
I cheekily said, 'We're not Britpop, we're Clitpop,' and this
became 'clit rock', a phrase I scrawled across my forehead in a
photo shoot. By that time, in the mid-1990s, I was so tired of
Britpop, which was like a humpback whale, mouth wide open,
swallowing all British music in a single gulp then shooting out
a marketing jet stream of floppy-haired white indie bands trying
to make it in the USA. I coined the phrase clit rock to mock
male rock and indie boy posturing, and subvert the concept of
cock rock, turning it into something I described as 'wet, swollen

and full-on'. Let's be naughty and promote the clit! The *NME* loved it, and clit rock was born.

I love how the term has been used over the years. I've spotted it on playlists, T-shirts, newspaper headlines and, in a more serious way, in festivals like Clit Rock, founded by UK punk musician Dana Jade in 2011. At the time of writing, Clit Rock have staged ten events raising money and awareness of FGM, working with organisations like Abandon the Knife, and Daughters of Eve, which was founded by writer Nimco Ali and my friend and fellow FGM campaigner Leyla Hussein.

Now also defined by the Urban Dictionary as 'lesbian rawk', clit rock has come to encompass any female music that is against the mainstream – from female-fronted rock bands to underground girl-rock. That female fist-pumping positivity makes me smile, and reminds me how, back in the early 1990s, we were claiming the outside track of British music for ourselves. We were in the race but not competing with the jet stream. We were creating our own story, and in the process became an antidote to what was considered hip. Skunk Anansie were neither lads nor ladettes, not Britpop nor Britrock, just part of a new, alternative scene that was political, aware, caring and diverse.

There's a line in our *Anarchytecture* song 'Bullets': *See the girls with no vision for themselves.* It was very important to me to have a vision, not just with my music and the message I was communicating, but also with the visual image. My mad onstage looks always start with my friend and stylist Kim Howells, a mischievous, edgy fashion stylist writer/designer from South Wales who started off assisting legendary stylist Nicola Formichetti before branching out on her own. She specialises in smashing the freshest of fresh designers together with the best of the legendary labels. I met her when I modelled a recycled wedding dress for Dr Noki at his Fashion East show in 2008, and we still work together on Skunk Anansie live tours, photo shoots, events, anything to do with me making a fashion moment. We're like two Macbethian witches hunched over a boiling cauldron of looks, rubbing our hands together in glee at what we can do next. Kim finds it liberating not having to create looks just for the catwalk, and sees our tours as fantastical projects. One year, for instance, we got the knitwear designer Craig Lawrence to make a huge gold and silver headpiece with metallic yarn, so when I came onstage it looked like I was in the middle of a giant fireball. My outfits are now part of the stage design, looked after on tour by my friend and wardrobe person Sylvia Mottram, who makes sure their glory never fades.

I love being creative with fashion, and have my own personal relationships with designers, like my friend Liborio Capizzi, whom I originally met when he asked me to model in a campaign for Italian giant Gianfranco Ferré. He's a bit of a genius! He was Ferré's head designer, and has created so many beautiful pieces for me, for both on- and offstage I'll be working a lot with Daniel Pollitt, one of my favourite up-and-coming designers, and I've collaborated with Keko Hainswheeler for many years. He created the iconic feathered plumage outfit for our 2009 *Greatest Hits* tour that reappeared on the album cover of *25live@25*. I'm obsessed with Jivomir Domoustchiev's sculptured PVC designs, which work wonders with the lights onstage, and Gareth Pugh, who made the futuristic stage outfit for our 2019 tour. The line between menswear and womenswear is slowly dissolving, and I've always worn both. I love the tailoring and modern crispness of the suits at Dior designed by my long-time friend Kim Jones. It's been lovely to see him flower and grow into one of the greats. It was a great honour when he opened his show at Art Basel with our song 'Hedonism'.

I think it's important to create your own internal barometer of cool and build on that. I love the way my girlfriend Lady proudly displays her armpit hair. It might not seem so radical now, but in the 1990s it was truly shocking for a woman to have a shaven head or hairy armpits. We both have similar memories of people constantly staring and pointing. My shaven head made me stronger and more proudly defiant, and it was the same for her. I get my power from shaving my hair and she gets hers from growing it. The juxtaposition of her chic femininity and her hairy pits is confusing for people. Even now, I've seen extreme reactions to her armpits, and when you break it down you have to ask yourself, why? Social norms about women's bodies have always been strangely controlling.

I like Lady's defiance and strength, and the fact she's secure in her identity. Lady creates her own path, and we are very similar in many ways. She's always waved her freak flag high. When she was a teenager she followed the band the Grateful Dead all across America, and we love a bit of classic rock when the mood takes us. She sold vintage clothing for years and loves the creative side of fashion, and dressing in over-the top looks is something we both enjoy. Not only a clubber like me, Lady is the one throwing the parties I want to go to. With Lady, our worlds collide beautifully – it makes me feel secure, and with her I can be truly myself.

The year that I got back with Lady I turned fifty years old. When I was forty I rented a couple of villas and had a massive, week-long party in Ibiza, with friends coming from all over the world. At fifty, I wanted to do the opposite. I had a more 'civilised' sit-down dinner with friends. At the beginning of the year, I thought hard about what I wanted my life to look like – maybe it was the last chance to do some mad and unexpected things. Firstly, I decided to get fit. For 2012's *Black Traffic* tour and the *Anarchytecture* tour in 2016, I hadn't done enough pre-tour training and was prone to injury. After years of stage-diving and throwing myself around in concert, my injuries had begun to mount. I'd had a compressed disc in my spine, twisted ankles, chipped bones, countless cuts, bruises and muscle strain. I did a whole tour in intense pain because of compressed discs in my neck, and eventually had to cancel a gig to get some surgical treatment, which wasn't fun. For a long time I had a Peter Pan complex because I've always looked younger than my years – but by then I felt less like Peter Pan and more like Captain Hook!

My first promise to myself was to find a good physiotherapist and commit to a proper recovery and fitness schedule, which I continue to this day. Next I drew up a Fuck-it List, a list of things I had always wanted to do. Fuck-it! Why not!

SKIN'S FUCK-IT LIST

1. Skydive – see that terror described below.
2. Learn how to ride a motorbike – easy! Done. Now I ride all the time on my 125 Mutt motorcycle, and after the Covid pandemic I'm going for my big bike test.
3. Buy a piano and learn how to play it. Done, loving it, but it's safe to say Stevie Wonder has nothing to fear!
4. Join a choir. Failed. Never in one place long enough, still dreaming.

5. Visit a country I've never seen before, hard for a touring artist! Done. Mexico is heaven, can't wait to go back.
6. Learn a language ... properly. Done. I now speak Italian, even though maybe I'm a little rusty.
7. Secret that shall eventually be revealed, or not.

The skydive came first. Knowing it was on my Fuck-it list, Lady had surprised me with this gift of possible death. When she booked it she had Googled 'statistics for dying during a skydive' and was not impressed. I persuaded my friends Richelle and Len to join me on my trip to the heavens (the fools!) and in September 2017 we drove to the skydive centre in Cambridgeshire. We spent the morning dressed in some very unflattering jumpsuits that creased in all the wrong places, and learnt basic skills like how not to die, how not to kill anyone else if you're going to die, and the quietest way to panic. We all had tandem instructors, one of them with a particularly dark sense of humour who cracked the most abominable jokes, but he met his match in Lady, who took his schtick and shot back with added sass.

I must confess my reason for this lunacy is that I don't like heights, and think that if I continually try and face it I will scare the fear away. To prove this to myself, I've climbed many tall structures like the Eiffel Tower and the Duomo in Milan, and I've skyrocketed down the longest zipline in Costa Rica. But still, fear of heights wraps around my throat like a hungry anaconda, sadly not the Nicki Minaj kind. This was my final chance to bitch-slap the fear outta me. If I fail, I thought, I'll accept defeat and just avoid heights. Maybe at fifty there is no joy in being scared shitless.

Before we went up in a tiny plane, we had to wait for hours for cloud cover to clear and the waiting around made everybody nervous, especially Lady. In fact, I had never seen her so subdued, and her death banter with Mr Naughty-pants had ground to a halt. And she was extremely quiet – highly unusual for a woman so gifted with the gab she could charm the knickers off a nun. I realised that while I was scared of heights, she was absolutely bloody terrified.

The flight took about fifteen minutes to get up to an altitude of four thousand feet. Then it hit me; white-cold fear crawled up my spine, wrapped around my throat and choked my scream. It was time to jump. I wanted out. I would have committed blue murder for it all to stop. Then *BAM!* My instructor took the initiative and jumped. We were falling through a cloud and it was glorious! I've never been inside a cloud before. They look soft and fluffy when you see them curled up in the sky but, strangely, inside the cloud it was freezing cold with a mass of tiny icicles hitting me in the face. Quite lovely. Then all was clear and we could see for miles. As we fell back to earth Superman-fast, it struck me how small I was in comparison to how huge the earth was. How could a tiny speck like me be falling so quickly, moving at 125mph? When prompted I pulled the cord, the parachute came out and I floated down over big wide fields like a baby feather. I loved it. Would I go again? Hell no! But what a great way to start a Fuck-it list!

Becoming fifty also made me re-evaluate my role as a singer and musician.

After years of being happy to wear the badge of an outsider within a music industry I knew found me difficult to pigeonhole, difficult to market and therefore difficult to give awards to, on 8 November 2018, I was shocked and delighted to win Most Inspirational Artist at the *Music Week* Women in Music Awards. At the awards dinner, *Music Week* editor Steve Sutherland leant over to me and said, 'We're so looking forward to your speech.'

FUCK! What speech? I thought, suddenly feeling unprepared. I noticed everyone who went up for an award had a proper speech planned. *Why didn't I think of that?* So I scribbled down a few notes. The Mercury-nominated indie-rock artist Nadine Shah gave me a lovely introduction, and up I went to collect my award.

'I haven't got many awards in my career, so this is extra special,' I said. 'I was thinking, back in the day, 1992 or '93 I wanted to be a rock singer, and it's been very hard being me. It's been a very difficult thing being a lead singer of a rock band looking like me, and it still is. I have to say, it's been a fight and it will always be a fight . . . but that fight drives you and makes you want to work harder. I want to say to any new artists out there, man, you're in for a ride! It's not going to be easy, it's not supposed to be easy; it's the friggin' music business and you're women, and some of you are black, and some of you are gay like me. You've got to keep moving forward, keep striving for everything you want to be.'

To my relief, everyone burst into applause. It was a moving moment, receiving that award. There was no template for me when I started out, no easy marketing category that I would slot into. I had to fight to be understood and respected. Sometimes the obstacles aren't always apparent – racism and sexism in the music industry can work in slippery, insidious ways. People don't need to be overt; they just exclude you from a festival line-up, or don't play your songs on the radio, or say they don't like your voice. That's why, when the recognition comes, it feels so sweet.

It felt that after years of striving, Skunk Anansie were receiving validation. We have always been a killer live band, so early in 2019, we released the triple album *25Live@25*, a celebration of the twenty-fifth anniversary of our first gig at the Splash Club in Kings Cross. We created a special limited-edition album with a photobook of personal memorabilia and pictures. We had no idea that it would capture people's imagination, but in June we won the *Kerrang!* Hall of Fame award. Previous winners include Rage Against The Machine, Green Day and Iggy Pop, and I was so delighted I posted all our *Kerrang!* covers on Instagram, including one where they'd spray-painted me gold.

That summer, we did a 41-date tour of the UK and Europe, and it felt like one of the best tours we had ever done. But right at the start of the tour I had a Twitter exchange with UK grime/R&B artist Stormzy that accidently went viral. Prior to his headline slot at Glastonbury, he tweeted: 'I am the first black British artist to headline Glastonbury . . . I'm overwhelmed with emotions; this is the most surreal feeling I've ever experienced.' I saw it and posted on our Instagram: 'Sorry, Stormzy, but we beat you to it in 1999! 20 years ago! And while we're on the topic I was the first black woman too! @Beyonce. Wishing you an awesome nite tho, bro. Kill it! You're amazing and we're all very proud!'

My comment went viral, and some of the UK tabloid press tried to start a beef between us, thinking they had a way to slap down Stormzy at his greatest moment – 'let's use Skin to put him in his place'. But we know their tricks. He tweeted an apology, adding, 'Thank you for paving the way – love (and) respect.' I sent Stormzy a friendly text back. It was always cool between us.

The man is pure class. I was on the judging panel in 2018 for his Ivor Novello Award for the album *Gang Signs & Prayer*, so I'm delighted to see him conquer the world. If anything, Maxim was there before all of us, when the Prodigy headlined in 1997. I didn't want to detract from Stormzy's performance. My point was, why was there a twenty-year gap? That should be the discussion, the fact that black British artists are still considered a risk by festival organisers, seen as not big or important enough to top the bill. And when we do, look at us battling to remind the public of what we have achieved, jostling for position to be the first, the biggest, the greatest. As black artists, it seems like we have to crow from the rooftops to get heard.

I like to think the world is trying to embrace diversity, but we are still fighting racism. We see it in every country we go to – in Japan, for instance, I'd walk down the street and people would literally cross to the other side. And we had horrible incidents in Russia. Once, in Moscow, Cass and I went to a shopping mall to have some food, and at one stall they refused to serve us, blatantly saying to our faces, 'We're not serving you.' In the end, Cass and I found a café that was playing Bob Marley, and we said, 'Ah, they'll serve us here.' We went in and sat down for thirty minutes, yet no one came to take our order, so we left disgusted. There was me thinking being gay would be the issue. Russia was hard work.

We wrote a song in 2018, the pile-driving funky Skunk Anansie anthem 'This Means War', that became one of our biggest moments on the *25live* tour. Usually it takes a while for people to get used to new songs, but that song smashed every night from the very beginning. When I sang, *I'll fight hard till I fall/'Cos this means war, fuckers!*, audiences kicked off with an incredible response, a blast of pent-up emotion. The song was more like a rallying cry, a call to arms.

It's really scary to watch how organised the extreme right has become around the world. Look at LGBTQ+ rights – we may win battles against fashion brands on social media but atrocities against gay and trans people are being committed in the real world. In 2017, for instance, ISIS fighters in Syria released execution videos and an image of a gay man being thrown from a tower as part of their homophobic propaganda campaign. And in 2019, the Russian LGBT Network alleged that gay people were being tortured in camps in Chechnya, while gay refugees from Uganda spoke of being tortured by police. We need to find solidarity, and *together* become a stronger fighting force against such horrors; thoughts and prayers are not enough.

On a local level, there's a lot we can do. As well as working with the campaign against FGM, another charity I have been involved with as a patron is Baobab Survivors, an organisation for child refugees run by campaign worker and psychotherapist Sheila Melzak. There are kids who come to England as illegal immigrants – child soldiers, or girls who might have been trafficked here from rape camps in war-torn places where young women are imprisoned and systematically raped by enemy forces. The kids are all under the age of fourteen, but they look older because of everything they've been through. Often they have no family, cannot prove their age and are not believed. The government makes it difficult for them to apply for asylum because the term 'asylum-seeker' has bad connotations, but children are fleeing from countries where they have been slaves. Sometimes they're so deeply traumatised they can't speak.

Some of these kids have been soldiers since they were four years old. As a patron of the charity, I remember meeting one child in particular – a girl from the Congo I'll call Tilly. Her parents had been killed by soldiers in front of her, then she had been raped and had given birth to four babies before the age of sixteen. She was brought to the UK and denied asylum because her experience was 'not state-sanctioned torture'.

I have been involved in the charity in a number of ways – raising money through gigs, contributing to the kids' summer holiday every year, and inviting kids to our soundcheck. For three years in a row, Cass was Father Christmas at their Christmas party.

Sheila also suggested I work with the kids as part of a therapy programme, so I did some music sessions, playing guitar and finding melodies for things they want to say. One boy wrote lyrics saying that he couldn't find his mother and hadn't seen her for ten years. Sheila told me that he had been forced to kill his own mother and father to become a soldier. That's how insurgents indoctrinate the children – orphan them, brutalise them and then give them opiates to make them dependent, so that they follow them around as child soldiers. It's so sad. I like to work with kids directly, to try to help them cope with their struggles and find a way through music for them to heal.

In 2018, the healing power of music hit me in another, very personal way. Renowned designer and dear friend Riccardo Tisci invited Lady and I to go with his family to Christmas midnight mass at Notre-Dame Cathedral in Paris. I remember looking at the flying buttresses on the outer walls, like a giant dragon's claw holding the building together. Then, inside, I was transfixed by the vaulted ceiling and the famous, stained-glass rose windows flanked by wooden carvings at the end of the nave. The workmanship was incredible.

I remembered lessons at Teesside when we studied classic architecture, structures built for worship like Notre-Dame, or La Sagrada Familia, Gaudí's cathedral in Barcelona. Since early civilisation people have built places of devotion to their gods, or for spiritual reasons, all with the same desire to impress. As a result, religious buildings have some of the most resonant architecture still standing.

For me the most touching moment was the sound of the huge organ, a rumbling mass of notes vibrating through the wooden benches. And over the volcano of sound were the delicate voices of the children's choir, soprano harmonies drifting in circles above our heads and echoing around the arches. It was so magical that we all wiped away a tear. It reminded me of being a young girl listening to Frank, our wonderful organist at St Matthew's Church in Brixton. He was actually a concert pianist, and played on Sunday just for fun. Man, he was so good you could see he really loved being in control of this massive yet complex musical instrument.

That night at Notre-Dame, over 9,000 people crammed into the cathedral, all quietly moved by the Christmas atmosphere. I'm not a deeply religious person, but as the choir sang you could see why they felt God was in the room, summoned there by the power of everyone's belief. I thought about my childhood faith, and being raised a Christian. As a teenager I rebelled against religious indoctrination, with all the rules you couldn't question, but over time I've made peace with it. I can see how religion has been a spiritual guide for my people through what was sometimes daily hell, enabling them to be strong.

But four months after that Christmas Eve, on 15 April 2019, in the middle of reconstruction work, a fire broke out beneath the roof of Notre-Dame. The whole world watched live on TV as the spire collapsed into a gulf of red and yellow flames. I was in shock, gutted. Medieval craftsmen had constructed that building, making it their life's work. Many had worked with their hands doing intricate carving, creating a piece of high art that had stood for 800 years, and now that part of the cathedral was gone forever. It was the first and last time I would see Notre-Dame in its original splendour, a memory that has stayed imprinted on my mind, and a personal reminder to slow down and take in the moment . . . we have no idea what lies next on the horizon.

TWENTY-ONE

I GOT YOU

I'm strong, I'm free,
My confidence is burning the fear . . .
The sweetest thing is you baby,
The sweetest thing that I can breathe

'The Sweetest Thing'

I still love pushing myself out of my comfort zone, and I did exactly that when, early in 2020, I appeared in the first UK series of reality competition *The Masked Singer*. The show involves a group of celebrities who compete anonymously on the show in costumes, performing covers of famous songs. I chose the duck costume because, quite frankly, it was ridiculous and funny – no one would ever imagine that Skin from Skunk Anansie would dress up as a giant rubber duck! It was perfect!

It was also bloody nerve-wracking, but not for the reasons I expected. I've never been that far out of my comfort zone.

I wasn't able to use any of the tricks of the trade I'd gathered during my thirty-year career, and I was singing in completely different styles. I was nervous about my credibility, when in the end that didn't matter because the hardest part was the singing. But I saw it as a weirdly fun way of changing the view England has of me as an artist. The image people have of me is that I'm super-tall, aggressive, political and serious. I just wanted to show that I'm also quite goofy and love to have a laugh. My friends and family loved it. My mum had no idea it was me until I took off my mask. I nearly ended her life! Surprisingly, even Cass – gatekeeper of cool – liked it. Apparently he was in his kitchen when he heard my voice, ran into living room and saw a giant rubber duck on TV. I would have loved to have seen his face. *The Masked Singer* was a world away from my role as lead vocalist for Skunk Anansie.

When I look back at all I've done in my music career, it's only natural that I reflect on the time the band spent apart from each other. Do I regret the band splitting up? Yes, part of me definitely does. Part of me wishes we had done what Ace suggested, and just taken a break. But I also know I learnt many things during those solo years, as did Ace, Cass and Mark. I gained so much knowledge recording those solo albums, honing my songwriting, which with hindsight gave the band legs that have taken us to twenty-five years, something few 1990s bands have managed to achieve. I also think the break made everyone value what we have so much more, treasuring the band dynamic we nearly lost. Skunk Anansie changed all of our lives for the better, and after the 2019 tour, we again found ourselves on the up, reaching out to more and more fans. I enjoy the special rapport between our band and the audience. A gig is like a film or a story – it has to have a beginning, middle and an end, and between those points you can experiment and play.

I trust our audience – they're gagging for us to do a good gig, so we're in it together. For instance, I've lost my ear monitor crowd-surfing many times. I just ask them to find it for me and, amazingly, they always do. I drop my microphone, it comes back; anything I lose comes back. I think our audience comes to entertain as well as to be entertained, and we attract some characters: outsiders who want a different life and who abandon themselves to the experience. I search them out sometimes because they're magical!

Onstage I don't just follow what's planned; sometimes I completely change the structure of a song or the tempo of the gig. I look at the boys and they know it's time to go off script. We don't restrict ourselves to the setlist; we can change the running order, add or subtract songs, and we have different songs for different towns. In the Paradiso club, in Amsterdam, I climbed up on the balcony and walked all the way round the edge, and everyone was freaking out, especially our crew. The best gigs are where something unique happens. Once, during our 2019 tour, I was thinking, *Why is there a big gap in the audience?* All of a sudden, out of the gap, bursting like a volcano, comes a guy in a wheelchair, beaming with joy and held aloft by about six people. Everyone went ballistic while I walked across the hands of the audience to him, and they held me up while I sang right into his face. A similar thing happened two gigs later, except this time it was a ten-year-old girl, sitting on her father's shoulders. We screamed every word of the lyrics at each other, eyeball to eyeball, straight into the mic, both of us loving every second.

Those are the things that I remember, and they are the whole point of live performance – the reason why I do what I do. Gigs for me are about creating moments, so we set everything up with enough flexibility to be able to ride with crazy as it comes. We love it when madness happens. Spontaneity is key, because that's where the magic is. It's through singing live that a song evolves. In the early days, 'Hedonism' made me really sad, because it reminded me of the hurt, and that was how I sang it, but that sadness died aeons ago. Now that song makes me feel really happy because everyone loves it so much. It's the reason people love us, it's our legacy, and now I can just enjoy it and maybe show off my voice a little.

Of course, I haven't totally spilled the tea. Some delicious little cookies are just for me – for this book was not supposed to be a list of loves won or lost, but a reflection on the blood and guts I needed to get here. If you were to ask me what was the most important part of my career, firstly, I'd say it was my time in Mama Wild. That was because it laid the groundwork. We had two years of being unknown, unsigned and out of the public eye, to make every conceivable mistake a starter band could make. In those days we were rubbish. I know that, because Mick Jagger came to one of our early gigs and left mid-song. But I also knew we were onto something for him to be there in the first place. We were fast learners, and made sure all our mistakes were new.

For example: that very first gig in 1992, when we supported Edwin Starr. I knew it wasn't good – the electronic samples we used were at the wrong sound levels, and I could feel it wasn't working. The polite applause of the 500-strong audience said it all. But what put fire in my belly was that unforgettable cutting quip of Edwin Starr, shading us over the mic at the start of his gig, declaring, 'Now we're gonna play *real* music.'

Okay, he was right, we were lame. It was our first gig, and you have to start somewhere. What we needed was some pointers, but instead we got a kicking from Mr Edwin bloody Starr – ouch! It's like when you wear a crap outfit and you're already on the bus, thinking you really shouldn't have put on a yellow tee with a yellow baggy pant, and the bus driver with his two-pence worth says you look like a squashed banana.

I still wear yellow; I just have thicker skin.

It's easy in the era of social media to create something quick and stylish, but when people listen more deeply they need to find something with substance. The songs must be authentically *you*, whether you write them or not, and my advice is not to share on your socials too early, don't give people power over your material while it's in the early stages because one negative uninformed comment can lead you astray. Get proper feedback from people who know what they're talking about. Be patient and let record companies come to you. Don't be too thirsty. Executives are a weird bunch. If they reject you, they'll reject you forever; they don't like to go back on an earlier decision and be seen to be wrong. At the same time, fresh ideas work, so don't be afraid to make it up as you go along. You might be pleasantly surprised.

We had great songs, but we had to learn how to translate them live and communicate their power to an audience. Some of them got lost on the way, but some of them sparkled, and that's what we built upon. Being good live is still very important, but you also need to be aware that different music genres have different vibes. If you do pop, you gotta have a banging live show; with rap, banging attitude; and country, banging voice. Your style must shine, and in Mama Wild our style was too bluesy, not fresh enough for the rock world we wanted to be part of.

With Elisha Blue we had the wrong guitarist – an incredible player, but one who in his soul came from a different era. Sadly, Blue died in 2020, while we were finishing this book. Cass told me about the heart attack Blue had in October 2019, while they were hanging out at his house. Blue felt unwell but refused Cass's help – luckily Cass didn't listen and our great NHS paramedics arrived in time to save his life. That changed Blue's life and gave him another few months to do what he did best, which was to play the blues to a London crowd that loved him. Being in a band with him was a wild ride that I will never forget, and I'll always be weirdly grateful for. He was a modern-day blues king, another great gone too soon.

Although some good music has come out of gargantuan battles, it's important to have chemistry and harmony. If you're playing or writing with people you detest, yet you make great music, I'm sorry, but the stars aligned like that for you, so good luck being bloody miserable. The virtuoso players are not always the best songwriters. I've learnt that twice: once with Blue then again with Robbie France. They were wonderful musicians, but you don't need that to write great songs; you just need a good ear and a talent for communicating your ideas to others in the band.

In Mama Wild I learnt to step back and take a good harsh look at our songs, building up a mental database of what worked and what didn't. If something shined I needed to know how and why, and if it blew chunks I needed to know the size and flavour of them. I'd think about the audience, and try to imagine what the girl in the third row was thinking. Being objective is hard, but sometimes you get close enough to weed out and reject your worst ideas, leaving room for better ones to grow. There is no quick way to being good – it's a long road.

No matter how excited I am about a new song, the best test is to play it in a room to other people and *feel* their reactions. Unless they're in the music business, it's difficult for them to put into words what they think. I read people's body language, like when they look up and smile and start tapping a toe or, conversely, when they fiddle with an arm-rest or look around the room for help. If they pick up their phone mid-chorus, I know I've lost them, it's over – *throw that song away!* In the very early days, when people didn't know my voice, I'd play tracks in the background with friends in the room to see if anyone started nodding along. I did that when I was living in the housing co-op in Brixton, and when I was DJing at parties – a cute, sneaky way to see if I was on track.

The writer Malcolm Gladwell talks about a 'tipping point', the moment someone makes what appears to be a split-second, instinctive decision – but it's often one based on years of practice and experience. When people tell you to trust your instincts, it's like being told to 'just love yourself'. Well, how the fuck are you supposed to do that? You need tools. I don't always love myself. I don't look in the mirror every morning and hit my head on the ceiling jumping for joy. For me, loving myself even part-time came with age and experience, and is rarely easy. It's the same with trusting your instincts. You have to find and train them, and that's what happened in Mama Wild. I learnt how to read an audience by doing a hundred thousand gigs, including one for a man with a dog-on-a-rope who turned out to have wandered into the wrong venue.

Mama Wild gave me tools that I'm still using – some of them are now like arrows that go straight to the point, like ditching something when it's not working, and being rigorous about what you save. When I'm working now on a Skunk Anansie song, I know when a section is a bit off (usually the middle eight) or where the chorus isn't good enough, whereas in the past I would prevaricate and feel unsure, and need to test out ideas. That's why Skunk Anansie was so strong so quickly – it wouldn't have been Skunk Anansie without Mama Wild, or songwriting with Len, or Cass, with his years of valuable experience, or Leigh, who had worked for a management company and could smell a timewaster before they finished brushing their teeth. From the beginning we'd write a song and send it to Leigh to see what she thought. We wrote five songs a week for a solid year before she said, 'Okay, that one's not bad, keep writing.' She still has that brilliant shit-o-meter now.

In 2020, I gave a songwriting masterclass to students at Leeds Arts University, and was asked a great question: 'What would you say to your eighteen-year-old self?'

'I'd say fuck all,' I replied, 'because at eighteen I wouldn't have listened.' I wouldn't have listened because I needed to make my own mistakes, and I was a late starter with a lot of catching up to do. That understanding came to me much later, after the attack in Brixton, when I was on my own trajectory. I went from being really shy to shouting at a guy in the street at the top of my lungs and finding my strength.

I'd have some words, though, for my 28-year-old self – her

ears would have pricked up. I'd have said, bitch, you need to chill. In the late 1990s, success came so quickly, going from sitting on the sofa to being in a Hollywood movie within six months. I'd have said to myself, relax and enjoy the moment. I missed so much, running to get to the top of the mountain, that instead of sitting down to take in the view, I fretted over conquering the next one. I was a working-class Brixton girl figuring out which fork to use in the Palace, and everything was brand new. I'd say to her, yes, be concerned for the future, but don't forget to find the joy in the present.

Also, most importantly, I'd tell her to always see herself as equal to everyone in the room. Do not think you are better or worse (and we all do it sometimes) – that's what ruins your spirit and your sense of community in the world. No matter the size of the wallet, the cut of the suit or the volume of followers, everyone is equal. For me, as a shy person, it was important to reach out and talk to people. I've learnt it's not so scary, and that most people are good. I'd also say, learn some business acumen. The music industry teaches you a lot about creativity but nothing about the business, so I'd tell my younger self to learn from everyone you can about how that side works.

Then, if I could talk to forty-year-old me, I'd say don't be anxious about settling down. Because I was – and I made a huge mistake. Society tells you you're supposed to settle down, and if I hadn't given myself that pressure, I wouldn't have taken a wrong turn.

And lastly, to that little ten-year-old Brixton girl . . . I'd look at her and say don't worry. It's gonna be okay. It's all gonna be okay. A child needs an adult to make them feel safe, to take away the worries at the age you realise the big wide world is a scary place. I love that black American thing, where they look you in the eye and say, 'I got you'. I would have loved to have heard that.

People always ask me for my definition of success. Success to me is waking up and being happy with the day in front of me. Okay, sometimes that means a shitstorm, and sometimes it's pure bliss, but it's my shitstorm that I've curated for myself, and my bliss to enjoy. I haven't been bored since 1988. At the time of writing, in spring 2020, I'm sitting in the apartment I share with Lady in New York, with the Covid pandemic at its height. It's scary, because 70 per cent of what I do as a musician is dependent on a crowd and, for the moment, I can't tour or sing live. I can't do the thing I love. My situation would be a lot worse if I hadn't been well managed. We're not from wealthy families, but Leigh made sure that each of us in Skunk Anansie could afford a house. As a musician, your manager is the most important person, because they pick your team and run your team and do the financial planning, and for that I am so grateful.

I'm finally happy in an exciting relationship with Lady, someone who understands me and with whom I can travel the world. On Valentine's Day 2020 we got engaged! And are planning our next steps in life. I have people in my life that I've known for over thirty years, people I value because I know we've all got each other's back. That's my definition of success. Some things I like doing better than others, but I don't do anything I truly hate.

My life has given me heartache and houses, prestige and disappointments. It took blood and guts to be this way, but I'm so glad this Brixton girl didn't end up a cliché.

ACKNOWLEDGEMENTS

SKIN

I'd like to thank Lucy O'Brien for being the calm to my storm when I was the storm to her calm; Leigh for remaining a wonderful example of a human being, even when surrounded by lizards dressed in chinos; Lady for constantly pushing me to be that little bit better when I was happy to be a lot o' bit worse; Kathy for being an intelligent ear right when I needed it; and my mum Pat for never ever muting *Top of the Pops*.

I'd also like to thank everyone for helping us put this book together. To my boys Cass, Mark and Ace for always being the best boys in boyland, and to my dad Ken for being a true original. To my family for being proper fam. To Maxine Clarke, Richelle Donigan, Carole Walker, Michelle James, Angela Robson, Tom Minney and Kim Howells for letting themselves be subject to interrogation.

And to my editor Fritha Saunders at Simon & Schuster and copyeditor Kerri Sharp for not cracking when I did.

LUCY O'BRIEN

Thank you to Skin for your warmth, humour, words and insight. You are such an inspirational force. Thanks also to everyone mentioned above, and also my family, Malcolm Boyle, Erran and Maya, for their love and support.